sleeping with BAD BOYS

A Juicy Tell-All of Literary New York in the Fifties and Sixties

"This is an outrageous book—and it's all true. It's wild, about our wild youth, but profound. Denham catches the undercurrents, the meaning as well as the misery."

—Adele Mailer, author of *The Last Party: My Life with Norman Mailer*

"A deft yet rollicking yarn about sleeping with bad boys—'50s and '60s male writers and editors who thought they had the world by the tail. Denham shows them otherwise in often hilarious send-ups. Denham's ear for dialogue and her trenchant descriptions of the social milieux of New York publishing and downtown Bohemia rival Mary McCarthy's. Acutely observed and finelywrought."

—Mary Dearborn, biographer of Louise Bryant, Peggy Guggenheim, Norman Mailer, and Henry Miller.

At the still point, there the dance is . . .
there is only the dance.
I can only say, *there* we have been:
T. S. Eliot, *Burnt Norton*, II

The cock crows but the hen delivers.
The Dixie Chicks, 1991

sleeping with BAD BOYS

A Juicy Tell-All of Literary New York in the Fifties and Sixties

alice denham

BOOK REPUBLIC

❧ about Alice ❧

Alice Denham's first novel, *My Darling from the Lions* was published in 1967 by Bobbs-Merill and reissued in 2003. Her second was the cult novel, *AMO*.
Denham is the only *Playboy* Playmate with a story in the same issue. In 1989 that story was made into a festival prizewinning movie. She became a Playmate to get that story reprinted, originally published in *Discovery*, a hot fifties literary review. As a founding member of *NOW*, Alice appeared on the Walter Cronkite CBS News show in the first national TV interview with feminists in 1970, and participated in the famous feminist takeover of the *Ladies Home Journal*. Her stories and articles have appeared in *Great Tales of City Dwellers*, *Best of the Missouri Review*, *New York Times Book Review*, *Village Voice*, *Washingtonian*, *Cosmopolitan*, *Publishers Weekly*, *The Nation*, *Confrontation*, and others.
Alice Denham lives in Greenwich Village.

BOOK REPUBLIC PRESS
An imprint of Cardoza Publishing

First Edition
Copyright © 2006 by Alice Denham
All Rights Reserved

Library of Congress Catalog Card No: 2005930781
ISBN: 1-58042-206-3

For a full list of titles, visit our website:
WWW.CARDOZAPUB.COM

❧ contents ❧

Dedicated to John Brady Mueller

Thanks to:
My dedicated skillful agent, Martha Kaplan; Jeanine Johnson Flaherty; Susan Brownmiller early on; Mary Dearborn throughout; David Markson; Adele Mailer; Lisa Dierbeck; poet Angelo Verga, curator at Cornelia St. Café; John Flood, Director Hudson Park Library; American PEN Women's Literary Workshop, Authors Sala and PEN chapter in San Miguel, Mexico. Also to Avery Cardoza, my innovative publisher and poker authority, and Sara Cardoza our talented associate publisher. Most especially to James Jayo, my first inspired reader and brilliant editor who is as passionate about the book as I am.

❧ 1 ❧

MEETING BOHEMIA...ESPECIALLY BALDWIN
SUMMER 1951

Dressing for Gabriel that night in the leafy Washington suburbs, I arranged an old rhinestone clip to lower the cleavage of my black crepe gown, a hand-me-down with weird wavy chiffon sleeves, and raced to the door when the bell rang.

Mother spun me around as I passed. "Where do you think you're going?" She'd confined me to quarters for two weeks for coming in loaded after a date with Gabriel. I wasn't allowed to drink.

The doorbell rang again. I dashed for the door.

Mother grabbed my arm. "You're not leaving this house with that no-good scoundrel."

Mother often slapped my face when I sassed her back, though I'd just finished my junior year at Chapel Hill. I felt it as a deep insult, which was why she did it. She pinched my arm and I jerked away. As I did, Mother slapped my face and I spun away from the blow, twirled around, and to my own amazement slapped her back in perfect rhythm.

I slapped Mother back.

We were both stunned, unable to move. I had equalled her. She'd never dare hit me again.

"The day I leave this house for good will be the happiest day of my life," I spat out.

Mother glared back with equally dependable coldness. "It can't be too soon for me." We didn't mince words, we two. Our hatred had turned so cold it burned.

Our quarrel was simple. Mother wanted me to be her, and I refused.

I marched past Dad reading in the easy chair. "See you later, Pop."

"Have a nice evening, sweetheart," he said mildly.

Leaning over, I pecked him on the forehead, greeted Gabriel on the porch, and off we went.

That night Gabriel and I ran away to New York.

৵৵৵৵

Old Kiss/Kill, I called Mother. Mother's face was so expressive that every shred of feeling that rippled through her revealed itself. Yet she thought my face too bold, too raw. "How could I have borne a daughter who doesn't look like a lady?" she asked me. She ruined her thick curly brown hair with permanents, belabored her body with girdles and garter belts and stockings and polite dresses. She never wore flat shoes. Both Mother and Dad looked excessively well bred in a way that their generation did.

Poor Mother! Still furious at not having money any longer, Mama with her hot eyes and mouth pinched with propriety. She ruled Daddy with the threat of hysteria and tried to smother me. She'd lost her father, the money, and now her eldest daughter.

Dad looked impeccable in his English suits, his scholarly high forehead and aquiline nose fit for a coin of the land. His prominent eyes emerged in startled blue innocence. Dad was playful. When I was a child, he called me "Alley-Oop, Stick stack stoop, Dominicker tin-toed, Bowlegged goop." He still called me Oop. My father, my intellectual companion and mentor.

৵৵৵৵

That night Gabriel and I ran away to New York. I ran away from Washington with Gabriel the guru mainly because he was a writer. He *told* me he was a writer. Scrawny white ghost Gabriel with his crazy black eyes and hippie beard looked like a Jesus freak, long-haired poet, and rock star. Beat, oh was he Beat.

"You'll never be an artist, Ali, till you immerse yourself in experience, squalor, and excess," drawled Gabe from his hollow El Greco face, a sublime face for suffering and madness. I thought he possessed the secret of creativity.

At Union Station I sent a night letter to my parents:

> June 25, 1951
> I'm off to N.Y. with Gabriel to seek my intellectual freedom. Will write. Don't worry. Love, Ali.

On the blue dawn train to New York, Gabe snapped his fingers. "Like that, I'll land a job on the *Times*, since I took a walk on the *Washington Post*. You can transfer to NYU for senior year."

"Where will we live?"

"We'll get a Village pad with fireplace and balcony," he squeezed my fingers, eyes lit.

I didn't like his cold hands.

We emerged in Greenwich Village in musty morning light.

"These are tenements," I said.

Gabriel hooted at my simplicity.

We landed at the San Remo where we each had two beers for breakfast.

Though the Village didn't look like Montmartre, I imagined it, hyped it with Utrillo streets, Pirandello souls, Joycean geniuses disguised in jeans, Toulouse-Lautrec saloons, and layabout ladies strolling through Max Ernst and Kirschner canvases. By nightfall that *was* the Village with its crooked cobblestones and snuggled houses, little colonial borough with old taverns and still humble stores.

San Remo at the corner of Macdougal and Bleecker was our watering hole at the center of the universe. It was desirably seedy with a plateglass view of its own hip corner. The dark mirrored bar smelled of booze. There were booths on two sides and rickety chairs by infinitesimal tables, small black and white tiles on the floor.

Above the bar in its place of honor was a photograph of our desiccated patron saint, Maxwell Bodenheim the poet. I'd read Bodenheim in my modern poetry anthology, edited by Louis Untermeyer. The beginning of "Old Age":

In me is a little painted square
Bordered by old shops with gaudy awnings.
And before the shops sit smoking, open-bloused old men,
Drinking sunlight.
The old men are my thoughts…

The walls were crammed with violent paintings, poorly done, by lesser patrons. The bartenders were rough waterfront types, maybe even junior mobsters, not slightly awed by literati. Joseph Conrad said to plunge into the "destructive element" of the city to learn. The San Remo was my existential leap to freedom.

Still, I was unprepared for my first sight of old Max Bodenheim with his crumpled little face, utterly undone by alcohol, a walking wavering ruin.

"What do you know of despair, of frenzy," Gabe laid it on me at the bar, "of the eternal pain of creation?"

Mouth agape, I watched Bodenheim who tippled over and asked me to buy one of his poems.

"Set up Max," Gabe said to the bartender at our favored bar perch, the outside corner.

"Hey, you're an ace, ace," Max toasted us. He was a dear old slob, beloved by all. Had poetry ruined him or booze? Had insistence on purity in poetry led to poverty then drink?

I took a dollar from my purse and Max pocketed it. He recited a short poem into the general din.

Everybody dressed like cowpokes or pirates, gypsies or sluts, and worked hard at seeming different. We slouched most casually, we advocated the overthrow of, we toked, we screwed. We special few hung out there by the dozens. Nobody looked clean and pure and stupid: I loved it! Nothing I'd ever do would shock these people—what a pity, what a relief—refugees like myself from the tyranny of provincial America.

We special few hung out there by the dozens.

"I have been true to thee, Cynara, in my fashion," Gabe gestured with his bottle and poured deeply into his throat. Then he borrowed the last of my money for two more.

SLEEPING WITH BAD BOYS

"See those university types," Gabe indicated two men standing nearby. "That's Philip Rahv of *Partisan Review* and Eugene O'Neill, Jr."

"Really?" They were nice looking straights in regular shirts and pants. I'd read O'Neill, Jr.'s *The Complete Greek Drama*. Here I was, afloat in a boozy rainbow-hued fishbowl of literary light. Milton Klonsky, poet and critic, asked me to live with him. Gabriel, meantime, flirted with Klonsky's girl.

Joe Gould, legendary Gould, stopped by to peddle his *Oral History of the World*. Gould was aged, alcoholic, grizzled, and more crazed than Bodenheim. He spouted gibberish and divulged the meaning of life for a free drink. Somebody sprung and he informed us grandly, "Life is a fountain."

"Life is a beer fountain," I hollered, silken fire drunk, "in a pot garden."

Gould began to yawp.

"What is he doing?"

"Gulls," said Gabe. "That's his seagull cry."

For years Gould collected drinks for his forthcoming opus to end all opuses. After his death it turned out, fittingly, that the pages were either boring or blank.

৵৵৽৽

After three days living on beer and pretzels, I was weak with hunger. Gabriel had lost interest in getting a job.

"The true artist," he informed me, "must undergo the most unbearable extremes in human experience."

Gabriel thought he spied William Burroughs. "Nope. Probably a real undertaker. Burroughs just dresses like one." Then he told me the story, one of the first everyone heard in the Village.

"Burroughs and his wife were living in Mexico. Burroughs played William Tell with his wife. She placed an apple on her head, he aimed his gun, and shot her dead."

"Jesus! Were they stoned?"

"Totally wrecked, out of it. He still likes guns."

"I hope he's on the moon."

No one was left at the bar who could put us up. We spent a night in the park, outdoors from 4 a.m. to morning huddled on a bench in Washington Square Park. Somebody had lent us a blanket. We were able to bum two doughnuts off a black guy. Then back to San Remo for a beer on Gabe's tab to staunch my hunger. Gabe seldom got hungry.

"You're such a bourgeois, Ali," he sneered.

かめ〜ゆめ

That evening at San Remo I spent in a booth chatting with a young black writer with light eyes, Jimmy, whose guppylike appearance raised ugliness to a high art. He was James Baldwin, whose first book would soon be published. His bulging eyes were a lovely light aqua, and swam with true humble artistic sensitivity. Not like Gabriel the poseur. Jimmy's words dragged behind him like a train.

At last, a real writer. I plied him with questions and he was patient. He talked about working on this first novel, which would be *Go Tell It On The Mountain*, about his experiences as a teenage storefront preacher. He'd come in from Paris to deliver a chunk to his editor.

"How can you afford to live in Paris?"

"I've been lucky with grants," said Jimmy.

I was overcome. Jimmy was talent, Gabe was a blowhard.

Jimmy examined me closely. "Would you like a hamburger?"

"My prince, would I!" I clasped my hands then blushed. "But why spend *your* money?"

"Listen, I've been up against it." Jimmy's large eyes were soothing. "I'm flush. I just got an advance."

His spaghetti and my hamburger came. "It's beautiful." I took several big bites while Jimmy watched me eat. Suddenly nausea churned inside because I was unused to food. If I didn't eat slowly, I'd get sick. I took tiny bites, chewed well, got pale, stopped. "Rest awhile."

"You've been hungry?"

He nodded.

James Baldwin told me if you have a proclivity for writing, fine, otherwise, it's hard. More people have talent than the will to sweat out the learning process. You teach yourself. In those days we didn't have graduate writing centers that spoonfed you novel construction.

"Will power is no problem," I shrugged, evidence—Gabriel—aside.

Jimmy bulged his huge eyes at that.

"Talent may be." I told Baldwin, "I was born on the banks of the only river that flows north, on a bed of Spanish moss under a live oak."

Jimmy chuckled, "You have a writer's temperament." He indicated a painter we knew. "How would you describe him?"

"He looks like a butcher disguised as a pirate."

He nodded toward a pitchblack-tressed gal.

"This is silly. She looks like the space queen of dope."

"That's how you write, sillybilly."

My head lifted with the thrill of recognition. With it came resolve, tiny green shoots, still weak, but there. Not duty but discovery, not leaden but shimmering. "Thanks, Jimmy."

"Your boyfriend, the messiah, now and then he shows up with a new disciple," Jimmy swivelled his spaghetti, "but you're the smartest." He arched a questioning brow at me.

۶-ʔ~ŝ-ŝ

At 4 a.m. closing time, Gabriel and I trudged west a long way with a handsome would-be writer named Jack Kerouac, to the apartment of a gal he said would put us up. The woman answered the door stark naked, mumbled yes, and fell back into bed before we settled on the sofa. Jack locked the door and joined her in the bedroom.

In Washington we always used Gabe's aunt's place in Cleveland Park while she was at the movies. We hadn't made out since our night at a dumpy Bleecker Street hotel, where bums sloped against the walls. Sophisticated Gabe was no match for my redneck college boyfriend, Beau. Gabriel loved literature awash with booze. Beau loved me drenched with sex. My former life seemed only a vague memory, a blur drowned in drink.

۶-ʔ~ŝ-ŝ

The next lavender dusk, I waited for Jimmy Baldwin. I could understand why he was happier in Paris. He was a target—intense, slight, willowy and black. When Jimmy came in, I went right over and captured him in his booth before the friends arrived. I adored talking to him. I could ask him stupid and obvious things, and he enlightened me, gently.

"Jimmy," I said, "it occurs to me that imagination is the ability to see what's there?"

"Without shame, without ducking."

I blushed scarlet.

Jimmy's pals came and I joined Gabe at the bar.

❧❧❧❧

My *father*! How could it be?

My own father walked into San Remo, my darling genteel daddy in his English suit. He'd traced us through Gabriel's aunt and parents. I stiffened. He wanted to throw his arms around me but didn't dare.

"We've been so worried, angel. Don't you want to come home?" Small proper Daddy looked like an Episcopal cleric, which my brother would be. He didn't belong in this nest of vipers.

"I'm happy, Dad," I lied. "Gabe's job starts next week."

"Righto," Gabe smiled on cue.

"You're thin as a rail," Dad's eyes popped with bruised innocence. "Let's get some dinner."

"I'm not hungry."

The bar bunch smirked. Parents were, of course, comic relief.

Dad begged me to come home and I refused. He pressed money on me, pled with me to get on the 8 p.m. train with him, and I got haughty.

With a gasp of grief, Dad turned abruptly and left San Remo. When he passed the plateglass window, his face was contorted by agony, plastered back in a frozen scream.

When I saw his face, I burst into tears and ran out to catch him, but he was gone. What had he done, except to be my dear affectionate father? While Mother warned me to button my lip or I'd never land a man, my father taught me the value of learning, the moral necessity of independence. For those gifts, I had slung him cold black deadly denial.

Very late I phoned home. "Dad, can you meet me at Union Station 7 p.m. tomorrow?"

❧❧❧❧❧

"Good luck, Dorian Gray," I kissed Gabriel goodbye as I slid into a cab. "So there you are," a stout prosperous businessman shouted at Gabe, hands on hips. "My god, my father," Gabe turned green. Giggling, I waved and yelled, "Goodbye, goodbye," so his father would know he had his son back.

❧❧❧❧❧

At Union Station I darted along the platform to the iron gate. I spotted my father, small and tidy in his summer pinstripe. Daddy lit up like an excited boy, his bluey-blue eyes leaping with joy.

"Daddy!" I threw my arms around him and he embraced me tightly and my tears dripped on his suit. "Oh, Daddy."

"Baby, I'm so glad you're home." Dad stooped to pick up my (nonexistent) suitcase, as he did when I came home from college. "Whoops," he laughed. We strode to the car with our arms around each other's waists.

As we rode up Massachusetts Avenue past rococo embassies, I foresaw Mother glaring at me with her terrifying intensity and whiplashing me like I was fifteen. Suddenly I went cold: I wouldn't be listening. I'd become a strong reedy Henry Moore woman, spread out and containing infinite space.

"You lost your job," said Dad.

"I'll get another one," I sighed. Every summer I worked for the money to go back to college while my gang lounged at country club pools.

"Alley-Oop, do me this favor," Dad's no-monkey-business tone. "Don't go in hollering at your mother. I persuaded her not to yell at you, not to criticize you in any way, if you'd do the same. Understood?"

"Fine, Pop," I passed it off breezily, then realized. For the first time, my father had truly stepped in between us and arranged a truce. When it mattered most, Daddy came through.

"By the by," Dad said, "the *Washington Post* has never heard of Gabriel. His aunt said he didn't work."

"That fits," I agreed.

I marched up the walk to the porch.

Behind the screen door stood Mother, my poor little mother whom I had never tolerated, in Daddy's old bathrobe and bunny slippers, looking like an old child. How often in my life there'd be Mama waiting—in a window, in a doorway, in a lobby.

"Hello, Mama," I said softly, and we embraced gingerly.

"I—I'm glad you're home safe." Mama clutched a linen hanky. She'd been crying. She cried a lot. We all did.

That was my crucible, my dark night of the soul. Evidently I had to dive into the abyss in order to rise as my own phoenix from dross. I had to break free. I had to break the mold. I passed through the valley of the shadow, and I did.

❧❧❧❧

At Chapel Hill for my senior year, I cut my hair, worked three campus jobs, refused to go out with Beau, switched my major to English, drove to the woods with Beau every Sunday noon when I couldn't hold out any longer, retaught myself to type in a week, made Phi Beta Kappa, got a scholarship to graduate school at University of Rochester, and decided to be a writer if it killed me.

❧ 2 ❦

FAMILY

"My father was richer," Mother said, "but the Denhams were aristocratic." She pushed up the tip of her nose to look snooty and giggled. I was not only Mother's scapegoat but also her confidante, being eldest girl. "You know why I married your father? Because I could control him. I couldn't control my other fiancés."

Mother had lost control of her life when she lost her father and destroyed her mother Nena's marriage. At twenty, she'd just graduated from St. Mary's in Raleigh, and come home to Jacksonville. On the downstairs phone, Mother heard a strange woman thank her father for the diamond necklace and earrings. She ran to tell her mother, Nena, who listened in. This patriarch, who slept with a gun under his pillow and a pint of whisky on his bedtable, denied he had a mistress. Then one day he didn't come home from his office. He left his family without a cent and Mother had to walk downtown to beg him for food money. Nena filed for divorce. WIFE OF LUTHER MEGGS FILES FOR DIVORCE screamed the 1922 headline in the *Jacksonville*

Journal. Luther, who was city commissioner, resigned and moved to a hotel he owned in Miami Beach with his mistress.

Once I heard this story, I began to understand Mother's impossible desire to control and her rage that she couldn't. But why did it have to land on me?

❦❦❦❦

We sat down to dinner with Limognes china and dimestore glasses, there in Washington in the late forties. Then we were treated once more to this.

Mother's famous dinner table story, neck arched, eyes gleaming, "I had four diamonds, you know. I was engaged four times."

Dad's cue: "Many dragons I had to slay."

"You were a Southern Belle, Ma." I winked at brother Palmer. She hated being called Ma.

"You *too* can be a Southern Belle." Palmer leaped up, swept me into his arms, dipped me into a bend, we swirled, and sat back down at the dinner table. We were great buddies. Sister Bunny and husband Ben and baby daughter had moved to Fort Lauderdale where he worked for his brother's plumbing supply firm.

Grandmother Nena, Mother's mother, lived with us. Sweet Nena was so gentle and shy I often held her hand at table. Nena wore her long gray white hair in a French bun on top, used a *pince-nez,* and dressed in old-fashioned pale voile and chiffon prints. It was Nena who loved me, in place of Mother.

❦❦❦❦

In the Southern houseproud competition, the old Denham house in Jacksonville was on the National Historic Register. It had a French parlor, formal parlor, sun room where everybody really sat; porte cochere, calling cards handed to the butler who placed them on a silver tray for Madame's cognizance on her return from chairing Daughters of the American Revolution or Children's Aid or Mount Vernon Ladies Association. The gold piano in the breezeway was topped by photos of Queen Marie of Romania and tiaraed and uniformed personages with ribbons crossing their chests. Grandmother Denham had been Official Hostess for Queen Marie when she visited Florida: Mamie's vaulting triumph. Mamie dominated—she did the carving. Grandfather ran the bank.

If Nena taught me love, Grandmother Mamie Denham taught me strength. "What do you intend for your life?" she asked. When I said I wanted to be a writer—she wrote poetry—she said, "You have a good brain. If you don't use a *good* brain, it rots." Mamie wore trailing gowns and Chinese pumps on tiny fat feet. "It may help you to know your grandfather Denham claims descent from the once-famous English poet, Sir John Denham." I didn't encounter him till graduate school.

Daddy's brokerage business made money in the booming twenties when skirts flounced and curls bobbed and moonshine liquor flowed and they were dancing along with Fred Astaire and sister Adele. Dad and Mom were rich. Through rich Yale classmates, who were also in the air service in World War I, Daddy himself arranged a million-dollar loan to his father's Atlantic National Bank. Daddy had flown those rickety open-cockpit planes over France.

Then came the infamous stock market crash of 1929. Daddy lost it all—his brokerage, his money, the money of his family and friends. He walked Mother down by the river and told her they had to sell the big beautiful house they'd designed and built, and become renters. They both cried.

⁂⁂⁂⁂

"No better than white trash," Mother said. Mother had gone from being spoiled rich to poor twice, with her father and now her husband. Men you had to rely on but couldn't depend on. Why didn't his rich family help out? Daddy had fallen out of favor when he called his own mother a snob. There was more show than money.

Then I came along, adding to the burden. Then Bunny and Palmer. Dad became property manager for a big national company and we moved to Coral Gables. We lost Jacksonville, Daddy lost his money, Mother lost her status, we were poor.

Mother raged at me, ignored Bunny, and doted on Palmer, her baby boy. I was a nuisance, the scapegoat.

ALICE DENHAM

Swat, she hit me in fury with the bamboo switch. She made me go out into the yard and break off the switch. If the bamboo wasn't thick enough, I had to go get another. I almost just wandered away in the dark. Bunny and Palmer wailed as soon as they saw the bamboo in the air and never got hit. I'd look Mother in the eye and refuse to cry.

"I don't care if you kill me," I said, "I won't cry."

This made Mother furious. She hit me harder. It was a contest of wills and I would not give in. This made her feel she was cruel, and she hated me for it. I went to my room, wounded, and wept buckets. Nena came in and held my hand.

"Your mother is angry—at the world," said Nena.

When I got too old to spank, she began slapping me hard across the face. She meant to humble me. It didn't work. It infuriated me.

⁂

When we moved to Washington after World War II for Daddy's Federal Housing Administration job, we lived in a furnished rental house, smaller than any previous, but in the best school district. Trees arched over our block like a cathedral. Beyond Westmoreland Circle were the Maryland woods we kids explored.

The good furniture, including the gold loveseat, was lost to the storage company because we couldn't afford to have it shipped up. Mother waved away the furniture. *Things* didn't mean much to her. Money was Status. She had no interest in knowing any living soul in the bureaucratic middle class of Northwest Washington.

❧ 3 ❧

THE REAL JIMMY DEAN
FALL 1952 - FALL 1953

The one I came to know best and loved best—the one who moved me—was James Dean.

Before graduate school, I visited my old friend, actress Christine White, an Eva Marie Saint lookalike, who was also from Washington, on far East 82nd Street. I visited Chris in New York to delay *my* performance anxiety. I was the only English graduate student on scholarship at U. of Rochester who was not Ivy League. Heading for the frozen North, the North where all Southerners hear *they* are smarter than we are.

❧❧❧❧

We first met when Jimmy and Chris were practicing for their Actors Studio audition at Chris's apartment. Actors Studio, sacred hall of Method Acting, taught Stanislavsky immersion, whereby actors learn to live their roles. All the big stars were Actors Studio—Marlon Brando, Montgomery Clift, Julie Harris,

Geraldine Page, Tony Franciosa, Shelley Winters, Paul Newman, Joanne Woodward, Gena Rowlands, John Cassavetes, director Elia Kazan: the crème.

"Why did you pick this kid to audition with?" I asked Christine. "He doesn't seem able to remember lines."

"Yes, he can. I hope." Chris seemed scattered.

This Jimmy boy looked like an adolescent, like my kid brother, with surprising maturity and great swaths of infantile petulance. He wouldn't rehearse. He horsed around. Jimmy Dean was short, five foot six, with a brown-blond pompadour poufed way too high to add height, well-built and limber as spaghetti, wearing the thickest glasses I'd ever seen. His regular features were perfectly proportioned but utterly unexceptional. You'd pass him on the street without a glance.

Achieving Actors Studio was equivalent to getting a first-rate literary agent. You were with insiders with contacts. Chris and Jimmy were visibly nervous. It meant too much to them.

Rather than Shaw or Ibsen, they were using a scene Chris wrote about a boy and girl who meet on a deserted beach. Distrust and attraction pull between them, till he asks her to his cabin and she streams off into the night. They practiced at Chris's apartment and at Jimmy's place. They tried the scene on agent Jane Deacy who handled them both at the Schurr Agency. "Work on it," she'd said noncommittally.

"Can he act?" I whispered to Chris.

"They say so," she mouthed back. "Let's run through again, Jim."

Ignoring her, Jimmy stuck something in his mouth to pretend to chaw and rared back on his elbows, detaching himself and watching me. Trying to look rangy and loose only made him look smaller.

"Southern Belle, eh, Miss Alice?"

"Ding-a-ling," I declared and rared back too.

Jimmy tittered and danced around, sloped his shoulders and flexed, bent his head one way then the other, then laid his head practically on my shoulder, his eyes on me like a trust. He seemed very familiar, like somebody, like Marlon Brando's little brother.

"You should play Stanley in *Streetcar*," I arced a brow. "You're imitating Brando."

Jimmy executed a bad ballet twirl then blushed. "You know Marlon?"

"I barely know where the corner is." Uptown was new to me.

Jimmy ruffled his hair, pouting. "Probably because I admire him so much. He's my idol."

"Everybody knows Marlon," Chris said, losing patience. "Let's go, Jim."

They completed about three interchanges then Jimmy mouthed his lines, then got bored and wandered the apartment.

Pushing him out of the bedroom, I dressed in a light blue linen sheath dress and heels, to visit my rich Aunt Sara and Uncle Lingan, who lived in California but kept an apartment at the Sherry-Netherland. As I emerged, he spun around.

"Wow, are you stacked," said Jimmy. "Want to watch our audition?"

"Sure."

We arranged that I'd go with them and they'd check out a door I could crack open, and observe.

"Good luck, Chris," I said pointedly.

❧❧❧❧

At Actors Studio we waited with other hopefuls mumbling lines. I thought how dauntingly opposite this dark drafty corridor was from the spotlit magic of the stage. Rather like the distance between my graduate scholarship and a master's degree. Right before they called out, "Dean," Jimmy dashed downstairs for a beer, greatly agitated. At wit's end, Chris put their names down under hers, White.

"Oh, he'll be back," I patted her, wondering.

The judges were Actors Studio founders, director Elia Kazan and producer Cheryl Crawford, and mentor-teacher Lee Strasberg, who sat dead center in the unlit first balcony. Jimmy returned calmed down and escorted me to a nearby door which we opened warily. The name "White" was shouted, they ducked out, and Jimmy almost tumbled onto the stage in his eager rush.

As the scene was original, Chris and Jimmy hoped for credit on that score. Chris's scene was naive and touching, filled with youthful angst and desperation.

Jimmy astonished me. He was marvelous, inventive, communicative, and emotionally true.

Jimmy appeared to be the kind of actor who saves it for performance, walks it through but doesn't let out the passion till the moment, then lays it on other performers like an eruptive improvisation based on the script but without practiced cues. He made Chris struggle and seem rather flat. Hardly fair. He controlled the scene and seemed far superior by comparison. Half the Marlon playacting fell away and James Dean blossomed—vulnerable, sympathetic, intense, and young. I was fascinated. His transformation made me shiver with thrill, and feel at the same time that I was rising within my own body.

I had to get to know this young man with the plain name. This James Dean possessed the creativity I sought like manna. Could I imbibe it from him?

❧❧❧❧

Afterward we went to Jimmy's dumpy digs which he shared with Dizzy the horse-faced dancer, as he called her. Way up the Upper West Side we tunneled along on the subway to the 70s. The hallways were tiled like a giant bathroom and the tenants looked like worn blankets.

"How'd you do?" It was Diz at the door, excited.

"Great," I answered. "They really did."

"Pray," said Chris.

"How's my horse-faced amour?" teased Jim.

We entered a large square grungy room with a crumbling dusty wood floor, graced by a couple of mattresses. It smelled musty, like an unused storeroom.

"Flop," invited Jimmy and we opened our six-pack.

By now I was so used to the Greek Revival charm of colleges that it didn't occur to me I'd be living in a room very much like this one when I came to Manhattan myself. Chris's one-bedroom was a palace compared to this dump.

Among the chosen few accepted by Actors Studio were James Dean and Christine White.

❧❧❧❧

It was late 1953 when Jimmy Dean took me to dinner at his favorite restaurant, Jerry's Tavern on Sixth Avenue at 54th. A few blocks away on West 55th, I now lived in my own dear old dump of a studio. Furnished, weekly linens, in an old brownstone. I now had my master's degree. My MA, plus a token, enabled me to model, once I let my hair grow long again.

Jerry's had checked tablecloths and candles dripping over Chianti bottles, and a waiter named Louis who was fond of Jimmy. When Louis saw Jimmy, he put on Beethoven and Jimmy whistled along. We had linguini with clam sauce—lots of real clams—and red wine. Antipasto to begin. Dining out was the ultimate wonder of Manhattan.

We were both a year older. Had Jimmy gained maturity? Now he seemed to have a noble head on a short body, and looked something like my father must have when young. A statesman's head, as Dad's secretaries said; he should be tall. The same staunch hurt look in the eye, as if every time he stood beside a woman, she looked down, not up. Not me, of course, but I was as tall as Jimmy in heels. His high forehead with the lofty pompadour and thick glasses made him look studious. But he had devilish eyes and a billygoat cackle.

"How come you're modeling?" Jimmy asked. "You got your MA, right?"

"Yep. I wrote my thesis on T. S. Eliot's poetic dramas—his verse plays judged by his own dramatic criticism." I was proud of that.

"Wow! How'd he come out?"

"Not too well," I laughed. "Too talky, not enough action."

"Then, why—?"

"Jimmy, I can't get my foot in. Not with publishers or ad agencies or radio or TV. Or magazines. I wrote copy for NBC in Las Vegas when I got my divorce last summer."

"What was it *like* in Vegas?"

"Like a neon campfire on the moon, with all the palefaces circling the slots."

"Great line!"

"It was wild—the hoods and Hollywood." I didn't know Jimmy well enough to tell him about the CBS announcer, the family man who almost strangled me to death because I wouldn't kiss him. Jimmy knew about my graduate school marriage and divorce from Chris White. I couldn't talk about it yet, with anyone.

"NBC—you'd think that would count."

"They want *men*. When I say I don't have shorthand, they say no." As my doting father had trained me for independence—over Mother's objections—job discrimination astounded me. I took it as personal rejection. I always felt if I were *better* I could move that eight-ball the size of a planet that blocked women's way. "At Chapel Hill, they warned us to take shorthand so we could be secretaries." I'd refused the insult.

HELP WANTED was separated into male and female in those days. Guess where the good jobs were? My education didn't matter. If I were local, if I'd gone to school here, I'd probably have contacts. But all I had were the want ads and the phone book.

"Modeling is better," said Jimmy.

"It's faster. I have time to write."

I made light of it because I didn't want Jimmy to know how embarrassed and disappointed I was that I couldn't get a decent job. All my fine education—the three scholarships, the endless college jobs, the milkshake for lunch. I was hungry but I couldn't spare more than twenty cents for lunch. Didn't graduate school qualify me for the professional world? Besides writing copy for the NBC in Las Vegas, I had an on-air interview show. But what did New York care about my two months in the desert West?

Daddy had said he could get me a good government job in Washington, where my Master's would matter and I could advance. But no, I had to make it in Manhattan. Mother saved a long letter I wrote home about how hard I was trying to land a job. I had failed my parents and myself. I didn't want the University of Rochester to know I'd failed. I should've written Dr. Katherine Koller, English department head, the *only* woman in the department, and asked if any of them knew anyone here who could help me. But I was ashamed.

"Your hair looks great red."

My newly red hair, formerly brown, did bring out my green eyes. "You approve?"

"I do."

Jimmy told me the TV dramas he'd been in—*Kraft Theater, Danger, U.S. Steel Hour, Robert Montgomery Presents*, numerous others. Occasionally I did walk-ons and one-liners on these shows, in that lost age of worthy live TV drama.

"I don't have a set," I said.

"Me, either," giggled Jimmy. "But but but," he paused, "I also had a juvenile lead on Broadway!"

"No!"

"Yes, in a play called *See the Jaguar* that didn't last."

"Still. I'm impressed. You're moving right along." I felt easy with Jimmy. But it was hard not to be jealous. It seemed so simple for him. But that was stupid. I wasn't an actor. "What did you play?"

"A demented youth in a cage."

"Played yourself, eh?" I cracked.

"Turn profile."

I did.

"Your best feature is your nose," Jimmy inspected me.

"Ha, with this bump? Photographers complain they have to shoot around it."

"That's a high ridge, aristocratic."

"My father's nose. They tell me to get a nose job, but I won't."

"I hate my nose, short and straight." Jimmy showed me his perfect profile.

"Want to trade?"

"Men should have strong noses," said Jimmy. I tended to agree with him. He fingered the bridge of my nose, "Very fine."

Then I remembered Jimmy's idol, Marlon Brando's great broke beak.

We talked shop. What do you think of Camus? Do you like Sartre's *No Exit*? You should read *Intimacy* and *Nausea*. What about Tennessee? He sounds like home to me. We both loved Williams. I think most of O'Neill is boring. So do I. *Salesman* is fine but *The Crucible* is even better. Have you read Flannery O'Connor? Virginia Woolf is unearthly.

How I envied his pitch of dedication. I ached to absorb his creativity. I saw glimmerings, perceivings, like bright fast fish that slithered away as I reached for them.

"How do you *act*?"

"You get inside the character and feel it—how does he think, what does he want, how does he move, act toward others?"

Jimmy loved to talk acting, elbow on table, fingers ruffling his pompadour. "Which is most important?"

"What does he want?"

"Right."

"Sounds like a story I'm working on," I flushed. Four drafts later this was the story the hot new literary review, *Discovery*, would buy.

"Show it to me." Jimmy sloshed ruby red into my glass. "Acting, writing, it's the same—you act it onto the page and I lift it off."

❧❧❧❧

Up flights and flights to Jimmy's top floor studio in a West 68th Street brownstone. Jimmy and Dizzy Sheridan hadn't been together for a year or so. Jimmy put Beethoven on the record player as I gazed out the porthole windows at black pinhole night, small lights in invisibly shaped buildings across the street. Jimmy's place spilled over with books and records as mine did. We had the same music—classical, bebop, African tribal and Latin. A matador's cape and horns adorned the wall.

"Another aficionado, I see." Papa Hemingway had driven New York *corrida* crazy. *The Sun Also Rises* had made Spanish calvados as exotic as French pernod. *Death in the Afternoon*, about the fatal goring of Manolete, had been republished in 1952. *Life* magazine ran photos of famous Spanish matadors Dominquin and Ordonez in action and Ernesto reported on their *corridas*. Classes in Caping were so popular that people chose from dozens of ads in the *Village Voice*.

Jimmy pulled out Carson McCullers's novel, *The Heart Is a Lonely Hunter*, which was a mutual favorite. We opened it and read parts we liked. That he liked women writers endeared him to me.

Before long we tumbled into each other's arms easily, without haste, tasting and feeling. Jimmy had smooth baby-smelling rosy white skin with very little hair except for the blondish-brown pad around his privates. He was lightly muscled, his high school sports muscles turning into longer slimmer dance muscles because he studied ballet. Jimmy smelled like vanilla.

"You're so huge for a small girl," he said. Jimmy was a tit man and he loved to nuzzle. As a tit lady, my ravenous pair loved it back. We fingered and tugged. Then went to the core of the plot, the confrontation that twisted with escalating tension to the gory grinding climax. Me first, he was skilled. Satisfied, we folded together briefly.

I never thought of sleeping with a man as starting an affair. I was testing, testing. Checking out his priapic prowess, his real "feel" toward me and sex and women. If he was narcissistic and only interested in coming, forget him. Jimmy Dean was tender and considerate. We were lusty; we fit. His dimensions were neither disappointing nor thrilling. They were average, perhaps the only thing about him that was.

We cuddled up together like the kids we were and slept till noon.

Jimmy Dean was still more like a boy than a man. Women weren't panting to go to bed with Jimmy. He made out all right but he was no ladies' man. He didn't excite desire when he entered a room. Like Marlon did. It was, "Hey, Jimbo, what's up?"

❧❧❧❧

Back at Jerry's Tavern for lunch, Jimmy Dean was manic. Last night he was vulnerable, a tender friend, but today he was a sardonic wiseass. He annoyed me so I ordered shrimp fra diavolo because it sounded fiery. Jimmy was off in his own world, making faces, talking to the past.

"Are you my mother?" Jimmy asked, rared back in trance, hot-eyed and haunted. "You are, I think. You look like her. I lost her, you know, when I was only nine, and I still miss her. I've wanted my mother ever since." He pushed back his wavy pompadour, eyes wary and tormented. "Truth is, I've never forgiven her for it."

"For dying?"

"Yeah, that." Jimmy squeezed his fists hard, then pounded the table again and again, so that people stared. Jimmy couldn't bear to go unnoticed. "My mother died, and left me behind. She had no right to do that." He glared at me for vindication.

"You had your father, Jimmy."

"You think so?" He tossed his head, curled his lip, and moaned. "I didn't. But it's not the same."

"I doubt your mother wanted to go, Jimmy."

"Don't you understand?" Jimmy rose in his seat. "I *am* my mother, my mother is me."

I folded my arms, sat back, and stared at him. "You were lucky, Jimmy. Your mother loved you. Mine didn't." Jimmy saw I was tired of it. He squirmed and guffawed as if he'd done a great put-on, heeheehawhaw. But I knew he meant it, half meant it, tried it on, used it as a release all at once, as actors do. As writers do. That homeless lost boy appealed with sexual tenderness to the screen.

"You're a wicked boy, Jimbo."

"Oh, Mommy, I am," he giggled. He loved to playact.

After that when he phoned, he'd tease, "Hey there, Mommy."

೭ೕ೭ೕ೭ೕ೭ೕ

James Dean was canny, unusually so for his age, a sense that developed early, perhaps, because he was shifted about so. When his mother died of breast cancer, Jimmy's father stayed with his job in Los Angeles. Nine-year-old Jimmy went back with his mother's coffin to Indiana with his grandparents. He was raised by his aunt and uncle in Fairmount, a small town near the grandparents' farm. He didn't see his father again till he went west to UCLA and met his new stepmother. His education was spotty—a bit of UCLA, a bit of theater arts, classes with actor James Whitmore. Apartments shared with other hopefuls, before long commercials and bit parts.

Jimmy had street smarts. He knew how to ingratiate himself with people who'd give him a leg up, help his career. He headed for New York with TV producer Rogers Brackett. Many young Hollywood hopefuls have to pay with sexual favors. Was Jimmy an exception? Possibly he didn't mind. Jimmy was experimental. But Jimmy was *not* gay.

His fast rise came because he was just plain good. Jimmy was acutely perceptive—finely tuned—and able to externalize emotion fluently and with absolute conviction. T. S. Eliot called externalizing emotion in poetic images the objective correlative. Actors call it the Method.

Still, I was amazed when Jimmy got a lead in *The Immoralist*, based on Andre Gide's novel, which was headed for Broadway. His second Broadway play, imagine!

೪೪೪

James Dean was the first really creative artistic boy I ever got to know well. Jimmy let it all hang out, like I did. He was willing to talk about art. We talked earnestly about creativity. What was it? I longed to know, fearing it was a magic secret I didn't possess. It was so fine to have a buddy who wasn't macho.

Jimmy Dean was, in a sense, a literary mentor because he taught me creativity wasn't magic. You thought it through. You delved to discover. You immersed yourself in your character—your story—which became deeper and more complex as its outer shells fell away. You didn't rest till you had it. Then you relaxed, forgot about it, and it took shape.

"I am my mother, my mother is me." I kept hearing that line in my head after he died.

ᴁ 4 ᴂ

JAMES DEAN THE STAR
WINTER 1954

Jimmy Dean phoned and invited me to *The Immoralist*, the adaptation of Gide by Ruth and Augustus Goetz. In *The Immoralist*, Jimmy played Bachir, the decadent Arab boy who tempts the husband (Louis Jourdan) away from his wife (Geraldine Page) on their honeymoon. Thus, in February 1954 homosexuality was confronted on Broadway.

Jimmy was so tempting that he won the Antoinette Perry award—the Tony—and the Daniel Blum award as most promising newcomer for the year.

"How's tonight?" Jimmy asked.

"Love to! I've been dying to see you in that play."

"No, I'm *taking* you."

"You mean, I come backstage afterward?"

"No," said Jimmy, "I mean, we sit out front."

"How—?"

"I quit."

"Quit? But you just won the jackpot, Jimmy." I was disappointed. "But I want to see *you* in it, Jimbo."

Jimmy cackled, "I just won a bigger jackpot."

"Meaning—?"

"I'll tell you tonight."

Jimmy raced up the two flights then sauntered into my studio, one humble room like his.

"*How* big a jackpot?" I said, posing in my little black cocktail dress and pearls.

Jimmy zoomed like a racecar, spread his arms into a diving plane that toppled me onto the bed, then hollered like a banshee. "I got it, I got it!"

"Do tell."

"Gadge just offered me the lead in *East of Eden*. I'm gonna be in the movies!"

"Wow!" Gadge, everybody knew, was Elia Kazan, famous director who made a star of Brando in *Streetcar* and *On the Waterfront*.

"It's based on John Steinbeck's novel. Father-son conflict."

"Jimbo, you're going to be a movie star!"

❧❧❧❧

We sat down front and center so Jimmy could check out his replacement's performance. Would anyone recognize him as the young Arab Bachir in his unadorned face? Without makeup?

"That's what they wanted me to do," Jimmy stage whispered. "Ham it up, for laughs. I said no."

According to reviews, Jimmy had been intense, devious, fascinating.

Several people nearby looked him over and said, "I think that's—" but subsided.

"What do you think of Bachir?"

"I think Geraldine Page is marvelous."

Afterward we went backstage where he introduced me to Louis Jourdan and that sublime actress, Geraldine Page, who was a freckled blue-eyed blonde, tall and bosomy. She radiated kindness. Gerry and Jimmy seemed to be buddies. He squatted down beside her dressing table and told her how to improve her performance.

"You lost concentration here," Jimmy said, and at another place, "you watched Louis when you should've turned to the threat, Bachir."

I was astounded that *she* listened to *him*. Young as he was, Jimmy had a good reputation among actors.

※※※※

We went back to Jimmy's place, in case Gadge called. Jimmy showed me his Bachir stills from the show.

"You photograph great, even in Arab makeup. I hate all the makeup I wear as a model."

"The thing about makeup," Jimmy said, "at first, it feels awful. Then after about an hour, your face adjusts to it and you feel natural."

"Only enhanced."

"Yeah."

"You photograph better than you look," I said.

"So do you." Jimmy had checked out my latest model shots.

"That's what photographers tell me. Aren't we lucky?" No one glanced at me on the street unless I sallied forth in full makeup regalia.

"Good bones, babe."

We had a couple of drinks then fell into bed. Jimmy and I were sexual friends. I've read he dropped gals after one-nighters. He never dropped me. Perhaps because he never had to pick me up. I never fell in love with Jimmy. He was never in love with me. We were compadres, soulmates, incestuous brother and sister.

In the middle of the night I told Jimmy about the middle-class man who tried to kill me. Jimmy was the only man I ever told, because he wasn't macho. I was afraid it would incite other men, make them flare up, because society said in those days that women were masochists, asking for it.

> I met him in Las Vegas at our NBC station party. He was a CBS announcer, a small thin fellow. We went out to dinner with another couple then he drove me to my car on the access road between the station and the Thunderbird Hotel. His hand, dawdling along the top of the seat, moved idly up and down my neck. I sat

forward to lose it politely. When he tried to kiss me, I brushed him off inattentively. And he strangled me.

I almost laughed in disbelief but his fingers choked it off. His steel hands squeezed my neck. His fingers were like steel cables tightening and I couldn't pry up even the tip of one. I looked desperately into his eyes—wide open, staring straight at me—and knew he didn't see me. He stretched his body away from me with his arms stretched way out in front, so I couldn't touch him.

I must've blacked out because when I came to, he had my head crammed under the steering wheel, face up, his hands choking tighter, harder, pressing in. I struggled till my head was up. Suddenly I knew I was fading. In less than thirty seconds he'd succeed and I would die. Fury possessed me and I went wild. Like a hooked fish pulling the boat about, I thrashed and kicked in aimless rage till I toppled him over and I was back on my side of the car, he stuffing my head into the passenger seat.. I kicked frantically, ferociously into the air till the hard toes of my high heels broke his windshield.

We both heard the windshield crack. He loosened his hands and blinked like somebody waking up. "Alice, I'm sorry—I didn't mean—"

Chunks of glass were stuck in my legs as I jumped out of his car. I limped into the hotel's back entrance. My boss and his wife took me to the doctor. The doctor yanked glass out of my legs and staunched the bleeding. He felt my neck carefully and said I'd have the world's worst sore throat.

My boss begged me not to go to the cops. It would hurt the station's reputation. They'd think I was a slut who'd let him go so far, then cut him off. Exactly what I had always assumed when I read about attacks in the paper.

A blurry little woman appeared at the station the next day. It turned out my attacker had a wife. When I told her I would sue, she groaned and begged me, "Oh my God, you can't do that. We have three kids to feed. If they know at CBS, he'll be out. It's happened before. He'll lose this job and where'll we be?" Her eyes swam with tears.

"He's done this before?"

She hung her head, "Yes, yes. He doesn't mean it, he just can't help it."

"Christ, woman, he ought to be in a mental hospital. How can you live with him?"

"He's all I've got." My lawyer asked for five hundred dollars, my attacker offered three hundred dollars. That poor woman's face. I told my lawyer to accept three hundred.

That was when I realized a man could kill me.

Jimmy held me, hugged me, as I cried wildly like a child. Letting someone else into it, at last. For several years, the strangler became a man deep in the night under my bed, rocking the bed just enough for me to be *sure* he'd reach up and grab me.

❧❧❧❧

My affectionate, witty, gentlemanly father did not possess violence in his nature. Mother did. But I knew she could no longer injure me physically. But men were strong enough to kill women with their hands. I absorbed the bitter truth all women learn sooner or later. I had thought I was safe with men I knew, men I dated, men on the streets. But I was not equal in the world's streets and blissful hills, in open spaces where I liked to roam.

Every time I went to Central Park and reclined against a rock, men gathered and watched, each alone watching. I couldn't relax, I couldn't read without that small nagging fear. I had to watch where they were, each man. When my head was in my book, several would move forward a couple of feet. Finally I'd give up and walk home, furious that I had no real freedom.

❧❧❧❧

I didn't think Hollywood would go to Jimmy's head. He didn't have that much respect for it. *His* veneration was for Marlon and Gadge and Tennessee.

Next morning when I awoke around eleven, Jimmy was on the phone.

"Marlon, hello Marlon, this is James Dean."

Jimmy paused and I perked up my ears.

"Marlon, did you see *The Immoralist*? What did you think?" Jimmy waited, and all I heard was silence.

"Marlon, did you know Gadge offered me the lead in *East of Eden*? I wondered if you could give me some pointers," Jimmy paused, "um, on Gadge, you know?"

Still, silence.

Jimmy's voice got thick. "Marlon, please say something. I know you're there. I hear you breathing." Jimmy sounded like he was going to cry. "Why won't you talk to me, Marlon? Why won't you ever talk to me?"

Jimmy sounded exactly like me begging my ex to love me, on my knees, nose in the dust. Neither of us should've begged.

Jimmy said loudly to me, "Marlon's on the line but he won't talk to me." Jimmy handed me the phone.

"Hello, Marlon," I said, hardly believing I was speaking to the vaunted Brando. I did hear breathing. "Your spiritual father doesn't want to claim you," I said, hoping that would elicit a response, but the breathing remained steady. Shrugging, I handed the receiver back to Jimmy.

"Okay, Marlon, I'm going to hang up now. Sorry I bothered you." Jimmy rolled his head back and around on his neck, a la Brando. "If he only knew how much it means to me."

"Maybe he thinks you imitate him, and he doesn't like it," I suggested.

"He's my idol," Jimmy wiped his eyes with his fist, like a kid.

❧❧❧❧

Before Jimmy flew to Hollywood, I introduced him to my favorite bistro, the Brittany, on Ninth Avenue in the 50s. It was funky French and cheap, but then living was cheap. Dining out was cheap, wine was cheap, rents were cheap.

"I'll have coq au vin and you have boeuf bourgignon," I said. These sophisticated French names improved the flavor.

"Why not?" said Jimbo.

"One night here I sat next to movie star Constance Bennett," I said.

"What did she look like?"

"Old and unhappy."

"Lenny got the music," he said. Jimmy had introduced his special buddy, our pal, composer Leonard Rosenman, to Gadge, who'd commissioned him to do the music for *East of Eden*. Lenny would also do the score for *Rebel Without A Cause*.

"Wonderful, he deserves it." I paused for effect. "Remember that story I showed you, "The Deal?" The editor of *Discovery* phoned. And asked to buy it. *Asked*, imagine!"

"Great," said Jimmy. "You can write."

I was excited, "At least, there's hope."

We were on our way to celebrate at Lenny's but we stopped downtown at Louie's Tavern for Dizzy the dancer and actress Chris White. Everybody hung out at Louie's, down in the dank light of a half basement right on Sheridan Square. This secret underground was inhabited by actors, as it was next to Circle in the Square, and by writers, as a halfway pond between the San Remo and White Horse watering holes.

In those fabled fifties days, the arts overlapped. Writers went to the Cedar on University to gas with Abstract Expressionists de Kooning and Pollock. At parties painters danced, writers crossed verbal sabres, actors preened and tried out personae. Norman Mailer dropped in Louie's now and then as did Jimmy Baldwin. Actors Studio fell by. I met Ben Gazzara and Steve McQueen and Joanne Woodward and Ralph Meeker and Marty Landau there through Jimmy and Chris White. The world was smaller. There were not too many of us to mix.

At his big loft, Lenny pounded the ivories and we all got bombed to celebrate their success. Lenny and Jimmy were the same small stature, though Lenny was leaner, less muscled, and wore a huge shock of thick black hair. We sang dirty blues and danced fake flamenco. Instead of a conga line pass-through, we played matador and *toro*.

Next noon Jimmy left my place and I watched him bolt to Eighth Avenue to walk home. Jimmy was forever bolting and dashing and looping and turning, from studying dance. He turned to wave, a slim fellow with straw-colored hair and sharp features, in khaki pants and white T-shirt and windbreaker, like everybody else, fading into the crowd.

❧ 5 ❧

JIMMY BECOMES MYTH
SPRING 1954 - FALL 1955

After shooting *East of Eden,* when he flew back briefly to New York, Jimmy told me he was in love with Pier Angeli, soulful young Italian actress with the ethereal Renaissance face of a Botticelli. His Madonna, his angel. Pier Angeli was Hollywood's latest European import, with a difference. She wasn't a sex bomb, she was virginal purity. Her overpowering mother accompanied her whenever she met the press. Pier was only eighteen, shy as a young nun, with glorious dark eyes suffused with feeling.

"It's the first time for me," Jimbo blushed, "that I've ever been truly in love." His eyes, often so troubled, danced with simple joy. "Her innocence, her beauty. . ." he sighed, in awe.

"I'm thrilled for you, Jimmy," I said. "It's not easy to—love someone." As I'd loved and lost, I knew.

"She loves *me*," he said, as if this were a major miracle. Jimmy was so enthralled with Pier he was transformed. He glowed with a crystalline light, a deeper awareness of life. He seemed more serious, more man and less boy.

"Love." My eyes watered. The glimmer in Jimmy's eyes reminded me of how I'd felt at first, as the white light of discovery opened me to the ferocious intimacy of love that I'd always known existed and only now found. "I thought it would never end, hoho." I laughed raucously but tears erupted. Jimmy hugged me tight.

I told Jimmy about my ex who was a dynamo. "He played Beethoven on the piano, skied off the high jump at Lake Placid, wrote short stories and edited the literary review at U. of Rochester, got a sculpture scholarship to art school in Michigan, and left me for a docile goddess who modeled there. He rescued her from her husband, was his way of putting it. I begged him to come back, I'm ashamed to say." Pleading on my hind legs after crumbs, shrinking with damp dog cringing. I lost his respect and my own. "He had everything except the desire to love me."

"No, he had accomplishments," said Jim, "which didn't include the ability to love."

"Thanks, Jimbo."

Carlos and I were married in late winter of 1953 by a judge friend of his father, a Rochester lawyer. He moved into my room at the dorm where I was assistant housemother. I had a separate entrance. Carlos typed half my thesis. As he was a senior and I a scholarship grad student, I hid our marriage from the English department for fear they'd think I was wasting time on romance. When I took Carlos home to meet my family, Mother said, "He's handsome. But he's still a boy." We were both twenty. "Mama, he's Byronic and romantic," I laughed, "and he adores me."

My past was a long-term illness I had to cure. I suffered the constant pain of inferiority and unworthiness. My ego—my very useful protective ego—had been blasted away. I was struggling to recover by analyzing the loss of my first love, in my cathartic novel. I routinely took notes on the marvelous and horrid in our marriage, to try to understand it. As I read them over, I began to wonder if he was really so grand or was I simply obsessed? I wanted Carlos but did I really want to be married? Being a wife, a little wifey, revolted me.

"Later, Jimmy, he left *her* and asked me not to divorce him. To protect him from his attraction to women." Jimmy snickered. "At least, I've got my own name back."

We didn't hop into bed. Neither of us wanted to violate his newfound love.

Jimmy flew back for the summer with Pier. Pier was reputedly virginal, so possibly Jimmy was her first. But in the *mano a mano* between rebellious Jimmy and Pier's protective Catholic mother, he lost out. In fall 1954 Pier Angeli married pop singer Vic Damone, more to Mama's liking. I was shocked that this evidently sensitive young starlet, as finely tuned as Jimmy, would accept such an ordinary fate.

Jimmy lost his great love, just as I had.

Jimmy, rather more sardonic and savage and hurt, returned to New York till shooting began in March 1955 on *Rebel Without A Cause*.

When Jimmy left Manhattan, it was the last time as an unknown. In April 1955 *East of Eden* was released to tumultuous public acclaim that astounded the reviewers. Jimmy became an overnight sensation, an international movie star.

SPRING 1955

In *East of Eden*, with its Cain and Abel rivalry for the father's love, Jimmy was no longer his plain self. As Cal/Cain, he looked glamorous, much younger, then in tense scenes older than he really was. Handsomer, tormented, sensual, vulnerable, and I realized the camera picks up nuances that move over the face so fast we react to them in real life without seeing them, without awareness of what each change looks like. On film, his head didn't seem too big for his body height. In scenes with Julie Harris and Raymond Massey, Jimmy had perfect emotional pitch.

Some say he *created* the disgruntled adolescent of the Age of Affluence who wanted love, respect and freedom, not success. *Rebel Without A Cause* reinforced this, with its tragic parallel of the chicken run in the car and Jimmy's car crash death. Every woman and man I know who was young then or in the next decade or two loved Jimmy, "who spoke for me."

As for imitating Marlon, it didn't come out that way. Jimmy seemed more *real*. Marlon was stagey. You watched Marlon play a role brilliantly, but you didn't watch the character. James Dean and Montgomery Clift played the character. To me, they were finer actors. All three, like Marilyn Monroe, had that burning focus that rivets attention. In the literary realm, that star quality belonged to Norman Mailer because he demanded it, and J. D. Salinger because he refused it, and later Jack Kerouac, flogged by Allen Ginsberg, PR creator of the Beats.

I left the theatre streaming with pride. I felt as if my own brother, my favorite boy cousin, had proved himself, had performed Shostakovich on his Stradivarius with utter purity and delicacy.

In spring 1955 my first story, "The Deal," was published in *Discovery*. It made me a novice artist among artists, I hoped, not a mere model.

When Jimmy was in town for a fast turnaround between *Rebel* and shooting *Giant* in Texas, he phoned. Jimmy shot *Rebel* in spring 1955 and *Giant* that summer.

"Can't see you," Jimmy sounded exhausted. "No time."

"Come by for two seconds," I insisted. "Something I *have* to give you."

Jimmy raced up the stairs, and hugged me onto the bed. "No time," he cackled, bounced to his feet.

"My story!" I had to validate myself. I handed him a copy of the blue *Discovery* paperback with writers names in Piet Mondrian squares on the cover.

"Great, babe." Jimmy turned it back and forth, held my chin and kissed me lightly on the lips. "So long," he leaped downstairs.

"So long, star," I teased.

That was the last time I ever saw James Dean.

☙☙☙☙

Jimmy was the first adolescent antihero of the Cold War that daunted the young with its atom bomb mentality. These were McCarthy red-baiting, Hollywood blacklisting days. If you thought air-raid practice portentous or the Russian bomb a threat to get military appropriations out of Congress, you were suspected of Communist leanings.

In the fifties—outside Bohemia—we ladygirls were supposed to be virgins. Mailer got in trouble for using the word *fug* for you-know-what. Senator McCarthy pointed a finger and a person's reputation and work were thrust away. Abortion was not only illegal but you couldn't utter the word.

These words you could *not* say: sex for sex (except as opposite sex), homosexual, lesbian, gay, vagina, penis, pussy, prick, cunt, cock, breast, butt, navel, orgasm, menstruation, rape, menopause, whore, damn, hell, and, of course, shit, ass, fuck. But we said them anyway.

Living together was living in sin. There were no single mothers, only fallen women with illegitimate children. Women were girls. Women like me who liked sex were sluts and nymphomaniacs. Women were arrested on beaches for wearing bikinis. As a pinup model, I posed in bikini panties that covered more than today's underwear.

During college if I had told my parents that I was pregnant, they'd have kicked me out of the house in disgrace. I was more terrified of my parents than of losing my life. So I endured a painful illegal abortion, the first of three. Parents were God, marriage the only option for girls, breadwinning for boys. Authority ruled.

That's why Jimmy made such an impact. *He was all of us.* The causes for rebellion were legion.

☙☙☙☙

My first foreign adventure, I spent the summer of 1955 writing in San Miguel de Allende in the cool Sierras of central Mexico. With my last sixty dollars, I bought a second-class ticket on the Aztec Eagle from Mexico to the States. My Brazilian girlfriend and my Mexican *novio* and I sat on a tree stump at the train station passing the tequila. We kissed goodbye and they waved me onto the clanking train. My beautiful Otomi, how we'd pretend to miss each other. Mooning, I wrote Spanish poetry.

On a seat I found a *Time* magazine and idly flipped to "Milestones." I read about his death on the train. I couldn't believe it. There it was, at the top. James Dean killed in a car crash. Jimmy was dead. It must be a mistake, I thought, eyes wet as I read it again and again. There was no one I could ask.

☙☙☙☙

His startling bright meteor crashed to earth September 30, 1955. His new silver Porsche Spyder screamed head-on into another car as he zoomed along California highway 466, now Route 46. He and his mechanic, Rolf Wuetherich, were on their way to a car race in Salinas. Amazingly, he had won six races. I remembered his thick glasses and wondered how he could do it. No one with eyes like Jimmy should race fast lethal cars. But there was no risk Jimmy wouldn't take. He always got away with everything. Pushing limits. People tried to warn him.

Jimmy died of being a kid.

That last moment, charging down the dusk road—road turned to dun haze by dusk—and suddenly knowing that black-and-white speck will hit you who are going eighty-five miles an hour on the straightaway. He's turned into your lane to make a left at an intersection you can't see. Eighty-five—too late. "He's gotta stop!" you yell then collide, and the silver Porsche crumples into you and breaks your neck. Terror then death.

The mechanic survived and the other driver bore hardly a scratch.

☙☙☙☙

Jimmy, long gone.

A dead hero is worth more than a living hero, even the Ancients knew, and a young dead hero is worth ten old ones. Churning young Icarus of the sensate media, revolving without rest. Once you've known a legend, you watch it grow till the famous stills—brooding, intense, haunted—become graven images of popular angst. Yet another death of the strident dreams of youth. To gain eternal fame in America, die young. The useful dead, so much more exploitable than the living who still own themselves. The beautiful corpses of James Dean and Marilyn Monroe sit enthroned on each side of the media god. Every year or two a new biography appears promising to tell the true James Dean story. Nothing's the same from the inside.

Jimmy, with his boyish casual T-shirt carnality, now a fond memory. Jimmy never looked as if he could grow up. I couldn't imagine him at forty, a short man turning beefy with middle age. Jimmy's timing was always perfect, twenty-four and prime.

Jimmy was my fury and rage too, everybody's youth, the precipice most of us pulled back from. In our day the young internalized rage, no one blamed society, and few took it out on anyone but themselves. Icarus, the only believable Apollo to a generation, antihero as martyr. Immortal Jimbo, a demigod on posters, a permanent icon. I seldom mentioned Jimmy to friends because all they could see was a god. He was such a boy.

What would Jimmy have thought of his ongoing celebrity? Probably found it a tad silly. Still, deserved. We know from George Bernard Shaw about actors' egos. Shaw said actors have naive egos compared to the monumental egos of writers. Actors only want attention, writers want to change the world or, at least, record it.

I know this: Jimmy would've doubled up, cackling his wild billygoat laugh, when I became Playmate of the Month.

Back in Jimmy's day, celebrity lacked the power—the glitter—of today. In restaurants and on the street, movie stars were glanced at but nobody mobbed them. Jimmy's legend accelerated as the power of celebrity did, as the media's power to create permanent celebrities did. Or instant celebrities. Whatever makes money. When they ran out of things to say about Jimmy, I began reading that he was gay. First, Sal Mineo admittted an unrequited crush on Jimmy. Then various unsuccessful actors claimed affairs in a last lunge for the spotlight. Everybody who knew Jimmy back then knew him as straight. The actress who plays Seinfeld's mother on TV wrote that she had an affair with Jimmy. If he also had affairs with men, no one I knew seemed aware of it. Of course, there have always been sexual beings who moved in the gay world without the straight world suspecting. Jimmy's appeal never seemed androgynous to me but simply boyish. Marlon had sex appeal, Jimmy had boy charm.

One writer, Paul Alexander, reprinted a nude shot of a young man, supposedly James Dean, in a tree stroking his erection. The instant I saw it I knew it wasn't Jimmy. Jimmy's penis was not that long. His was a perfectly acceptable medium length. Jimmy didn't have a dark thatch of pubic hair but rather a soft light brown muff. He had more chest and shoulders, a more masculine body. That photo, oddly enough, is the only one without a photographer's credit.

Jimmy Dean's great love was Pier Angeli. Sometimes after a great loss, a person becomes careless with his life. Losing Pier to Mr. Ordinary, Vic Damone, was probably Jimmy's greatest loss after the loss of his mother. Jimmy was used to gambling and winning. Here he played for real and lost totally. Pier's marriage to Damone ended as her career faltered. Pier Angeli disappeared from the news. When she was interviewed late in life, she said that James Dean had been her great love. She committed suicide.

I wonder if they could have saved each other.

These days, Jimmy, I see you everywhere—in the video store window, on the beauty parlor wall, in restaurants, in chic boutiques. Here's looking at you, Jimbo. You've lasted.

ॐ 6 ॐ

MAILER THE MAULER'S STRIP SHOW
SPRING 1954

In those fabled fifties days three celebrated young novelists vied desperately for Hemingway's crown—the lightweight slugger, the middleweight puncher, and the large drunk. At college I'd mooned over their handsome photos on the backs of their famous first novels, which were my first contemporary reading. They were my movie stars—James Jones, who wrote *From Here To Eternity*; Norman Mailer, *The Naked and The Dead*; and William Styron, *Lie Down In Darkness*.

The triumvirate was predicted to overcome the previous iconography of Hemingway, Fitzgerald, and Faulkner. I was beside myself with desire to meet them. For we literary romantics of the fifties, film stars—with few exceptions—were cheap-shot celebrities. Writers were venerated.

Tonight I'd meet the middleweight puncher. I was invited to Norman Mailer's party.

As I stepped off the stairway into Norman and Adele's loft, the Liontamer towering beside me, I shivered with stagefright. I wore a lowcut clinging blouse for fear I wouldn't be noticed. A good white crepe blouse with black crepe skirt and high heels, plus one earring, a silver spike, an affectation that came from losing earrings. The Liontamer wore his leopard-skin shirt open over his immense chest. His eyes were gold-flecked and leonine and his arms resembled lion's limbs. After a bad clawing, the Liontamer was working as a model. We met on a model shoot where he had to carry me over his shoulder into the forest for a paperback cover, my head and bosom and long curly hair dangling down his back.

Our cab drove downtown through the dark glamour of Manhattan. Eyes whirling night lights like street stars in black canyons. The shimmering thrill of action, life, motion everywhere. For two years I was high off the city. My feet hardly touched ground. I glided the pavement on a pillow of air, buoyed and cloudlike—meeting, seeing, learning. Becoming sophisticated. How I longed to be sophisticated.

Abruptly we were in a squat squalid section, cab bouncing along the cobblestones of the Lower East Side, not yet euphemized into the East Village. The Mailers lived in an old shabby six-story building that I now knew not to call a tenement, at 41 First Avenue near 2nd Street. As we trudged up five flights of old wooden stairs, I thought, Paris garret, grungy peeling brick, ascending to art. True artistic sensibility was never elegant, never ultramodern, never "done." Art, not furniture, dominated the atmosphere.

Everything in New York frightened and exhilarated me— writing, modeling, literary importance most of all. My ego had been blasted, shattered, when my ex left me for Karen. I felt I was climbing a steep rock face, with hardly holds for my toes, to get up to myself. I'd slip and fall and break, huddle at the bottom broken in self-hatred, revulsion at my lack of worth, then start to climb again. If I'm not happy by the time I'm forty, I'll commit suicide, I comforted myself, before entering the party on the arm of the Liontamer.

Where was Norman?

Around the foyer slouched a group of pale gray anxious young men—far too serious for small talk—who guarded the entrance. Arms crossed, eyes wary—editors, critics, social scientists and bluffers—they inspected applicants as they entered. I tried to saunter and smile.

"What don't *you* do?" a gray carnivore shot at me.

"I don't sleep with men for money," I said with deadly aim, gaining provisional acceptance amidst chuckles. Once I started modeling, my studious scowl lessened and my graduate school back straightened. I was getting used to focus, acting important for the camera. I pretended to be secure: I acted. That photographers paid me for my looks astounded me.

I'd been invited because of my short story in *Discovery*, the avant-garde literary review edited by Vance Bourjaily, author of *The End of My Life*. *Discovery* also published Norman Mailer and Hortense Calisher, Saul Bellow and May Swenson. When Vance bought it, I wept. It was my first published short story.

Where was Norman?

Norman and Adele's loft was jammed with people looking picturesquely undone—shaggy hair, bright scarves, black leotards, ethnic beads, cowboy boots, cleavages to there, jeans hugging genitals, slitting vulva. Ambience of ancient sofas, old dirty floor boards with faded Oriental rugs. At the edges people sat on different levels, a living theatre propped on pillows. Those who sat upright were more uptown proper than the sprawled slouching Village Bohemians. The Liontamer headed for the bar. "Tequila," I called.

Someone behind me said, "You come into the room like a Christmas tree."

Laughing, I whirled, and it was the middleweight puncher himself, our host, the esteemed novelist Norman Mailer, who looked shorter than I'd expected. Poor Norman, everybody expects him to be as huge as his reputation. A bright-eyed jujube, Norman postured about like he longed to be a tall blond fighter pilot, or even a liontamer. He just missed being a Jewish dumpling, having large shoulders and a sturdy-legged build. Norman had tender canny blue eyes, a halo of dark brown curls that shone, and pimples. Over thirty, with pimples. A literary hero with pimples? He looked boyish.

"You look like a Southern Belle," Norman said in the Texas accent he'd ingested in his Army unit.

"I am," I teased, "a decadent aristocrat." My exemplars were Katherine Anne Porter and Tallulah Bankhead.

"Fabulous smiles, you Southern girls."

As a proper Southern girl, I was bred to be good at men. I was, too. Good at getting them, not keeping them.

Norman's bright blue eyes danced with scintillating light. Norman liked Southern girls even more in later life, first Beverly, his third wife, then Norris, his sixth. He perched beside me, curls artistically tousled, and flirted.

"Vance tells me you can write."

"Thanks," I blushed. "I hate to fawn, but I loved your novel."

"Which one?" I was unaware of *Barbary Shore.* "Wait'll *Deer Park* comes out, you'll like *that*," he grinned.

Norman stood like a fixed pole of the magnetic North. People sucked up to him, salaamed, and peeled off. Literary celebs floated through the flowing booze. *Who* were all these important people madly chatting together? I didn't know a soul. Then I spotted Vance Bourjaily with Anne Bernays and Bob Kotlowitz, editors at *Discovery.* I ran up to them like saviors and huddled in their protection till they whirled away into other friends. There was director Elia Kazan. I went up to Gadge to say I was a friend of Jimmy Dean's. But it turned out to be critic Alfred Kazin who looked like Elia Kazan, and writer Anne Birstein, his wife. There were editors Linda and Aaron Asher, Barney Rosset who put his money where his mouth was with Grove Press, critic Dwight Macdonald and wife Gloria, Budd Schulberg who made *Sammy Run*, Victor Navasky, Anatole Broyard, Jules Feiffer, Joe Flaherty, Ed Fancher, Art D'Lugoff, Nat and Margo Hentoff, Gordon Lish, actor Mickey Knox, boxer Jose Torres, plus ladies.

A year or so later I knew a few of them and who the important others were. All those were at various Norman and Adele soirees, and many that memorable steamy night. Actor Mickey Knox, Norman's buddy, was the guy I got to know best—funny, clever, without pretentions. A great guy.

As we were decor back then, few women stood literary tall. I have a writer friend who says she didn't know any women before the women's movement. Neither did I. Except Chris the actress, my literary agent's assistant, Helen, and Nancy the ballet dancer who lived in the back apartment in my building. We weren't pals, we were competitors for the men. Alas.

Up came the Liontamer with my tequila and his Scotch, and I introduced them. Norman felt the Liontamer's arms, using both hands to embrace his biceps. Norman loved the Liontamer, who, I'd soon discover, looked far more like Sergius O'Shaugnessy, six foot three, blond blue lightheavy hero of *The Deer Park*, than Norman did.

I wandered off and kept angling to meet writer Anatole Broyard. But he was always surrounded by *femmes*. Anatole, the legendary Village lover, was easily the most handsome man at the party.

Norman's wife, Adele, fiery Brooklyn Latina, talked animatedly to a group nearby. Every once in awhile Adele's black moon eyes strayed, sought out Norman, and observed him narrowly. When he caught her at it, he lifted a shoulder and swooped away.

❧❧❧❧

Booze, of course, was the fuel of imagination. Note our stokers: Hemingway, Fitzgerald, and Faulkner. You were a sport, a big man, an intense tortured soul who contained his demons with this fluid of creativity. We ladies—us girls—kept up with the boys, but not drink for drink. We drank, and held our liquor. We had to hold our liquor, drink without getting drunk. The boys got falling down drunk, we got supple and smashed. No one liked the sight of a woman drunk—so gauche. Meanwhile the men crashed into furniture, slumped against walls, and when their ire was up, punched each other out. Especially Norman, famed literary mauler.

Norman had never met a guy like the Liontamer.

At Norman's insistence, he and the Liontamer squared off for a little shadow boxing. It was like a ferret trying to fight a lion. Every time the Liontamer cuffed him with a forearm, Norman almost fell. The Lion would steady him and Norman would charge again, the middleweight puncher of the literary set. Norman slung punches the Lion batted aside with his arms, carefully not using his fists.

His wife, Adele, sauced-up, well-stuffed tamale, jumped up and down, "Give it to him, Norman! Cream him, baby!"

Everything stopped and everybody watched. "Get him, Norman, go for him!" they yelled and clapped.

Talk about your literary fantasy.

Somehow the Liontamer managed to keep Norman on his feet. Mickey Knox declared a draw before tempers got out of hand.

Suddenly a furtive fellow, a critic, handed me a note and ducked away.

I opened the note. "Meet me by the bathroom. I have something to ask you. Norman." Since flirtation is a way of life down South, I didn't take it personally. I met Norman, who was toweling off from the exercise, outside the bathroom door off a narrow hall. The only hiding place in the loft.

Norman put his finger to his lips and whispered, "Can I call you?" He wished on me his best sexy pimply leer, like a college kid.

It never occurred to me to intrude on a marriage, even if intrusion were invited. But it was flattering, so I gave him my number and wandered back into the melee. Norman spotted Adele's suspicious glare and marched off away from both of us.

In those days I was horrified by the notion of sleeping with a married man. An adulteress had broken my dear grandmother Nena's heart and marriage, losing her a husband and my mother her own father. It was betrayal, it was cruel. Mother always said adultery was worse than murder. Then, with Carlos, it happened to me.

❧❦❧❦

A group of smallish New Yorkers clustered around the Liontamer, embracing his arm muscles, looking up at his gold-flecked leonine eyes with very unliterary appetite. We all got properly polluted on the elixir of our choice—sip, gulp, slug, or drag. Ardent spirits charged the atmosphere. Joints passed in small groups. Waves of blissfully wiped folk washed back and forth, giggling, guffawing, gamboling.

Suddenly up came Adele Mailer, the fiery Latina, who was flashy and fetching, spilling out of her red satin blouse.

As I smiled, she grabbed me by the upper arm. Hard.

"Hey, there," I wrenched my arm free. Mother always grabbed me by the arm, and I don't like it.

"Hey, my ass," said Adele, totally zonked.

"Pardon me?"

"You think you're pretty fucking cute, don't you?" hulked Adele.

"Now that you mention it," I huffed back, loathing the rudeness that seemed the order of the day in New York. New Yorkers were crude. They had no imagination when swearing. All they could manage to utter was: fuck, ass, shit.

Maybe Adele thought I was interested in Norman. Intensely, but only as a friend and literary buddy. I was too insecure to know I could inspire jealousy. As a novice in the Big Apple, my main concern was to keep my anxieties from spilling at everyone's feet.

Suddenly it was quieter. Friends glanced at Norman and Adele. Friends left in great bunches, especially proper couples, as if they knew what to expect. Now there were only about twenty guests left.

Adele was clearly out of her skull with boozy anger. She paced back and forth, raving drunkenly, as Norman smiled and we blinked.

Adele stopped in front of me and shrieked, "Take off your clothes and we'll see who's the best woman."

"What?"

"You're some damn fancy-ass model. You come in here and think you can suck up all the men. You think Norman's up for grabs, eh, you?" She hollered this, pacing away and returning.

"I'm a writer," I broached, praying it was so, tossing my long mane with a model's hauteur.

Now that I modeled, everyone assumed I was rich and beautiful. I made a bare bones living at it, and nobody in my entire life had ever called me beautiful before. Now it was automatic, a certificate of validation: model meant that female hero, the beauty queen, equivalent to the sports star. Marilyn Monroe equalled Joe DiMaggio, Ava Gardner equalled famous matadors.

"Writer, shit! You make me laugh," Adele paced away. "Norman's a writer, *that's* a writer." She gestured grandly at her man.

This time Adele slipped out of her tight jeans and kicked them into a corner.

The Liontamer watched amused, leaning on a paw, exchanging smiles with Norman.

"A madwoman," I said, "absolutely insane," as Adele wheeled

up on me again. She had that sultry Latin intensity that my ex, Carlos, had.

"Yes, you, who are you?" roared Adele, ripping off her sexy low-cut blouse, and tossing it to the winds, as she undulated again to the far end of her stage.

"Looks like we're in for a strip," I mouthed to the Lion, wondering why Norman didn't stop her, save her honor and all that.

"Very unprofessional," the Lion whispered. As models, we got paid for this sort of thing.

Arms crossed, Norman wore a well-pleased smile of infinite masculine superiority. Suddenly he was clapping. "Take it off, baby! Go all the way!"

Norman pushed Adele to extremes. She was trying hard to please him and found she liked going ape-shit wild.

"Yeah!" she shouted back, "yeah, baby." Adele unhooked her bra and slung it in Norman's general direction. Then she stepped out of her panties.

Jouncing and bobbling, she charged back toward me, cursing and yelling, arms flailing the air. Rather billowy, I thought. Being model-thin, a tiny person with tits, everybody looked huge to me. But Renoir liked it too—voluminous and quivering, flesh love. Plunge through her suffering with shock, that's why. Adele was terrified of losing Norman.

જ્જ્જ્

My first strip was for an affable bug-eyed photographer, with enough equipment to shoot game in Africa.

In opaque robe, I'd apologized for my humble furnished studio apartment. But Larry pronounced the light good and setups multifold: the bed, windowseat, desk, bookcase, marble mantel, the bed. This was my Desert Period: sand-colored Cambaya curtains, butte-rust upholstery cloth bed cover, and fifteen dimestore pillows ranging from mesa-rose to purple. The wall behind the bed I'd painted violet-mauve as the last gaudy gasp of a desert sunset.

"Thank God the other walls are white," said Larry. "For light."

I'd kissed a perfect stranger for a romance magazine, shot a faithless lover for a detective mag, and died gorily in an alley for a paperback cover. But I'd never posed nude, only pin-up jobs in bikinis. Miss Olivia, agency head, had said, "Do you want to make a living or not?"

"Would you like a bikini—bottom?"

"No," said Larry, fiddling with equipment.

"How about a sheer shortie nightie, or negligee?" I asked hopefully.

"No—nude." Now he looked up, and we blushed, bright-eyed, at each other.

"I'll be right out."

Trembling, I whipped into the john to comb my hair and inspect my face. On stage—naked. I felt like I was peeling my skin off for a perfect stranger. Why did I have to be in this side of the business? Because at five foot two with a showy display case, you cannot do fashion.

Out I flounced, tossed the robe aside, and crawled among the pillows, arms covering my breasts, legs tucked up defensively.

"Good, very good," said Larry, and shot from several angles.

I changed to arms over my head, revealing breasts, staring evasively out the window.

I expected him to leap at me.

Then I kneeled at an angle, front leg bent higher, chest lifted and back arched, supporting myself with my arms, glancing suspiciously at Larry, who sweated.

In the finished shots, I shrank into the wall, a frightened dewy-blossomed virgin, smaller and more scared than the smallest, scaredest male in the world. That sold the shots right off, Larry said. They appeared in three different pin-up magazines.

Years later Larry confessed it was the first time he'd ever shot a nude model, and *he* was bug-eyed with fear.

❧❧❧❧

Here Adele performed for free. Adele with her black searchlight eyes, shiny wild tossing hair, nonstop energy. Gash of scarlet lipstick. Adele was a de Kooning as dark lady.

Adele swayed and rolled, slid her hands over her breasts and hips, caressing her body in historical ecdysiast fashion.

I got paid for working out my fantasies—Cleopatra, Balzac's

mistress, space queen in conical bra, our lady of the whips—while other people had to use social events. Of course, Adele didn't know I'd never go out with Norman. I was very strict not only about other women's husbands but also boyfriends. I was no sneak.

Now everybody formed a street mob around Adele, looking offended and eager. It was almost as hard to watch a naked stranger as to be naked. Neither effect lasts.

Shirt coming off, Norman sort of hipswayed like a rumba.

Adele swept up to me again and shook me by the shoulders, her bosom bobbing in rhythm. "Take *yours* off," she bellowed, "and we'll *see* who's the best woman."

I pushed her away.

The men were clapping, shouting, "Take it off."

Smiling at her audience, Adele started clawing at the buttons on my blouse.

Shouts, cheers, like a raucous street mob.

I karate-chopped at her arms. "Get *away* from me!"

"Scared to show, little Miss Nice Cunt?" Adele tripped away, wheeled about, then came at me with a rush, a charging bull.

Sidestepping, I gave her a shove. "I don't like to win so easily," I tried to sound cool.

"Let's go," I yanked the Lion's paw.

By then Norman was down to white boxer shorts. He jumped up and down on their double bed.

Suddenly everybody left except two awed Upper East Side couples, the Lion and me.

Norman dropped his shorts, shook them off his feet and slung them away. Then he jumped higher to make his wad go up and down for the visitors. Adele climbed up onto the bed and jumped too.

Something strange happens when people take off their clothes at parties. They mean to shock. But instead they appear helpless, vulnerable, oddly shaped beggars pleading for love.

Tears rimmed my eyes. Why? Something I'd seen in my parents' marriage—the hunger within.

"At least it ought to be a good night for you two," I said whimsically.

Then I pulled the Liontamer out the door before he got any bright ideas.

I tried to remember what the world famous novelist, Norman Mailer, looked like naked. Norman was just square, no particular waist or pectoral definition, sturdy legs large at the knees, an ordinary penis, scared balls trying to hide from all this show. My introduction to the literary world.

෨෨෨෨

'Twas the Age of Affluence, of the Cold War and Ike, of the little black dress and the cocktail party. Governor Rockefeller wanted to build air raid shelters. The man in the gray flannel suit, the organization man who was part of the lonely crowd, was married to his suburban wife who cared for 2.2 children at home, fulfilling her feminine role.

Manhattan flowed with young folk, single women and men, escaping the Freudian drama of provincial America. Even at Norman's party, a tall distinquished psychoanalyst with commanding black eyes delivered societal judgments. Sophisticates looked up at him like children, hands folded, awaiting God's pronouncement.

Psychoanalysis ruled the fifties, and I didn't respect it any more than Norman did. What? You're not in analysis? *writers* said to me, in disapproval. The literary world was divided among Freudians and Jungians and Existentialists. The doctrinaire nature of Freudianism brought out the rebellious Jungian and Existential Absurdist in many. As I felt innately connected to the universe, and hoped to become a tuning fork of mass consciousness—as writers are—I felt I should think for myself. Though life was ravishingly absurd, my aim was to *create* meaning for mine. Kurt Vonnegut said humans were mud that got to sit up and look around. I couldn't bear to be mere ambulatory matter.

I was reading Sartre and devouring Simone de Beauvoir's monumental examination of women in *The Second Sex*, possibly the most urgent book I'd ever read. Revelation, confirmation poured through me—yes, yes, yes. That was woman's subordinate position, enforced by the male power structure. Simone laid it all out in scholarly historical analysis ten years before *The Feminine Mystique* of Betty Friedan. *The Second Sex* taught me to understand my chauvinist ex well enough to develop his character in my novel.

We were all busy creating ourselves. Norman resisted being a nice Jewish mama's boy from Brooklyn. James Jones, of the regular Army and equal fame as a war novelist, had once been a Midwestern farm boy. Like the third member of the triumvirate, William Styron, I was a renegade Southerner whose forebears had owned humans.

"Make noise in the world, son, you're a genius." You can almost hear Fanny Mailer, Norman's mother. With one thousand percent encouragement from tough Fanny plus his pa's gambling instincts, Norman got a jump start. Whereas I was bred as a proper Southern girl to hide my light behind a bushel. Don't call attention to yourself, don't be pushy. "Don't get too smart," Mother had warned. "Men don't like it."

Norman wasn't involved in being a Jew, any more than I was interested in being an Episcopalian housewife. Probably it had to do with going to war. Though he didn't see much action, his stint in the Pacific theater late in World War II was the bedrock of *The Naked and The Dead*. Norman tried on all-American personae— Texas trooper, tough Irishman, hip square, White Negro, literary self-promoter and big mouth. Also, finally, Mr. Macho, Mr. Retro throwback.

As for myself, I was in deep rebellion, high rebellion, total rebellion. My brother was now an Episcopal priest, my sister properly married with two daughters, and here was I, with my Phi Bete key and master's in English, modeling in the nude. In magazines. My father tithed to Chevy Chase Episcopal, Mother had wanted me to debut down home in Jacksonville. Though we had small money, Grandmother Denham was a grande dame.

When I visited her one debut season, my junior year at Chapel Hill, five debs I hadn't seen since I was seven gave me parties. Grandmother Denham wore her tiara and I wore my five hand-me-down evening gowns to a frazzle. My wardrobe came from Cousin Middie, daughter of Uncle Ling, who was listed in *Time* as one of the ten highest salaried men in America. Gorgeous clothes, in my shabby genteel life.

Cousin Mac was legal aide to Senator Claude Pepper, Cousin George would be a Marine Corps general, Cousin Lucretia married a multimillionaire, Cousin Freddie would soon be one, and I took off my clothes for a living. My own family were humble civil servants; that is, Daddy's FHA job paid too little to send his own kids to college, so Palmer and I had to work our way through. Daddy told me he didn't grow up till he lost his fortune in the Crash of 1929. Daddy warned me to use my mind. Mother wanted me to marry a rich man.

When we moved from Florida to Washington, Grandfather Denham's chauffeur drove us up because we didn't own a car. After his day at FHA, Dad got on the bus to go sell AAA memberships across town at night. I suggested maybe Mother could get work at the shopping center, and they both hollered in outrage. Eventually Daddy became head of Property Disposition with two hundred people under him. When he was halfway up the ladder, his boyhood friend, Charlie Merrill, of Merrill-Lynch offered him a job in New York. Dad's indecision gave him pneumonia. He turned it down because he feared he was too old to broker stocks and wanted to leave Mother with a secure government pension. He never forgave himself.

છે⌇છે⌇

'Twas the age of propriety, of premarital virginity, therefore of illegal abortion, of discrimination against women at colleges and at work. We women weren't allowed at Chapel Hill till our junior year. Graduate schools had ten percent female quotas. At *Time* and *Newsweek*, women weren't allowed to be reporters, only researchers. We were expected to marry, get a man to carry us. Wear tan, navy, or brown suits and defer, to keep your man. Having flunked marriage, I sought romance, sexual ecstasy, fun and games. Passionately I yearned to be a writer, as a nun yearns to marry Christ. No man could satisfy that desire. Not even the one I lost.

છે⌇છે⌇

New York in the fifties was like Paris in the twenties. Going to New York was scaling a skyscraper to a literary dream. Nobody wanted to be a movie star or a rock star. In the fifties everybody wanted to write the Great American Novel. Modeling, being part-time, gave me time to write seriously.

Simone de Beauvoir said it best: "Art is an attempt to

59

found the world anew on a human liberty: that of the individual creator."

᠅᠅᠅᠅

My risk-taking forebears, Southerners and Puritans, had settled the wild colonial forests of the New World in 1635. Three centuries later I made my foray into the Manhattan jungle. God exists in the imagination, Wallace Stevens said. My god was literature. Two of our potentates had received Nobels, Faulkner in 1949 and Hemingway in 1954. Fitzgerald, my favorite, had died of living in 1940, age 44.

The triumvirate of Norman Mailer, James Jones, and William Styron—they called themselves the three best young writers in America, said Mickey Knox—competed to write the Great American Novel. The Great American Novel was our literary altar. Could one of these brilliant boyos pull it off?

By the mid-fifties these seminal books had already been published: Salinger's *Catcher in the Rye*, James Baldwin's *Go Tell It on the Mountain*. Baldwin, who had been kind to me and inspiring a few years previous when I ran away from home and landed at the San Remo. Also Saul Bellow's *Adventures of Augie March*, Kurt Vonnegut's *Mother Night*, Nabokov's audacious *Lolita*, Ralph Ellison's *Invisible Man* and *The Recognitions* by William Gaddis. Also *A Good Man Is Hard to Find* by Flannery O'Connor and Katherine Anne Porter's *Pale Horse, Pale Rider*. Being women, Southern, and brilliant, they thrilled me with hope. *They* were my mentors. The literary decade was incredibly rich. The world still believed in the Word. Serious art was highbrow. Foreign films were middlebrow. Hollywood and TV were lowbrow. In those days there was choice.

The *Village Voice* was started by psychologist Ed Fancher and editor Dan Wolf, and Norman, mainly with Norman's money in 1955, the same year Art D'Lugoff opened the Village Gate. The *Voice* office on Sheridan Square became our magnet.

We began the sexual revolution in the fifties. Though we seldom lived together without marriage, we played around and changed partners and got laid constantly: a lifelong affair lasted two months and a serious involvement three weeks. Every month

I had a mad new crush, a fabulous new romance. I didn't deceive myself that it was true love.

Though provincials didn't dare, we New Yorkers were devotees of sexual freedom. For me, sex was a wild ride across the hinterlands and forests and meandering springs of distant psyches. Sex was my great adventure. Through sex I was learning the world. Margaret Sanger's clinic provided my diaphragm, we had penicillin for V.D., and antibiotics for the old bad diseases. Home free. Unless we slipped. Abortion was illegal and my own, in college, had been gruesome. Women died. I was very very very careful now.

In 1956 liberal New York was madly for Adlai and startled that our nation preferred Ike as president to a man of such literary acumen as Stevenson. Also in 1956 the Hungarian Revolution failed. We, the United States in the United Nations, had encouraged their uprising against the Russians, promising military aid. The naive Hungarians, naive as myself, stood on their rooftops waiting for UN planes. I felt personally mortified that our own leaders had lied.

The new word is dissembled.

•••••

When the 1955 reviews of *The Deer Park* were as bad as those of *Barbary Shore*, Norman printed them up in the *Village Voice* to pitch himself. He tried to get Hemingway to anoint him as his heir, crown prince of today's literature. Norman once told me he sent Papa novel after novel and letter after letter, to no avail.

Ernesto was our official Literary Giant, just as Marlon Brando was our Movie Anti-Hero. James Dean not only idolized Marlon, he adored him. But you can't expect an artist to nominate his replacement.

Like Ernesto, Norman haunted our age. Open the papers— Norman spouting. Once at a party, I asked his sister, Barbara, what it was like growing up with Norman. Incredulous, she laughed, "I was invisible."

ॐ 7 ॐ

MY REWARD: JAMES JONES
SPRING 1954

Norman Mailer phoned to apologize for his wife Adele's bull
rush.

"Where'd you get that madwoman?" I chuckled. Stripping at
a party, going wild like Adele did, could be fun. But my taking it
off for strange men, month after month, made me feel queasy, a
bit whorish.

"Who else would have me?" Norman said ingenuously.

"Tsk," I shushed, seeing his blue eyes crackle.

Norman acted as if he felt he wasn't physically attractive to
women, which, being Norman, he intended to change.

"She misunderstood," said Norman. "I want you to join the
gang, be friends."

"Me, too." I was touched by his affectionate tone. Norman
was capable of friendship without sex. By nature, he was affable,
outgoing. He liked people, high times, back then.

"Is Adele studying caping?"

"We both did, last summer in Mexico. Great fun."

Gracias to Papa Hemingway, everybody knew the revered matadors—Manolete, Dominquin, Ordonez. Writer Barnaby Conrad fought the bulls in Spain and Brooklyn's Sidney Franklin was a famous matador.

"Did you see Carlos Arruza?" Mexico's greatest matador.

"He was astonishing," said Norman. "We spent every Sunday at the *corrida*. You happen to know Bette Ford, ex-model?"

"No."

"Bette stayed, to study seriously. She wants to fight the bulls."

"Really? A woman!" A few years later *novillera* Bette Ford would be a big attraction, mainly along the border.

"Yeah, I wanted to fight," Norman wore his tough's voice, "but Adele wouldn't let me."

"Better a live writer, Norman."

"Here's why I called. To make it up to you, I want to invite you to our big bash for James Jones."

"Who wrote *From Here To Eternity*?" I could see his handsome photo on the novel's dustjacket.

"That Jones. He's single, besides."

"Oh boy, this is exciting." I wrote down all the particulars.

"He's coming from that writers' colony near the little town in Illinois."

"James Jones lives there?"

"Get him to tell you about it."

"Should I bring a date?"

"Hell, no. I'm inviting you to meet Jim."

❧❧❧❧

James Jones, I'm invited to meet him. I hugged myself, dancing at the mirror. James Jones, whose great war novel about army life in Hawaii, *From Here To Eternity,* seemed more profound to me than *The Naked and The Dead*. Jones was more deeply immersed in army life, as a regular. He who photographed most handsome and rugged in his jacket photo, with strong jaw and wavy straw-colored hair with bright blond streaks. He looked to be both tough and sensitive, morally strong. I'm invited to meet *him*.

Even the movie had been good, if not literally accurate. Montgomery Clift as Prewitt, who was most like Jim, Burt

Lancaster, Deborah Kerr. Hadn't it won Oscars? Jim Jones must've made a bundle between the movie and the bestseller. This literary hero of mine was, voila, single!

Seeing this handsome dude, my new love, in the mirror, I leaned against him and kissed the mirror.

๛๛๛๛

The fated day of the fete came, at last.

That afternoon I posed for an ad in a gorgeous fuschia bathroom in my new semi-sheer negligee. In one corner of Barry's cavernous studio was a complete shiny kitchen and in another, the elegant complete fuschia bathroom—pedestal tub, modern swoop basin and toilet, each with silver accessories. The color ad would run in the ladies' slicks. I posed combing my hair at the fuschia basin with the fuschia tub as backdrop. This was the sort of ad I'd send the family.

The stylist ran up to daub my nose with a touch of powder and place an auburn wave behind my ear. She stared at me as if I were a flower arrangement, and declared the perfection of my makeup and hair. Assistants rolled massive lights about, which were cleverly focused on everything but me—on basin and tub, thick pile rug, and ceiling. I knew what they wanted—a suggestion of breast, curve of hip. Classy not cutesy. Long neck, lifted chin.

Next to Barry stood a somber man in elegant suit with arms crossed, scowling: the client. Next to him, arms waving in explanation, stood the art director from the ad agency. Barry himself, with his thick glasses, furrowed brow, and pullover sweater, was the picture of school-boy seriousness.

"Less smile," he barked. "This is not a pinup."

"What do you want?" I was instantly insecure.

"Serene, serenity—the lovely woman at home."

"Ah." I flowed in calm materialistic serenity, the grand lady given to ethereal ballet expressions. A delight to drop the boopsy boo and goo-goo eyes. Modeling was miniature acting. You create the mood and freeze the pose.

"Perfect—great." Client dropped his arms, art director smiled broadly.

That was the sort of model job I enjoyed, with professionals

64

shooting for beauty, not nakedness. They made me feel worthy. My ballet training made it easy to swing into new stances. The model agency had gotten me seventy-five dollars for the hour. My tiptop figure modeling fee was one hundred dollars an hour, but if I didn't work for fifty dollars, I'd starve. I lived on two hundred sixty dollars a month. My rent was sixty-five dollars a month, utilities included. With luck, I could write for a week, uninterrupted, if I didn't get another call.

What made Bohemia possible: cheap rents, cheap bars, cheap cabs, cheap books. Hardcovers cost under five dollars, paperbacks fifty cents, the subway merely fifteen cents. Artists all over town lived off part-time work. Manhattan hadn't discovered money.

๛-๛-๛-๛

The phone rang as I walked in my door. It was Norman.

"Oh, Norman, I'm so excited about tonight!"

"Um, that's what I called about."

"Yes?"

"You can't come." Norman's voice was funereal. He sighed, "Adele says to tell you not to—you're *un*invited to the party."

"What? Why?"

He lowered his voice. "Adele doesn't—trust you. She thinks you're after *me*," Norman giggled at the implausibility of this.

"Can't you—can't you—?"

"Listen, I'm sorry."

"It's not fair," I bleated. "We didn't go out!"

"Yeah, well—"

"Doesn't she *know* that?" I was about to blubber.

"You're mighty tempting," Norman drawled, as Texas trooper. "She knows *that*."

"So, I don't get to meet James Jones," I raved. "That's mean, that's cruel."

"Yeah, it is," said Norman. "I've got to get off the phone. So long."

I could almost feel Adele watching him.

Wives have their ways. Adele didn't trust me. I was exiled from the literary world. I'd *never* meet James Jones now. I bawled like a baby.

Now I hated modeling. If I hadn't been a model, Adele never

would've focused on my green-eyed glimmer and auburn tresses. I pulled back my hair and gave the mirror my graduate school glare. What a somber face I had when alone and serious.

At my windowseat as dusk turned to dark, I stared at my mind's-eye view of James Jones who became more brilliant, glorious, and desirable by the starlit minute. I saw one star out my window, above the traffic screech. A dream. Obviously too good for me. Once in a while something lurched in me, and I felt I was in a prehistoric pueblo on a planet already ended. Dead stores and streets. Nothing. No one. I was destroyed.

At about ten I pictured the bash of the year in full swing, and wept buckets. *Everybody* was there, everybody who mattered, every witty gorgeous talented being in New York. There to honor one of their own, Mr. Marvelous James Jones. I felt so deprived I broke my golden rule about drinking alone. I had a shot of tequila. Two guys had phoned and asked me to dinner. But I was far too deprived for such simple pleasures.

࿐࿐࿐

At about eleven-thirty the phone rang. I sat and watched it ring. Sighing, I finally answered. It was Norman.

"Oh, hello." I didn't feel friendly.

"James Jones is here," Norman sounded tightly wired.

"So they tell me."

"He wants to meet you. He wants to talk to you. I'll put him on."

"Hello, um, Alice, this is Jim Jones," said a crackling voice.

"The authentic Jim—?" I suspected a nasty trick.

"Only one I know," he chuckled. "Listen, I know it's an ungodly hour. But could I come up?"

Norman grabbed the line. "Jim has almost no time in town. I told him all about you—"

"Gimme that phone," Jim laughed. "I really *do* want to meet you."

"How drunk are you both?" I was leery.

They guffawed. Jim said, "Only slightly soused, ma'am. Nothing to offend your sensibilities."

"What about tomorrow night?" I huffed.

"He may not be alive tomorrow night," Norman gaggled.

66

"Please," said Jim.

"All right," I let my guard down, lilted a laugh. "Please accept my invitation, suh, for a drink. Tout suite."

"Right away, ma'am. Got my horse revved up."

అఖఖఖ

Oh, I sighed, arms crossed over my chest, head to the empyrean. Such bliss. I was flattered to the skies, as I knew what it meant. That, in spite of all the dandy gals at Norman and Adele's bash of the century, the guest of honor wanted to depart the revelry *to meet me*. Norman must've done a dynamite job of talking me up. Norman must really find me fascinating, and how chivalrous, how kind, to want to fix me up with his good friend.

Now I was all loving kindness as I made up my face carefully, trembling. For luck, I donned the same clinging white top I'd worn at the Mailers' party. Plus tight jeans. We'd all just discovered the appeal of tight jeans.

Just before the witching hour, the second member of the triumvirate, the lightweight slugger and celebrated war novelist, James Jones, paid me a visit. He rang my bell.

"Up two," I hollered down the stairwell.

అఖఖఖ

I was delirious with power till I saw him. These fellows certainly didn't look like their book jacket photos.

James Jones had an abnormally long head front to back while, incomprehensibly, his features were bunched together in the squalling center of his face. Then I remembered he'd been wounded in the head at Guadalcanal. Though let down, I was rather glad. If he'd been handsome as I'd dreamed, I'd have been speechless. The cowboy duds worked though—suede fringed vest, checked shirt, jeans, and tight leather chaps over a hard wiry muscled body.

"Howdy, ma'am," James Jones doffed his Stetson, and we shook hands.

"Howdy-do, suh," I curtsied.

Jim Jones wore a wide turquoise wrist bracelet plus two huge turquoise rings and a turquoise belt buckle.

"Do you keep your royalties in jewels, on the person?" I giggled.

"Nah," he laughed. "That's so I have to win the arm wrastle ever' single time. If I don't, a gem gits crushed."

We perched at the rickety fold-down dining table. As soon as I steadied my arm, James Jones put it down. "Wait, wait!" I objected, settling my arm at a different angle. We tried again. Crash, my knuckles crunched.

"Ya see, nothin' to it." Jones swaggered about a bit, chest puffed and waiting. He faced me.

I made him wait two beats then said it: "You're strong."

Jones grinned, a lovable rumpled grin, and hoisted a pint out of each back pocket. "I brought us a little firewater."

"Want rocks?"

"If you please, ma'am."

Maybe I liked him. I tended toward weird dudes. I splashed firewater on the stones and handed him a drink.

"Bet you can't do this," I challenged. I shot my right leg straight out and did a one-legged kneebend with the left, down and up, without support.

"Great!" said Jim. "I can do that."

He tried it and toppled. He got his balance and did it the second time. Though stumpy, Jim had a well-tooled body, but he was easily as short as Norman.

"It's a ballet move."

We clicked glasses. I loved showoff athletic stuff.

Jim Jones twirled his Stetson into the corner, settled on the floor pillows, and dropped the accent. "Vance showed me your story—first rate. Interesting—whore's point of view."

"She wasn't a whore."

"She took money."

"Once," I blushed.

"You tried it, eh?" Eagle-eyed Jim.

I cocked an eye at him. "I'll probably try anything that doesn't hurt. *If* it interests me."

"Good girl."

We clicked glasses again. But it had. "It hurt. Like your book did. You led up to it just right—that monstrous war of my childhood."

"Thanks." We both blushed.

Drank, smoked, and talked as Jim Jones told me about competition in the ring. Jim had to admit he considered Norman numero uno, himself second, but Norman thought the large drunk, Styron, the lyrical member, was number one, which pissed Jones off, who thought in the long run, he would be number one, Norman number two, etc.

Norman was on his third novel, Jones explained. But he, Jones, had more and greater experience to grind, and so, therefore, money didn't matter. They all had huge advances and world fame. What mattered was who the real champeen was: *who* deserved to wear Hemingway's crown.

"Why does there have to be *one*? You all write differently."

"Because that's the way it is in the ring, baby. Somebody wins, somebody loses."

Sometimes it seemed Hemingway and John Wayne had fathered half the men of America.

Actually, Jim Jones, the sensitive boy from the bottom, was the only one who'd made massive moolah, between the *Eternity* novel and movie, which had made his publisher eager to throw more money at him.

Jones talked about World War II, how the army was home to a farm boy from Illinois. About the writers' colony in Robinson, Illinois, run by an older woman he had to lay to get his room and board. About how you make it if you're tough enough, enough man.

"Hold on, now—about this woman."

"My mentor, Lowney Handy." He flushed. "I really like her a lot. She's tough. What difference does it make if she's older?" He got defensive.

"None—to me." Did he have to defend his desires to other men? Probably.

"You live there, at the writers' colony?"

"Yeah."

"Why?"

"Why not?"

"You mean it's home, like the army?"

"Yep. But I sure need a vacation."

I told Jim how I was born with a silver spoon in my mouth that was yanked out before I learned how to use it. In Jacksonville, Florida. How I'd worked my way through University of North

Carolina to a graduate scholarship at U. of Rochester upstate. Thence to my heart's desire, New York. I told him a down home tale. My grandfather called Coca-Cola that silly syrup from Atlanta, when asked in as an initial investor. Every Southern family knows that anyone with one hundred dollars in Coke made a literal million.

"Was it hard to write *Eternity*?" I dared to ask.

"Awful—I had to live it all again."

"That's what you have to do, isn't it?" I was learning that myself.

"Couldn't have done it without Lowney riding herd on me. She knew I had it in me."

"Even when *you* didn't."

"Exactly," he laughed. "Yep, you're cursed. You're one of the tribe."

That made me very happy. Maybe *I* could do it too. I nudged his glass, caressingly. We were well into the second pint now, confiding time. "Here's the way I look at it. Writing is the *only* thing I want to do. I have my whole stupid life to do it in. Should I do something I don't want with my only life?"

"Nooooo," Jim moved closer.

"I don't care if it takes forever. I don't care *what* I have to do to feed myself." Was I ever bombed.

"Most girls want kids, Lowney says."

"Maybe *there*. But not in New York."

Jim looked doubtful.

"Why do you think we're *here*?" No husband would put up with a wife who wasn't primarily a mother. You had to choose.

We talked our way to intimacy in that ancient ritual of romance: getting to know you, feeling you out in resonating empathy and desire.

Suddenly I came to—where had I been?—and there I was flat on my back, every light in the place on, and Jim was going down on me. In a very friendly manner. We had intense drunken conversations now and again, then he'd go back to it. Our clothes were slung in a corner. His broad shoulders, deep chest, shapely legs splayed out.

Jim would stop, sip his drink, I'd sip mine. He'd lean an arm on my thigh with his fingers feathering the hair, other arm propped on his chin with his elbow between my legs. Spread-eagled, I put my arms behind my head, and together we considered the current state of injustice in the world. Then Jim lapped me up once more, his hands gripping my thighs.

I didn't know much about all this. My college boyfriend had done it once, but out of genteel embarrassment, we dismissed it. Several men had tried to pry my legs apart. Then I remembered. Even my high-school boyfriend had done it once, and we both liked it. Six years repressed.

Jim sniffed, pleased. "You smell delightful."

"I do?" Reassured, I let my legs flop. "I always worried that I smelled bad, and that men only did it as a favor and held their breath."

"Child, sweet child. You like it, don't you?" He was the kindliest soul.

"Yes, because it's mooshy." I was totally smashed, relaxed. "Can I ask you a question?" I felt down to the little-man-in-the-boat and put his fingers on it. "Is the little-man-in-the-boat the clitoris?"

Jim rolled with laughter. "I can't believe you!"

"I wouldn't ask if I knew." I turned my head aside and pouted.

"Yes, ma'am, it is—the precise same knob. Like on a saddle. You jist hol' on and we'll ride."

And ride we did, post and grab, lick, lap. Post and grab, lick, lap.

"What does it feel like?" Jim the writer, working.

I tittered, trilled, "Molten lava that oozes." Then I got curious. "How does it taste?"

Jim rubbed my newfound clitoris with his nose. "Like feathers in a trunk."

"Like dew on musk?"

"Like a sassy little pussy," the master said, placing his fingers around the rim, playing the vulva like a vibraphone. "You're coming nicely, you know."

I wasn't coming. With little rushes of spirit, I was relubricating. If it flattered Jim to think those were orgasms, some women— who'd never really blasted through—didn't seem to know the difference either. But I was getting impatient for the stick, which he showed small inclination to deliver.

Finally I said, "Don't you like to screw?"

"When I'm sure you're ready."

"Man, I'm past ready."

Jim wouldn't let up lapping. After a while I really got into it. The glaring out-of-place light, my sprawled legs with the grassy knoll I looked down on, where the male animal fed at the fountain over the cliff of the knoll. I raised my hips and rolled the knoll forward and back to tilt the fountain, with its many flowing knobs and rivulets leading to the main sluice. Slup slup slup softly and wildly, his eyes closed, his hands hanging on. I held his head with my legs and rocked it in my cradle, I the Queen Mother. I blasted through, I came, flowing all over Jim's face as he tried to suck it all into his mouth. Then looked up at me from that humble position to see if I was pleased. Yes, smiled my body, oh yes.

Jim moved off his stomach and up toward me, and I glanced down and said, "It isn't hard. You want me to get it hard?"

"Yes, it is."

I touched it, pulled it, and it *was* hard. Only it was the size of a man's thumb, no longer and no thicker.

Never had I glimpsed a penis so tiny. But I showed no shock. Moving around, I couldn't feel it even when I put my legs together between his and squeezed.

Afterward Jim asked if I came.

"I couldn't again," I said. One that size would never do it. But Jim knew how to compensate. As they say, he tried harder.

Next noon over jelly doughnuts and coffee, Jim told me his new novel would be about the movie stars and Hollywood goons he met when they made *Eternity* into a film. He was going to Paris to work on it.

I felt a pang. Would I miss James Jones? Suddenly I thought of another James. Jimmy Dean would soon be in town.

"Paris, where all writers long to be. And *you're* going." It made Jones seem very rich.

In Manhattan you get to meet celebrities and dispose of your fantasies. Icon-shattering was surely part of the fun. But I liked Jim Jones enough to be his girlfriend till he left town. Naturally, I assumed Jim wanted to be my boyfriend. Little I knew of the world.

We both had appointments downtown. In the cab as we bumped across 14th Street, I felt blissfully balmy. A sappy smile on my anxious face.

"I got a thousand things to do before I leave." Jim put his hand on my knee. "Don't get hurt if I don't get back to you."

Jim Jones did not phone again before he left for Paris. Not even once. After worshipping at the source, after creating a shrine. After making love like that. I wrote in my notebook: no woman is mature till she can sleep with a man once only, by his choice, and not be bothered by it. Still, it hurt.

Norman phoned and asked how I'd liked Jim.

"Fine," I said, "a real down-to-earth guy."

My ego was devastated all day. But I hadn't fallen for Jones.

I certainly didn't fall in love just because I slept with a guy. I'd only been deeply in love once. When I let out my full passion, it had turned him off, my ex. I feared true love would do me in. But I adored sex sex sex and men men men, romantic dining, fancy soirees, squalid garrets, literary chat, and parties, nonstop parties.

For me, sex was swimming in the seas of the planet, exploring the family of man—lands and races, occupations and proclivities. I was seeing the world. I flew out over steep cliffs in exotic lands and glimpsed paradise. During sex, paradise opened for me. *I saw it.*

But I was *in love* with art, *writing* was my passion.

"Who's throwing the blast tonight?" I'd ask my date, leaning on the bar at San Remo or Louie's. John Wilcock, *Village Voice* columnist, was the party-inviter, then Bill Manville wrote up the bashes in his "Saloon Society" column. For years in the mail, I'd get a list from John inviting me to open parties for the next two weeks. There were no closed parties. Except the single most sought-after invitation: the yearly *Voice* blast publisher Ed Fancher gave at his Village floor-through. We lucky revelers pushed from parlor to bedroom and back in a subway rush-hour squeeze of a hundred or so. We were at Ed's. We were In.

We all dated with a frenzy. My phone never stopped ringing. As a boring cook, I relished being taken out for dinner. Always on sacred Saturday night. No woman admitted she was alone on Saturday night, as that made you a wallflower. I never felt I had to put out to pay for anything. Brilliance lit Broadway—Anouilh,

Giraudoux, Shaw, Beckett, Sartre; Off-Broadway—Ionesco, Genet, Albee. Dates took me to all of them, and paid. Men paid for everything. Trained by my parents and the wacky wit of the South, I was an engaging conversationalist. My insecurities weren't about my social appeal. I could get men. But could I *keep* them? Did I want them? Our musical chairs moved so fast I couldn't judge. Manic Me.

Depressed Me: I needed attention from men to restore my confidence. Lots. Constantly. To smother my sense of inferiority. My fear I'd never write anything worthwhile again, that I could no more write a novel than climb Everest. So I created Ms. Southern Belle, femme fatale, thanks to modeling.

On Waverly Place I went to a great key money party. The host offered me his perfect Village apartment if I'd pay key money for the furniture. The rent was one hundred dollars a month. I couldn't afford it. My West 55th Street brownstone studio, between car showrooms on Broadway and Stillman's Gym on Eighth Avenue, was thirty-five dollars cheaper. I modeled in midtown and played in the Village. West 55th was funky showbiz folk and the old Hearst building. The Village was my neighborhood.

Did I feel poor? Poverty was romantic. Poverty meant dedication to art. I felt privileged to be part of the drama.

࿇࿇࿇

Later Norman Mailer told me Jim Jones met Gloria, who'd be his wife, fifteen minutes after me. Gloriously blonde Gloria had asked him to look at her novel. Jim told her, said Norman, the novel was lousy, she couldn't write, but how'd she like to be a writer's muse. Maybe the timing was not quite that. Possibly he met her before. But anyway, said Norman, Gloria bowled him over. I was far too naive for Jones.

Truth was, I liked the same sort of men Norman did—tall, lean, muscular Liontamers. My ex, Carlos, was six foot two, dark, vaguely exotic, and built. He also had brains and creativity. Not, unfortunately, standard equipment for studs and hunks. I was beginning to wish the Liontamer would go back to the ring. He bored me, as so many studlet actors and bar stars did. Brains *were* sexier. A brilliant remark could turn me on.

The third member of the triumvirate, Bill Styron, had married Rose, a department store heiress, and decamped to Connecticut, a quieter place to write. I regret that I never met him, as we came from the same South.

They set up their separate courts—Norman in New York, Styron in Connecticut, and Jones in Paris. The Jones salon on Ile St. Louis was a coveted invite, the host often attired in a smoking jacket.

Not one of them would cotton to a woman with a real career. Adele was a painter then an actress unless Norman wanted wild and crazy. Gloria seemed content being Jim's wife. Of course, they all had children to raise. They were very much men and women of their generation. I was *not* a woman of mine. Like the Beats, some of us lived the sixties in the fifties.

I have a soft spot for Norman young. For James Jones, too. Jim, alas, gone. We were all so dewy and immortal.

❧ 8 ❧

DOUBLE DATE WITH MARLON
SPRING 1954

Nobody told me the trysting time had been changed. As I dived
into Pavillon an hour late, Marlon Brando ducked into the entry
and did a double take. Just like an ordinary man when he sees
something he likes.

I was dumbstruck.

As I plunged through softly lit elegance toward the table,
he followed, grinning. I introduced myself to my blind date,
arranged by my actress friend, Chris White. He was Sam Spiegel,
famous producer of *On the Waterfront*, starring Brando. Spiegel
then presented me to Marlon and his sultry Mexican mistress,
Movita, and playwright Paul Osborn, author of *Bell, Book and
Candle*, and his wife. Osborn had just finished the screenplay for
East of Eden, James Dean's first movie.

Marlon Brando was Jimmy Dean's nemesis. Marlon was the
favorite actor of Tennessee Williams and Truman Capote and
most writers I knew. Marlon was a cult.

Marlon threw me a sneaky smile.

I got stage fright and began shivering. Everybody at the table looked at me pityingly, as my hand shook so that Marlon couldn't light my cigarette. I put the cigarette and my hand down, scarlet with shame.

"Funny how you never get over that," declared Movita, which I took to mean stage fright when meeting celebrities. What a phony I was—in awe of movie star Marlon, after all. My shaking humiliated me so I couldn't stop. I was bitterly disappointed in my character. A fan!

To my surprise, Marlon wasn't dark and dramatic looking, as he appeared in fifties black-and-white movies with their hard tones. His hair was light brown and his eyes blue, his skin a soft rosy white like Jimmy Dean's. His fine hair was the sort that balds young.

They had all waited an hour for me without ordering, inducing guilt. Spiegel helped me translate the French. In my starstruck dizzy state I couldn't see the menu too well. All that I remember distinctly that I ate was spinach. I adore spinach.

Sam Spiegel, the powerful fiftyish producer also known as S. P. Eagle, resembled a penguin in black-and-white tux. His high, balding forehead led to jowls to chin that merged with neck in a single penguin descent. However, he wore an urbane, sophisticated European eye and manner. Knowing, continental, Charles Boyer.

"What a marvelous gown," said Mrs. Osborn.

I smiled gratefully. These were nice people. They wanted me to be at ease, lighten up. I wore my black crepe Marilyn Monroe short evening gown with straps and form-fitting built-in bustier. Talk was general and easy. How I wished I looked like Movita, exotic, flashy-eyed dark with sweeping jet hair. Many men, Mailer included, liked Latins. I could understand that, having had a fling with a Colombian from Cali. The Osborns looked remarkably suburban.

Marlon seemed casual, laid back, except for his habit of lowering his chin, glancing up almost secretively and watching— me. Only, I presume, because I was the one person there not well known to him, and the only woman across from him. More observing than flirting.

After dinner the Osborns took their leave. The four of us repaired to Sam Spiegel's suite at the St. Regis for a nightcap.

Sam and Marlon talked current projects and Movita and I talked writing. By now I sounded reasonably recovered. I started to mention Jimmy Dean's phone call to Marlon. But suddenly I wondered if Jimmy was putting me on, and someone else was audibly breathing into the receiver. Later in the *New Yorker*, I read Truman Capote's interview with Marlon in which he told Tru that Jimmy haunted him with his persistent calls.

Marlon had taken to lowered-head spying on me again, only now he smirked knowingly, swung his eyes to Spiegel then back to me with a disgusted teasing sneer, as if he were thinking, I know your kind, you're going to bed with this ape for money.

I'm not a whore, I wanted to scream. I will *not* let your porcine producer touch me.

When Marlon and Movita said good night, Marlon wafted me a disdainful flirtatious leer, his head slightly to the side, nodding, as if to say, I know, I know. Marlon liked to intimidate people, disconcert them. Of course, I didn't know that.

"Thank you so much," I said. "I'd better fly." It hadn't occurred to me I'd be left alone with Spiegel.

"Sit down, sit down," Spiegel handed me a crystal snifter. "Try this fabulous French brandy."

"Yes, excellent," I agreed. Brandy was always too strong for me.

Sam Spiegel told me he got out of Germany in 1937 on the last boat before the Nazis clamped down. We talked about fleeing Jews and the Holocaust. Then Sam talked brilliantly about movies. Before I got too comfortable, I rose to go.

"Sit, sit, jumping jack," he chuckled. "I want to make you a serious offer." His large dark eyes got that bedroom look.

"Offer?" Stardom? Write a screenplay?

"I need a hostess," Spiegel took my hand, "for my Park Avenue townhouse. If you'd live there, I'd give you a thousand dollars a month for personal odds and ends."

"What?" I was flabbergasted, disappointed.

Sam covered both my hands. "I won't touch you, I won't ask a thing, only once in a while, if you'd let me lie next to you."

Spiegel pulled me to my feet. "Like this," he said, gripping both my hands and pulling me into the bedroom of the suite.

"I have a boyfriend," I frowned, trying to release my hands, which I accomplished as he flopped onto the bed.

"Let me show you," he patted the bed.

Annoyed, I headed back into the living room and grabbed my wrap.

Sam bolted up and caught me in the living room. "Please," he pled with his hangdog eyes, "only next to you. I only want to stroke you very gently. And maybe now and then I could kiss you?"

"Listen, I'm involved," I said, which wasn't true. I almost felt sorry for him.

Till Spiegel grabbed me in a massive strong-armed embrace and smashed my mouth open with the sheer force of his in a throat-scouring kiss, that left me all wet as I pushed hard to get away.

Furious, I found my purse and clutched my jacket and headed for the door.

Flustered, sweating, Spiegel bustled himself to courtesy. "I'll let you out," he said and palmed something into my hand. "Cab fare," he said. "If you should change your mind—" He handed me his card.

In the elevator, going down alone at midnight in my evening dress, among proper couples and men looking me up and down, I felt like a call girl. Was lipstick smeared over my face? Was my hair crazy?

In the cab I remembered to look at the bills—two twenties. If he had a townhouse, why was he at the St. Regis? Probably he'd have told me it was rented. Or he was just buying it, or whatever. Two twenties. That was my rate for amateurs—two hours for forty dollars. Let's just consider this a deviant modeling job.

What did my life have to do with these famous people? I thought as I climbed the slanting creaky stairs to my third floor studio. They were like icing on a cake that didn't exist.

How dreadful to desire youth so desperately, so fiercely. He should've sought a contemporary, but he was so obsessed with youth he wanted to buy it. Being a kept woman was an occupation of sorts back then, before there were decent jobs for women. Sam Spiegel ultimately married a young woman, though older than I, who looked in news photos more like a nurse than a glamour girl.

As for Marlon Brando, my actress friend, Chris White, phoned to invite me to a bon voyage party on the QE 2, which plied the North Atlantic to Europe. She'd booked on the same boat as Marlon, she said, on whom, she now confessed, she had a lethal crush. Marlon was there, all right. But as it turned out, Marlon was only there, like myself, to bon voyage a friend with champagne.

❧ 9 ❧

DOSTOYEVSKY THE PIN-UP GIRL
1955

My dear old dump on West Fifty-fifth was the shoddiest building from Fifth Avenue to the Hudson. During my longterm sentence there, it peeled, shredded, corroded, and caved, while the property manager knocked once a month to have coffee with me. The bannisters wobbled, stairs and floors slanted. On one was Mr. Connally, our super, a retired salesman who chain-smoked and was dying of lung cancer. On two were Jimmy the trombonist and Don the actor. On three with me was Nancy, the Metropolitan Opera Ballet soloist. On four were a machinist and an anarchist who always had a working girlfriend. Two furnished studio apartments on each floor plus two small rooms with hall bath rented by single men.

Mine was on the front with two windows looking out on the old Hearst Building, several brownstones, and a welfare hotel. When I sat on my bed reading, a Chinese man across the street would masturbate, a naked yellow Buddha aiming at me, bare bulb emblazoning his act. I painted the bottom half of that window white and decorated the ledge with a plant and a small Noguchi lamp. The place was seventeen-and-a-half feet by thirteen-and-a-half feet. I kept measuring it to try to make it bigger. I dreamed of being able to afford the room next door to have a separate bedroom. I had a swooping double bed and sagging dresser, circle chair, desk, and round Carrara marble dining table to replace the folding creature that came with the place. It was love/hate. Love because it was so cheap I could travel in summers.

Hate because I felt overwhelmed by my struggle to become a writer. A short story was one thing but a novel was vast, requiring—everything. When I couldn't make it work, I got so furious at myself that I banged my head against the wall till I wept. I scraped the wall with my nails and roared with pain. But I adored the writing process. It charged me up, it got me high so I rocketed whirling through the universe, like Kandinsky, creating new planets, moving from pettiness to profundity. Writing was my drug of choice.

I reread Dostoyevsky, *Notes from Underground* and the *Brothers*, and studied each page, each line and section of a page, to see exactly how he did it. He combined character, theme, action, and plot movement *all in one sentence*. How I yearned, ached, to be able to do that. Dostoyevsky thrilled me like Bartok—subtleties, interplays, ironies springing in human shapes from his ominous flow of words.

Dostoyevsky and I walked beside the Neva. He tried not to glance at Peter and Paul prison where, to destroy his soul, they had mock-executed him. Then we went back to his rooms to write at his massive dark desk. Did *he* have to punish himself by gambling? He wrote that the thrill and dread and fear of losing involved him more than the elation of winning. Tiny mock-executions. Tiny humiliations laced with fear and dread, like modeling. I hated modeling.

Fortunately, I bloomed at night in the lifting air from 11 p.m. to 5 a.m. I worked on my novel all night long. I got to bed about 6 a.m. with earplugs in and the answering machine on, slept through the ringing phone, and got up at 2 p.m. Then I phoned the model agency and Miss Olivia hollered, "Where were you all morning? You missed two calls."

"Give me their phone numbers," I said. I phoned and made appointments to see these clients at 4:00 and 4:45, saying I was booked all morning. As I was the last model interviewed, I often got the job. On the back of my composites I wrote "Model & Writer," so we had something to talk about that singled me out from the others.

Commercial photographers liked to book models from 4 to 7 p.m. when the advertiser could come after his workday. Amateurs liked to book 6 to 8 p.m. or 7 to 9 p.m. I'd come home, do ballet exercises while dinner cooked, eat, nap for forty-five minutes, get up and start writing at 11 p.m. My crazy schedule was entirely practical.

❧❧❧❧

Saturday they met my train, my real fans, the silent overstuffed daddies of the world. Don, the officious president of the Camden Camera Club, was backed by several bearish engineers, a kindly old master watchmaker, a sunny cynical Irish cop, a gray accountant, several splashy salesmen, and electronic technicians. Dedicated to the Art of the Camera, they shot nudes to Be Creative. They vied in telling me how many of my photos they'd collected from magazines.

"Don, I know one you missed," said Darrell the fuzz. "Four-page spread on Alice by Alex Heish in *Modern Photography*."

"This month, Darrell?" frowned Don, outdone.

"I missed it too," I laughed. "I'll tell Alex. He didn't know when it was scheduled."

"I'll mail you three-four copies, okay, Alice?"

"I still think your *Escapade* and *Nugget* layouts top 'em all," declared Bob the engineer.

Two salesman shambled over. "Would you mind autographing these, Miss Denham?" They handed me several eight-by-ten color prints from the last session at the clubhouse in Camden.

"Hey, these are great!" I knew to say. I signed them, "Besos, Alice."

We drove to the Pennsylvania woods.

❧❧❧❧

Glistening white maiden in bikini bottom perches on rock precarious in midst of gushing stream. Ten gents on one bank and six on the other click in unison box hung on their groins. "Hey, Alice, where ya hiding that sweet smile?" says salesman Sal.

"This is my classic ballet face, Sal."

"Ya look grumpy to me," offered the kindly old watchmaker.

I knew what they wanted. I slung my arms and tits into the air and whipped out the big grin with the big pearlies asparkle, ready to bite, and the boys came to with a jolt. Well, poor guys—if they had any taste, they'd shoot flowers and faces and ghettos, and I'd starve.

"Alice, I can tell you love your work," said Don. "You're so natural."

I guffawed at that one. I could put it on, off, at the drop of an eyelid. After all, I was brought up in the South, where womenfolk and blacks learn to needle Old Massah with dropkick wit, fast turns, and fleet insinuations instantly denied. Irony, some folks call it. Modeling forced me to glue on a smile, to plaster my face with coy and cupcake cute. My Southern girlhood surfaced in my smile and made it fetching. We Southern girls have the best smiles.

Sell, sell, sell—the American mantra. Sometimes I thought I'd collapse from the sheer effort of putting out such drivel.

I hated modeling. I hated throwing my clothes off for strange men. Week after week.

Was I punishing myself for losing the love of my mother and my husband? As if I had to expose my bare body to the elements like St. Simeon Stylites, and what was more, show patience, not chagrin. Do not hate those who devour you with their eyes, but love, and by loving, make yourself beautiful beyond their power to desecrate it.

❧ 10 ❧

DREAM BOY ANATOLE
FALL 1955

"Remember? We met at one of Norman's parties," Anatole Broyard phoned.

Adele Mailer had relented and invited me back.

Anatole! "Yes, of course." I shivered with delight. Anatole, reputedly the Great Lover of the Village.

"Were you away? I phoned before."

"I was in Mexico for the summer."

"I read your story—so daring," said Anatole. "I admire you for revealing all that."

"Well, thanks." I admire your looks, I wanted to say. But also, "Your "Cystoscope" story was—moving and courageous."

His story, "What the Cystoscope Said," was about his father's decline and death. My story was about an impoverished young woman painter who sleeps with an old Las Vegas gambler for money. There we were, in different issues of *Discovery*. Stacked on top of each other, cheek (soft) by jowl (strong). The sexy wild things we did between the covers!

Anatole Broyard was the very image of the Bohemian dandy. Anatole was straight-arrow handsome as a shirt ad. He didn't look quirky or weird as writers did. His family had moved to Brooklyn from the French Quarter in New Orleans when he was a boy. Anatole looked vaguely French, vaguely mulatto, exotic not literary. Yet Anatole was the most literary of all. He ate, slept, and talked literature. Unlike Norman and Jim Jones who talked about everything but. They were experienced. Apparently, Anatole was a beginner like myself.

We made a date. Though I'd long lusted after Anatole, I didn't think he knew I resided on the same planet. How could I stay out of this man's bed on the first date? Hoards of women had a lech for Anatole, and I felt foolish joining the queue. Still, Anatole was a turn-on. When he waltzed into a party, women became aware of their bodies.

We ladygirls were supposed to hold out till the second or even third date to gain respectability. To prove we weren't Easy. To make the suitor show he wanted more than a one-night stand. This was impossible for me, as I either burned with desire for a guy or not at all. Hot as a pistola, oversexed. Men told me I had a male sex drive. Which only meant I *admitted* I liked it as much as the boys did.

෴෴෴

The afternoon of our big date I posed for a bunch of hobby photographers at a seedy rental studio on Sixth Avenue at 24th. As I shined my nipples and cleavage with Vaseline, I sobbed. Fastening my lacy lowcut black bra too tight so my breasts would bulge over immensely, I kept from blinking because tears would smudge my savage black eyeliner. I hated this. I hated to model for amateurs. But I didn't earn enough from commercial shoots. Posing for camera clubs was classy compared to this, where guys just walked in off the street.

As I swept onto the set, I felt like a stripper, a stripteaser in a dive. The set was a white paper roll banked by rickety lights. Seven or eight voyeurs, gleaming phallic cameras hung on droopy guts, aimed their cameras at my covered crotch, tried to sneak around the side to see more. They stood five feet in front of the paper backdrop and I posed five feet back on the paper.

First I posed in my new sheer negligee with the lowcut bra and ruffly peach bikini panties underneath. They wanted less but for suspense I had to start somewhere. As a gruff voice muttered, "Take it off," I flung the negligee aside, jutted my hip out, lifted my hair, and wafted them a sultry Sophia Loren glance. Then I splayed my high heel sandals slightly, bent forward for cleavage display, and splattered them with a glittery Marilyn smile.

Then on my knees, I lowered a strap on my black bra and gave them a boopsy-boo Brigitte Bardot pout. Then the other strap—click click—as I twisted my back to them and unhooked the bra. Then rolled forward for their first bare breast shot, nipples stiffly alert—click click click happily as I swayed from pose to pose, combining ballet and flamenco and calisthentics and modern dance. Till shame fell away and I became a naked goddess, swaying my worshippers with my fierce erotic power. I was Ariadne, Isis, Coatlicue, source of life, I was fire, I was belief.

The hobby photographers almost forgot they wanted me to strip, wanted bottomless as well as topless. I posed with an elaborate silk flower bouquet covering Down There, and they shot furiously away, loving the suggestion they almost thought they saw.

Fortunately for me, it was illegal to show not only genitalia but an inch of pubic triangle or a shred of pubic hair. Censorship saved my remaining modesty. After I'd been nude modeling for awhile, I tried to think of my flesh as armor behind which I could not be seen. Maybe I had to run the gauntlet, humiliate myself, break my pride to be a writer. Like the *Flagellantes* I saw in Mexico, stumbling on the cobblestones, whipping their own backs.

๑๛๑๛

That night I dressed carefully for Anatole in my best little black dress. I wanted to look respectably chic to wash away the taint of the rental studio. I needed to talk literature to cleanse my soul. At night, if we didn't wear Bohemian black stockings and skirts and turtlenecks, we wore good black crepe cocktail dresses. Black was It, even then. Anatole also dressed up.

He came by in his tweed jacket and bow-tie and svelte form, toting Wallace Stevens's poetry. He looked as sartorial as an editor or agent. "Have you read Stevens?" Anatole read me a short poem. "He's wonderful, isn't he?"

"Marvelous," I grinned.

Some writers were brawling burly Hemingway, others were dapper Scott Fitzgerald. Anatole was Scott. Norman Mailer and Jim Jones were Papa Hemingway. The boys' club was good at cloning. Though large, Bill Styron was in the mode of small gentlemanly Faulkner. Anatole didn't feel dressed without a book under his arm. I never saw him without one.

We went for dinner at Chumley's on Bedford Street, which was wildly famous for having no sign identifying its heavy wooden door. You had to know. To know was to be In. We waved to Village artists and hangers-on we knew and I prayed no one would join us.

"Tell me about your story," Anatole's expressive soulful eyes spoke for him. "And how you come to be here."

Anatole Broyard was said to be a quadroon or an octoroon. His father, some claimed, worked in Brooklyn as an ordinary black man with a toolkit. But with World War II—he looked like an officer, which he'd been, on a troop transport—with the GI Bill and the New School, Greenwich Village and literature, Anatole had moved light years away. His skin was Latino beige, not as dark as my college suntan. Adventurous New York women were turned on by that heady dark possibility. Anatole was thirty-five in '55, older than his preppy looks, older than I expected. Yet he'd not published a book like Norman and Jim Jones.

"You wonder how I know about the Wild West," I said.

"Naturally."

I sighed. "I was married in graduate school, he left me for another woman, and I got a six-week divorce in Las Vegas. Then came to New York, which is what I wanted to do anyway." In those days only one state, Nevada, granted uncontested divorces. My copywriting job for KORK, the NBC station, was out on the Strip at the Thunderbird Hotel. Briefly, I was on-air interviewing show-biz celebs performing in town. I was happy to leave Las Vegas. I saw my Carlos's face everywhere.

"What was he like, your ex-husband?" Anatole's intensity made it seem he really cared.

"A deceptive charmer, multitalented. Left me for a docile

goddess—he was a sculptor." I was tired of describing her that way. I was tired of airing it.

Anatole's eyes showed pity. "Was it tough?" he said.

I was halfway up the rock face and didn't want to look down. My own suffering had become wearisome. "Las Vegas was like a neon campfire on the moon," I repeated. "I'd never imagined such a raunchy gaudy carnival—a giant Pop Art Hollywood whorehouse. Except sex played second fiddle to money. Money was sex. Hotels like papier-mache movie sets with cartoon facades." I paused. "I had to write about it."

"You talk as well as you write," Anatole seemed vaguely displeased. "Who do you like? I like Kafka and Celine and Lawrence and, specially, Stevens."

"Kafka and Dostoyevsky, Bartok and Thelonius Monk. I wrote my thesis on Eliot." I rather felt Celine and Lawrence were self-absorbed crybabies. Pity-poor-me types.

"You like Eliot?

"I *adore* Eliot."

"In the room the women come and go. Talking of Michelangelo," breathed Anatole.

"Let us go then, you and I, while the evening is spread out against the sky. Like a patient etherized upon a table" I replied.

"Oh, do not ask what is it. Let us go and make our visit," he said and we laughed. We talked writing till we glowed with camaraderie.

Anatole had something to show me before we went to Louie's Tavern. We walked to Patchin Place. "e.e. cummings lives there," he said proudly.

"There?" I said, amazed that he lived on solid ground. Cummings had read delectably at University of Rochester and shown his bad dreamy pastel paintings. Robert Frost, when he read at Chapel Hill, had seemed pompous, but Cummings was easy and welcoming. He was fetchingly elfin with a shaved head, pointed ears, and huge Buffalo Bill blue eyes. I shouted, "So how do you like your blue-eyed boy, Mr. Death?"

Anatole chortled. "If you only knew how many of us have done that." We rolled happily to Louie's on Sheridan Square. San Remo was boycotted temporarily. A tough Little Italy bartender, giving the bum's rush to a drunken customer, had taken the opportunity to beat him viciously.

We entered Louie's dank, jammed half-basement, which had a sordid furtive air. Suddenly I understood that the imported dirt that hung like moss from the low tin ceiling was there to make the bar look like a seedy dive. We artists felt that squalor equalled seriousness. How I loved to hang out. We found perches at the bar, ordered tequila and beer, and turned to check out the crowd. We both straightened. I stuck out my tits and he his manly chest.

Andrew Sarris, the tall lumbering critic, sped over. "That story of yours, 'The Deal,' that story changed people's lives."

"What?" I gasped.

"That was the first story any of us had read about sex from the point of view of the woman who takes money for sex. Instead of the man who pays." Sarris was excited.

"How did it change lives?" I asked.

But Sarris was important, and he'd already whirled away. Uplifted, I smiled a secret smile of pleasure, needing no one.

"Well," Anatole was miffed. "Chop, chop—a cut in time."

Mournful Milton Klonsky toodled up. Klonsky, poet and critic, was Anatole's great friend and my dear buddy.

Breathlessly, Milton said, "Have you read *Lolita*?"

"Nooo," we breathed.

"I'm awestruck. He's incandescent, Nabokov," Milton's hangdog eyes lifted and his face was beatific with thrill, as if he'd seen a vision he wanted to share with us both. "The best, very best novel I've read in ten years!"

"Really?" Impressed, I read it right away—we all did—and he understated it. Nabokov's sophistication was beyond American writers.

"Have you seen Genet's *The Balcony*?" I asked. They nodded. We agreed it was sublime.

Theatre was European sophisticated—Enid Bagnold's *The Chalk Garden*, Ionesco's *The Bald Soprano, The Madwoman of Chaillot* by Jean Giraudoux, Shaw's *Saint Joan* with Siobhan McKenna—and down-home American with William Inge's *Bus Stop,* Tennessee Williams's *Cat on a Hot Tin Roof,* and Arthur Miller's *View From the Bridge. Bus Stop* starred Ralph Meeker whom I dated off and on for several years. Off-Broadway in the Village, actor

Louis Gossett invited me to see him in Genet's *The Blacks*, still one of the greatest plays I've ever seen.

In November 1953 the great Welsh poet Dylan Thomas succeeded in poisoning himself with booze and died in St. Vincent's Hospital. In 1954 drunken old poet Max Bodenheim was murdered in a dingy Bowery room, he and his lady, by a jealous lover. In 1955 great jazz trumpeter Charlie Parker died, OD'd at age thirty-three, but Birdland lived. Also in 1955 atomic power was first used in the United States, in Schenectady, upstate. Another ladykiller like Anatole had just won the middleweight championship of the world, Sugar Ray Robinson.

Nicely lilting, not smashed, we walked to Anatole's apartment on Commerce Street. The Village was a triangulated maze you could cover in six to eight blocks. Anatole lived in a four-story Gothic brownstone at the elbow of Commerce Street where it swerved from the Cherry Lane Theatre to the Blue Mill Tavern on Barrow. At each flight my anticipation heated. I felt vaguely surreptitious. Usually I insisted on my place, to be at home. So if anybody wanted to leave, it wouldn't have to be me.

We were hardly in the door before we were in each other's arms in a mad passionate endless tongue-lashing. Tightly pressed against his body, I previewed coming attractions, heart pounding. Surely we were soulmates—we brilliant, gorgeous, talented two. Anatole made us a nightcap and I managed to notice his attractive apartment possessed more serious style than mine. Anything I liked got taped to the wall.

We kissed torridly, he clasped my breasts and licked them remorselessly, we dallied and twisted like eels into a nice fitting ying/yang—I was so moist I was embarrassed at my eagerness—and nothing happened. Anatole had a soft-on.

Men get nervous too, you have to be patient. Though I felt explosive, roiling, volcanic, tight as a drum—the female version of blue balls—I played calm. "Let's just rest," I said.

Anatole reached for a couple of joints, at the ready on a dish, and we lit up and toked. Certainly *he* seemed calm.

Everybody made a big deal about marijuana. Socially, I didn't like it. At parties, folks drifted into a state of dumb bliss with dim bulbs for heads. Nobody wanted to converse, just sit there grinning with clasped hands. It turned my head to cornmeal. If someone answered a question I asked, by then I'd forgotten the subject.

But grass expanded sound and physical sensation. Jazz slowed down so you heard every intimation. Colors and patterns and sex were enhanced. Every crevice and nodule I possessed became super-sensitive. My mind's eye could watch my vagina clasping his penis. But I feared depending on it because such effects seldom last, requiring more and more. But tonight was special. Already I saw us connected.

We talked quietly, then slowly and gently began to play again. I felt confident this would work because I'd been nonjudgmental, hadn't shown irritation. We tried again and again nothing happened. The same soft-on.

"I'm sorry, Alice," Anatole said. "I've never been able to make it with a girl who's my intellectual equal."

That was the fanciest rejection I'd ever had. "You don't like me?"

"I do. Want some brandy?" Anatole seemed perfectly normal, at ease, but vaguely distant. Not upset and not affectionate.

If he liked me, I was willing to wait forever for the sex. Trembling inside, thwarted, I said, "Let's just go to sleep." Trying to ignore my painful groin and hacked-up emotions, I felt I was being mature.

We went to sleep.

I was anticipating morning but the dawn rose without us. As I rolled toward him, hoping the night's nestling had made us closer, Anatole slipped quickly out of bed.

"Why, Anatole?"

"You're too much for me."

The most subtle form of discrimination: you're too much for me. Anatole considered me competition. If Sarris the critic had complimented *him*, not me, Anatole would've liked me.

꙳꙳꙳꙳

At parties Anatole was always with a new girl, either dazzling and distinctly dumb or very bright and rather plain. Hiding behind her, he'd flirt with me. At Fire Island, he'd duck behind her and fling sand at me, making eyes. Not once or twice but all weekend.

Anatole reminded me of my ex, who wanted control, not equality. Carlos had said he'd rather I sewed on buttons than become a writer, because I'd have more time to *do* for him. Control freaks, they're now called. It broke my heart that when I had everything in common with a man, that was too equal for him.

You're too much for me: the ultimate putdown. Check out the most interesting women from the fifties and sixties. They heard it from men who hated equality. Men did not recognize "female" accomplishment. We were called career women, disliked by men. But I was an Artist. Was that different? Superior women challenged male supremacy. Chauvinist pigs wallowed everywhere but no one had yet noticed the odor.

Anatole was a great lover because the boys did the grading. Because he posed as such, and they believed him. As Freud said, narcissism attracts. He was always with a new face. Quantity was all that counted. He did have one quality lady friend whom he lost by playing around, Anne Bernays, who became a published novelist of note and was a *Discovery* editor when they published my story.

As a secret notch carver myself, I kept a list, recording each man. Though I aimed for quality, my judgment was probably no better than Anatole's. I divulged no facts of character or performance, just a name to remind me as I flaunted about my humble digs. I wrote down Anatole and put 1/2 beside it. My votive carvings were hidden in a secret file with an innocuous name.

Anatole went on to respectability. He never wrote a novel. He married, moved to the Connecticut suburbs and became a daily book reviewer for the *New York Times*, able to cut, chop, and skewer novelist friends and foes at will.

❧❧❧❧

Sociologist Ned Polsky said that Anatole was famous for getting laid for ten years off one short story. If the girl said no, he'd say, You're prejudiced against me because I'm a Negro. That, said Ned, melted them because they felt guilty. Maybe the conventional lasses. But boxer Sugar Ray Robinson and poet LeRoi Jones, now Amiri Baraka, were in great demand. Even though LeRoi was married to Hettie, he had other white women as mistresses. The rich sister of a Wall Street trader I dated was Sugar Ray's envied girlfriend.

Belatedly, fellows and bedfellows, let me say you were all unnecessarily jealous of Anatole. Ask the women. It's not the show stoppers. It's the quiet guys that have it.

Anatole craved respectability, the opposite of imagination. To be creative, you must be willing to face humble reality. I don't think Anatole could bear revealing his poor family living the life of Brooklyn blacks. He'd passed. He didn't want to go back. He'd become white.

࿆࿆࿆࿆

When Anatole's posthumous memoir, *Kafka Was the Rage,* came out in 1993, it was about Greenwich Village in the forties, not the fifties when I knew him. Anatole died in 1990 of prostate cancer and wrote about it in a book of essays called *Intoxicated by My Illness.* Only after his death did the big poohbahs learn what we all knew in the early days. The *New York Times* reacted with shock that their esteemed book critic was black. Black, my, what a shock.

Anatole turned his back on his greatest story: how he successfully passed from one race into another.

❧ 11 ❧

LITERARY GANGS
WINTER 1956

"We need a model for 'Girl Gun Runners of Saigon.'" My friend, Alex Austin, author of *The Greatest Lover in the World*, phoned from Mag Man. Mag Man, or Magazine Management, was a book/magazine conglomerate before conglomerates. Half the young (male) writers I knew toiled there as editorial slaves.

"There are girl gun runners in Saigon?" I asked. This was 1956, long before Vietnam.

"Please, Alice," said twinkly curly squirmy Alex, "this is true adventure. We make it up."

Mag Man published men's magazines: *Male, Men, Man's World, For Men Only, True Action*. These were popular magazines before TV pounced on every petty war and revolution on the planet that permitted visitors.

Alex chuckled. He handled the book line: paperbacks and anthologies.

"You've noticed my eyes have an oriental tilt," I teased.

"Bring dark makeup," Alex said and we set the shoot.

෴෴

In the Mag Man studio at 655 Mad Ave, commercial artist Ralph Valenti shot photos of me that he'd sketch from to illustrate "Girl Gun Runners of Saigon." I posed as four Vietnamese women peering over a ridge, each with a rifle, bunched together.

For the first I posed peering through binoculars, the second aiming her rifle, the third shading her brow on lookout, and the fourth, supposedly tight against her, cocking her rifle, pistol on hip. Open-necked shirt for cleavage, clothespinned in back to pull tight as skin. Ralph would combine the photos for his sketch. I often modeled for commercial artists, for paperback covers, movie posters, and comic strips. I was Queen Zalita in Al Williamson's *Secret Agent X-12*.

Then I posed for a before and after ad, shot by Irv, the staff photographer. They'd booked me for two hours. This was the simplest kind of before and after ad, for a tummy-control waist-cincher. It was a mail order ad that garnered believers in surprising numbers. We shot it in bikini, in profile, which is most convincing.

"Slouch more," said Irv, the photographer. "Stick your tummy out more."

I did. "You want my jaw gaping so I look demented?"

"Don't overdo it," Irv laughed. Click click. "Now, stand up straight—straight as a die—lift your chest and tuck your tummy in."

Which I did. Click click click. Irv changed the lighting and we shot it several more times. As this wasn't nude, I got my normal rate of thirty dollars per hour, or two hours for fifty dollars.

Alex Austin whipped by and invited me to his next party.

෴෴

Alex was a partygiver like Norman. Everybody loved Norman and Adele's great rowdy soirees. Small genial Alex was cuddly and cute. He looked like a saner, happier younger cousin of Norman, like Norman at twelve.

Alex's apartment was on the fourth floor of a brownstone on 58th Street, right behind the Plaza Hotel, west of the Paris movie theatre. Did I know a human being who lived below the third floor? In the mid-fifties brownstones ran the cross streets from Fifth Avenue to the Hudson. The lofty office towers and hotels that dominate Avenue of the Americas didn't exist. It was plain old Sixth Avenue then. Not that Manhattan has ever conceded the name change.

As I was Alex's date, I met the rest of Mag Man at his party. The cast of characters included the *lover*, David Markson, managing editor of the book line, known as the house intellectual. David was starkly handsome with features almost as perfectly delineated as an El Greco. He was easily as handsome as Anatole, though far less aware of it. He was working on his first novel, *The Ballad of Dingus Magee*, a satirical western that Frank Sinatra would make into a movie. Naturally, I flirted with David.

Then there was the *wife-to-be*, Elaine Kretchmar, a gorgeous full-lipped blonde, who was executive secretary to the owner, Martin Goodman. Elaine would become my third literary agent and emerge as a big-timer.

Also at Alex's were Bruce Jay Friedman and his sexy redhaired wife, Ginger. Bruce handled Mag Man's *Playboy* ripoffs, *Swank, Bachelor, Stag,* and *For Men Only*. Bruce was goodlooking, conservative, riotously funny, always in a suit. He was working on his first novel, *Stern*. Later on, Bruce would handle the adventure line and buy "The Deal" for *Man's World*. The author—surprise!—he called Al Denham. Bruce and Ginger brought along Bruce's new assistant, Mario Puzo, who was working then on *The Godfather*. Puzo, a heavyweight, looked like the whole Mafia gang.

Also in the cast was the *introducer*, everybody's buddy, Joseph Heller, who was working on *Catch-22*, with Shirley, his curvy sexbomb wife. Joe, overweight and jolly, had a wild sardonic streak and bit his nails. Joe wrote ad copy at *Look* and wrote his novel after dinner and before breakfast, which is why *Catch-22* took ten years. His wife did everything else; he didn't have to pick up a plate or his underwear. Occasionally pat a child on the head. Originally he called it *Catch-18* till a book called *Mila-18* appeared.

The center of the drama that evening was the *agent*, everybody's agent but mine, the celebrated Candida Donadio, one of the first famous women agents of the fifties. Candida followed in the hallowed wake of Annie Laurie Williams and Audrey Wood. Candida was dark, melancholic, haunted, and overweight in Italian fashion. She did not move from the center of the sofa all evening, where she received supplicants. Her black eyes darted about wrathfully: a powerful figure. She handled Joe Heller, Mario Puzo, Bruce Jay Friedman, Alex Austin, and David Markson, and sold their first novels.

Joe Heller said, "Let me introduce you to my agent, Candida." We went over to her.

"You liked Alice Denham's story in *Discovery*, Candida." Joe carefully introduced me with credentials. "She's working on a novel you might take a look at."

"How do you do?" I leaned forward and stuck out my hand. "I've heard so much about you."

Famous agent Candida Donadio, the dark lady, looked me over, glared at me, went "Haruuumph," stuck her nose in the air, turned her head to the side, and refused to acknowledge my presence.

"Hello, there," I tried. "Candida?"

"Come on," said Joe and pulled me away.

"What did I do?"

Joe Heller shrugged. "She doesn't like good-looking women. I should've known."

"That's bizarre." I blushed.

Bruce Jay Friedman had watched the nonencounter. He put his arm around me and walked me over to his wife, Ginger. "Candida won't even speak to Ginger," he said and she nodded. "She likes to pretend she's having all of us, in her head."

Joe Heller joined us. "Well, so much for the mother of us all."

Candida's stable was all male. She was a queen bee, one of those women who don't like women. You see it all through the literary and art world.

Also at Alex's party was Stan Lee, who handled Mag Man's comic books and later began Marvel Comics, the most successful in the field. Blonde go-fer Rona Barrett came with Stan. Rona became a well-known TV Hollywood gossip reporter. Jazz authority and biographer James Lincoln Collier held forth. Freelancing for Mag Man were out-of-towners Mickey Spillane and Leicester Hemingway, younger brother of Ernesto.

Alex Austin was my buddy, as Joe and Bruce would be. Once

a week he played drums for the Stompers, who appeared at the Grove Street Cafe. Alex was single but I wasn't romantically inclined to him, yet he was kind and genuine enough to be my friend. I kept watching David Markson, who kept a running log of my movements. Finally I stood stock still and he ambled over and asked me for a date.

෴෴

The first thing David Markson told me, over dinner, was about Dylan Thomas. We strolled to Steak Pomme Frites on 56th west of Fifth Avenue. Cheap French restaurants lined 56th from Fifth to Sixth.

After Dylan Thomas gave a reading at Columbia, where David was a graduate student, on a whim David invited him for a drink. Dylan suggested the White Horse and they went various times. In Dylan's day the White Horse, on Hudson near Abingdon Square in the far West Village, was literary macho and longshoremen tough. Women preferred Louie's and the Remo.

"What was he like?" Dylan Thomas was the Bacchanalian patron saint of artists, revered as a demigod since his 1954 booze demise, after yet another galloping immortal drunk at the White Horse.

"Brilliant, when he wasn't too stewed to make sense," said David.

"He looked like a bloated angel fish in photos," I said.

"That was Dylan. You should've seen the crowd jam at the White Horse. People just stood and stared at him."

"Strange, how many writers just throw it away," I mused, as David played footsie with my ankles and his hand found my leg.

Markson and I were kindred souls. We were overliterary and oversexed, overvoluble, overexcitable, enthralled with literary Bohemian life. Unlike Anatole, David was humorous and fun. David was known to a select set as a stud lover-boy cocksman. Because he was literary and witty, handsome and hung.

I lusted so after David—we had such fun together—that it never occurred to me to fall in love with him. But it did occur to Elaine. Of course I thought he was dating both of us at the same time. We all did that. Noncommitment was the *cri-de-coeur*. If you pined for or demanded a monogamous relationship, you were square.

One night David brought over a huge novel called *The Recognitions* by William Gaddis. "This is the finest novel," David pronounced, "written by any member of our generation. Gaddis is astounding, the zeitgeist of our age." David was a generous enthusiast.

"I'd love to read it." Immediately I coveted it, a feeling I have only for books.

David bowed and presented *The Recognitions* to me. "Right away," he said, "because I need it back."

"What's it about?"

"You, me, expatriate life, the Village, sex, fraud, relationships—everything. You'll love his style."

I did love *The Recognitions*. I marveled at Gaddis's symphonic, erudite slangy style. Although I did weary of constricted Wyatt who treated affection as an obstacle to his art. A fashionable fifties and sixties stance among male artists was to consider the need for closeness an indication of female triviality. I hated that. It seemed to me an easy out. Wyatt was the veritable self-involved artist who communicates with art, not humanity. I loved the layered symbolic relationships and serious disgust with contemporary life. Though I did *not* feel the loss of religion severed human connection.

Alienation was the height of male literary chic. A refusal to reach out, disguised as inescapable human frailty. Each in his own cell, in solitary. I called it megalomania, suffocating self-love. Whereas ordinary men and women did manage to get close, to know and touch and relate. Even if they failed to make it last. What these hotsy male writers knew about love was *nada*.

Gaddis's novel became the underground cult novel of our day. The too-few copies in print were passed from one devotee to the next.

"Gaddis works over at Pfizer," said David. "I'll introduce you to him."

We met at the Remo, or was it Julius's? I'd finished the holy novel and David had it under his arm, grinning with the thrill of Gaddis's book.

"Indeed, I loved your novel," I said, "the philosophic exploration, the style."

Gaddis thanked me with a wan sparkle, lit a cigarette off the butt he discarded, and we ordered drinks.

Gaddis looked New England gothic, slight, rail-thin with a highboned narrow face, bony hands, yet an insinuating air. He was medium-toned with beige skin and beige straight hair. Willie Gaddis was a miniature—not tall but so thin he seemed taller. His amused glance was so aware and at the same time wary that he gave off a world-weary attitude that was not unsexy.

"You look like the poor man's Frank Sinatra," I let out.

Gaddis smirked rakishly. "Poor is right. I do copy over at Pfizer along with writer Dick Dowling. You know Dick?"

"Nope." A few years later I'd date Dick Dowling, who was working on *All the Beautiful People*. We often doubledated with Gaddis and his wife, Patty. "When do you write?" I was always astounded when anyone holding a full-time job turned out a novel.

"We put money aside and I did most of *The Recognitions* in Europe and Mexico. But Pfizer's not too bad. They let Dick and me write all morning on our own stuff and show us off to clients as 'our novelists.'"

"How's *that* for luck?" put in David.

"Not bad." Imagine, a *corporation* did that! In 1956.

Like many cadaverous people, Willie Gaddis looked debonair. He bought David and me a drink. Easygoing and friendly, tart wit of the Cole Porter sort, Gaddis seemed a tad more sophisticated, more mature, than David and me. He was older, more experienced.

Smoking like a chimney, he wafted goodbyes and went home to dinner with Patty and daughter, also in the Village.

David Markson did more PR for that novel than any PR firm could have accomplished. He flogged it. He carried it under his arm, mentioned it to every literary person he encountered, to dozens of important writers and editors. In a sense, it was David who launched *The Recognitions*. Few young writers were that ecstatic about their competitors.

❧❧❧❧

Wamsutta Sheets had hired me for the Linens and Bedding trade show at a Lexington Avenue hotel. Bright and early at ten-thirty every morning I took off my street clothes. I donned an elaborate lavender gown with lavender ribbon straps and climbed into the bed with its beautiful silken cover in a dark room with little twinkling lights. Customers looked at me through a giant keyhole constructed into a cardboard display door.

"Do you want me to actually sleep," I'd asked, "or just lounge about and pretend, with a beatific smile?"

"Really sleep, if you can," replied the sales director.

That week I wrote all night and slept all day and got paid very well for it. Once in a while I'd wake up, wonder where I was, and refrain from a big yawn.

Then I'd hear: "Is she real?"

"No, she hasn't moved."

"Wait—I saw her breathe."

"It's a doll, you dummy."

Slowly I'd slide an arm, and they'd gasp.

࿇࿇࿇࿇

Ad Reinhardt looked like the ad agency exec he'd been. He wore button-down pink striped shirts with white collars, silken ties, and vests over his large chest. Ad was natty. We met at P. J. Clarke's where the ad crowd hung out. Working at an ad agency was considered the next best thing to being an artist. After all, each agency had a creative department. Ad guys fondly spoke of great creative campaigns, meaning ads that worked. Andy Warhol and Pop Art originated in ad agencies. Pop was commercial art sanctified by *haute* galleries.

Ad Reinhardt showed his black-on-black paintings at Betty Parsons gallery, the hottest Abstract Expressionist showplace in town. Betty Parsons pushed Rothko and Pollock, Barnett Newman and Saul Steinberg, while pining for recognition as a painter herself.

"Now, explain to me this black-on-black," I said.

Ad burst out laughing. "I did it as a gag. I had no idea it would catch on. Smear it all—just what the art world deserves."

"You're very clever. You're a total hit," I laughed.

"Phony baloney," said Ad, "just like the ad game."

First, we had to get our Monk fix.

৯৽৽৽৽৽

Down into the low roar of the Five Spot to hear the great Thelonius Monk. The Five Spot was on artfully sordid St. Marks Place in the East Village. Ad and I sat at a tiny table for two in the dark urban forest beneath a pinpoint lamp.

"Round Midnight" followed "Straight, No Chaser."

I revered Thelonius, who was godly toward fans. Godly in a playful way, as he reinvented jazz piano with a flurry of intricate new sounds and rhythm. I owned all his records. My high-school years were spent in black jazz clubs when I was supposed to be at the movies. The new innovative jazz, bebop or modern, charged me up like Bartok's scintillating dissonances.

"This black-on-black," Ad said more seriously, "it's sort of like a stretched single sound."

"A mono-sound," I said, "like Monk holding a chord?"

"Good as any. Or an oriental gong."

New York in the fifties was the era of the sophisticated Negro, not the tough street black. Of James Baldwin and Ralph Ellison and, I would discover, Zora Neale Hurston. Of the Duke and Diz and Charlie "Yardbird" Parker, of Sarah Vaughan and Billie Holiday, Lena Horne and Harry Belafonte. Musicians and writers and artists, black and white, mixed. We were all, according to us, superior to bourgeois America around us with its prejudices and prohibitions. None of us white folk had any realistic notion of how really rough discrimination was for our black friends.

Black LeRoi and white Hettie were married at a time when interracial couples caused shock on the street. Though some of us, including me, dated black guys, marriage was uncommon. Occasional captions on news photos from the South would report that this black-white couple had been arrested for miscegenation. It was still illegal in thirty states.

৯৽৽৽৽৽

Ad Reinhardt and I walked up the stoop at 324 East 14th Street, and entered the large dark front room of LeRoi and Hettie's apartment. An immense mirror between the front windows gave back dark ghostly shadows of guests moving about.

When we adjusted to the gloom, we found LeRoi, who was slim and frenetic with huge bulbous tormented black eyes. His arm was draped around a pretty young white woman, not Hettie, whom he introduced to us as his chick.

"Go on back to the kitchen and get a drink," he said, grinning and wheeling to greet poet Harvey Shapiro.

"Hello, Harvey," I introduced Ad. Harvey's wife had already departed for the back. Harvey, with his wily sparkle, was the first poetry editor and ad manager of the *Village Voice*. Harvey would become the discerning and popular editor of the Sunday *New York Times Book Review* and a noted poet.

Circling through the romantic dark were half the poets in New York—wild-haired Allen Ginsberg, gaunt Joel Oppenheimer, sexy Diane DiPrima, my buddy Milton Klonsky. Husky *Voice* publisher, pale blond Ed Fancher, and blonde political columnist Mary Perot Nichols were there. Mary was credited with helping to save Washington Square Park when Commissioner Robert Moses wanted to extend Fifth Avenue through it. Ed had been Adele Mailer's first boyfriend. Also *Voice* writer John Wilcock, disheveled Englishman and our party inviter. Also *Times* writer Victor Navasky who would become editor of *The Nation*, suave and clever; blonde beauty Joyce Johnson, then Glassman, working on her first novel, *Come Join the Dance*. Joyce would win the National Book Award for *Minor Characters*, her haunting memoir of an on-and-off affair with Jack Kerouac.

Our genial host, LeRoi Jones, greeted his good buds and literary pals and the stunners with them. Ad Reinhardt and I separated. Every dating pair split on entering to foray for the future, to flirt and chat and, hopefully, argue the fine points of Joyce or Camus, or the poetry and stories in the new *Discovery* and *Partisan Review* and *New American Writing*. I headed for the kitchen.

Wives and chicks clustered around the kitchen table, harboring small children, infants in arms. Their resentful glances followed the free women circling the rooms and the men. Finally I figured which was Hettie because she got up and down and fixed drinks and shoved plates into the sink. Hettie Jones was not pretty but interesting looking in that intelligent way that makes pretty women, like me, feel she must be far smarter. I introduced myself. Overburdened and harrassed, Hettie had time to say "Hi." The former Hettie Cohen, though a fine poet, dedicated herself to LeRoi the poet and their children. Later she'd write *How I Became Hettie Jones*, a revealing memoir of their marriage.

The neglected wives and chicks wafted hateful looks at the gorgeous and mobile whom their husbands and mates never doubted their right to pursue. Several writers there, besides LeRoi, had established girlfriends on the side. It was not only rumored but you could tell by the intimate way they stood together, like a couple. If it was obvious to me, it must've been obvious to their wives.

Why did they put up with it? I wondered. They sat huddled together at the table in an angry knot that made them look ugly. The wives and chicks had the tribal glaze of the habitually and passively oppressed. I thanked my lucky stars I'd never let myself get into their position.

In those days LeRoi Jones was integrated. This was before he broke with Hettie, renounced the white world, and became Amiri Baraka, black activist and separatist.

Ad and I didn't fall into bed as we seemed not to have developed any special rapport. Though we liked each other, we'd been too distracted and excited to talk. Ali, babe, don't you know the rule? You're *always* supposed to sleep with famous men, so you can tell people.

Ad Reinhardt didn't become as famous as other Abstract Expressionists because, unfortunately, he died young. Overdid it, as we all did.

༺༻༺༻

At George Plimpton's party, writers and editors rolled on tall shoulders. Plimpton, at six foot three, gabbed with Joe Fox, six foot three, Random House editor, surrounded by various important-looking lengthy personages. Though American, they spoke French to each other. They seemed to have just blown in from Paris, and name-dropped Deux Magots and the Flore, Cloiserie de Lilas and Brasserie Lipp.

"Spent an evening with Jean Paul and Simone at the Montana," said some elevated aesthetic beanpole.

Glancing up at their heads in the stratosphere, I felt too small to be noticed. These writer and editor fellows talked to each other, as if the women present were invisible. Lovely tall women hovered around them, listening respectfully. They all possessed the flat, stylishly repressed, Ivy League monotone. Now and then a woman would launch forth, get going, be interrupted then ignored. Then she'd stand there quietly with that intimidated smile.

George Plimpton wrote books about trying out for pro teams and playing in a game or two. *Paper Lion*, about his fling with the Detroit Lions football team, was popular. Plimpton's literary stature, though, resulted from publishing the *Paris Review*, a leading literary journal. From Paris, Sadruddin Aga Khan backed the *Paris Review*, lending it exotic international cachet and perhaps money. Plimpton was scion of a rich social WASP family, his father partner in a lofty law firm. Quietly beside him now and then stood his tall classic blonde wife, then, almost bowing, she'd duck away to look after hostessing the party.

Many guests appeared not to have to work for a living, unlike the Mag Man editorial slaves and the Bohemians at LeRoi and Hettie's soirees, who scraped by with a bit of editorial or an article here and there, when they weren't moving furniture. The best job was working Wednesdays for Danny List distributing the *Voice* around town. Danny hired only (male) artists and paid each one hundred dollars for the day. Easy to live on four hundred dollars a month! At those parties I yapped my head off about writing and literature. But this wasn't a democratic party.

At last I spotted Vance Bourjaily, who'd invited me and introduced him to my date, sculptor Gardner McKay, who happened to be six foot five. Vance introduced us to Barnaby Conrad, who'd just written *Matador*, his bestseller about being a bullfighter in Spain. As a blond blue-eyed muscular matador, Barnaby had been a hit. Also there were others Vance had published in *Discovery*—poet Muriel Rukeyser, novelist Herbert Gold, critics Leslie Fiedler and Paul Goodman. All these appeared more approachable.

Gardner was surrounded by women, Vance wandered off. I approached Herbert Gold, whom I recognized from his photo on his novel, *The Man Who Was Not With It*, part of which had run in *Discovery*. Gold had fine precise features in a pale, bony, handsome face, set off by cold black wavy hair.

"How do you do, Herb," I said. "I'm Alice Denham. We've both had stories in *Discovery*."

"Who?" he scowled.

I repeated it, adding, "I liked yours greatly."

"I know who you are," said Herbert Gold, lip curling in disgust. "You're that pinup model."

"What?" I said foolishly.

Herbert Gold gave me a cold nasty glare and spun away, highly offended.

My date, Gardner, had watched our exchange and came over. "You want me to punch him out?"

"Leave it," I said, face scarlet.

Still, I felt the worse sin was to be respectable.

❧❧❧❧

"If you don't shut off that phone, Gardner, I'm going home," I warned. I'd known Gardner for two years. All he had to do to get women was to lie in bed and answer his phone, and admit visiting ladies at appointed hours.

During his brief spurt of fame, Gardner McKay was called the handsomest man in New York. He was very tall, dark, handsome with the bluest eyes and longest black lashes, perfect curve to eyebrows and sensual mouth. At parties he was prettier than all the women as well, but he looked macho virile. However, Gardner was a quiet solitary man who liked to tinker with his sculpture. One Christmas I helped Gardner hang a mobile he'd sold to Time-Life for the lobby of their building.

Photographers approached Gardner on the street asking him to model. When he ran out of money, he did. Instantly he appeared in major ads and on magazine covers, and in no time, he landed in Hollywood. He starred as a sea captain in a ballyhooed TV series called *Adventures in Paradise*. There was only one problem. Gardner couldn't act.

Never were a man's inside and outside so ill-matched. He'd tasted fame and it had moved him away from himself. I read that he moved to Hawaii and became a recluse. Eventually Gardner wrote an affecting sea saga drama that I've seen several times on public TV. He began to write seriously.

The war novelists, Mailer and Jones, plus Styron, were now bumped by younger male novelists—Saul Bellow, J. D. Salinger, Bernard Malamud, Harvey Swados, the lovely Herbert Gold, with three majors yet to come: Joseph Heller, Philip Roth, and John Updike. The gentility of the publishing world was jolted by dynamic new houses and editors.

Paris Review published incisive interviews with revered writers—Hemingway, Faulkner—plus Styron and Jones. In paperback anthologies called *Writers at Work*, they were marvelous instruction manuals for the boys.

❧ 12 ❧

LUNCH WITH GORE
SPRING 1956

I met Gore Vidal and Leo Kelmenson, my ad agency buddy, for lunch at the St. Regis in the King Cole Room. Behind the bar in a wall-to-wall mural, old King Cole made merry with his minions. As I crossed the room filled with exquisitely scented expensive people, Leo stood up and waved, and Gore rose too.

Once more, Gore Vidal wasn't the devastating stunner he appeared on the book jacket of his controversial novel, *The City and the Pillar*. We all, apparently, benefited from dramatic lighting and subtle retouching.

"Alice, this is Gore Vidal," said Leo proudly. "And, Gore, this is Alice Denham, a talented young writer herself."

"How do you do?" We shook hands, sat down, ordered cocktails.

When I told him I enjoyed his novel—boldface lie, I hadn't glanced at it—Gore waved it away. "Second-rate stuff," he dismissed it cavalierly.

"You let yourself off easy," I demurred. I'd heard Gore wasn't quite first-rate. But that was from the macho war novel boys. We pored over outsized menus and ordered lunch.

Gore was sardonic and witty and smooth. Unlike most young novelists, he looked to be gentry. His brown-blond hair waved with casual perfection, his skin was peerless. His almond eyes were seductive and his lips sensual, chin a tad short. His grandfather was powerful Oklahoma Senator Gore. His privileged family was part Southern political. His father was a World War I aviator, like mine. After that, his mother tended to marry rich, to Hugh Auchincloss whom she relinquished to Jackie Kennedy's mother.

"Sooner or later, I want to run for something," said Gore. "Country's in the hands of lethal nincompoops."

"Where?" asked Leo.

"That's the tough one," said Gore. "Time's not right, anyway."

"Start some prominent do-good project," I suggested.

"Sounds exhausting," Gore grinned.

We all marveled at *Long Day's Journey Into Night*, O'Neill's posthumous play. "His finest," I said.

"Absolutely," Gore agreed.

Then I sang the praises of the New York City Ballet, especially its leading male dancer, Jacques d'Amboise. D'Amboise was straight, not gay like so many male dancers. He got to me where I lived.

"Not only is he nimble and emotional," I sighed. "But his delicate turns with those long sexy muscular legs. Drives me wild." I laughed, "I'm in love with Jacques d'Amboise."

"Oh, so am I, darling," said Gore, leaning forward, not quite flapping his wrist. "I'm mad for the boy."

Then I knew.

My face didn't fall, but I plunged inside. It had never occurred to me that suave Gore was gay. He didn't hide it. He simply didn't broadcast it. Finally Gore declared himself bisexual, which everybody felt was the code for gay, back when homosexuality was barely tolerated and mostly denied. Though Tennessee Williams and Truman Capote were openly gay, flagrantly so. If I had actually peered into *The City and The Pillar*, I'd have known it too.

What I didn't know was that Gore Vidal had just written about my own famously gay cousin, Denham Fouts, in his 1956 memoir of expatriate days in Europe, called *A Thirsty Evil*. Denny was Elliott in "Pages from an Abandoned Journal."

Denham looked like a young WASP prince in the Cecil Beaton photo on Grandmother's gold piano. I was madly in love with my impossibly handsome cousin. He ran away from Jacksonville at sixteen with a rich man, around 1930. I'd never laid eyes on him. In his thirties, he looked like a teenager.

Truman Capote lived with cousin Denham for six months in Paris in the forties. Denny had fallen for Tru's seductive jacket photo on his first book, *Other Voices, Other Rooms*. He sent Tru a first-class ticket to Europe, saying come see me. Truman called Denny the "Best Kept Boy in the World" in *Answered Prayers*. Denny was the "Unspoiled Monster" kept by wealthy men in Europe including Prince Paul of Greece, who pensioned him off when he became King Paul. But the one who wrote most tellingly of Denham Fouts was Christopher Isherwood in his 1962 book, *Down There on a Visit*, in which he called him Paul. They lived together for a year in L.A., a celibate year before Denny served in the army as a conscientious objector, doing duty as a cook during World War II.

Denny's mother, Aunt Mamie, Dad's sister, showed us his exotic postcards from all over the world. Never an address. The family worried, but what could they do? In *Time* magazine, there was a photo of Denham lion-hunting in Africa with a rich Brit who belonged to the pro-German Bund before the war. For a while we worried that he was a Nazi spy. He'd posed in a Nazi uniform as a joke and got caught in Germany after the war began. Influential Brits had him flown out.

In Hugo Vickers's biography of Cecil Beaton, Vickers says, "Cecil hated Denham Fouts with what Truman Capote described as 'an unconsumed passion." The man he was in love with, Peter Watson, was in love with Denny. According to Tru, Denny knew how to torture Watson and other wealthy gays by making them pay for his opium addiction. An international gay star, my benighted cousin died of a heart attack in Rome at age thirty-five, on his second withdrawal from opium.

Gore had been a friend of Denny and I could have *asked* him about Denny. But I didn't know that till years later. I didn't know that Gore, Capote, Isherwood, and Speed Lampkin all wrote about Denny. In *A Thirsty Evil*, Gore wrote that Denny gave great parties and would receive visitors sitting up in bed, recovering from an opium bout, still looking like a teenager. He was a center of the European gay world.

Denham Fouts wrote himself. He'd planned to come home to Jacksonville in 1948 to recover from his second opium withdrawal. He sent his writing on to his mother, my aunt Mamie, a memoir of his life and times. After he died, she read it, discovered he was gay, and burnt every page.

How strange to unknowingly encounter someone who knew my own cousin, who fascinated me so as a child, whom I had longed to meet. In his memoir of his early days, *Palimpsest*, Gore says he wishes Denham Fouts had written a memoir.

He did, Gore, and it was destroyed. His mother burnt it.

Just as my own mother would burn my first published novel.

❧ 13 ❧

HEFNER HIMSELF & PLAYBOY
SPRING 1956

"John, I've got a dynamite idea." I phoned my literary agent, John Cushman. John was a gangly New England Brahmin, a perfectly sweet level-headed guy, the sort my parents wanted me to be interested in.

"Shoot," said John.

"I was leafing through *Playboy* magazine and came across Delmore Schwartz's great story, 'In Dreams Begin Responsibility.'"

"So—?"

"That means they take *reprints*. I read that story originally in *Discovery* or *Partisan Review*."

"I'm all ears."

"Why not get them to reprint "The Deal" and use me as Playmate of the Month? I'm modeling anyway. That way, they can say something more interesting about the gal other than that she takes her clothes off."

"Why not? Why *not?*" said John. "A great idea. I'll write them a very classy letter."

"And I'll come up with a couple of my best color nudes."

"By Jove," John laughed, "we'll get that story read by half the men in America."

Playboy bought the idea. Hefner loved it.

❧❧❧❧

Playboy flew me to Chicago to pose as Playmate of the Month in March 1956. I was to be their July centerfold, the naked lady with the stapled navel, who folds out into three full-color pages. My story would be in the same issue.

I was told to wear a red rose in my hair to identify myself.

Hugh Hefner himself met me at O'Hare. When he spotted my red rose and bustled over, he quickly escorted me to a limousine. As he rigidly bowed me into the limo, I assumed from his black suit he was the limo driver. I got in the back.

"I'm Hugh Hefner, how do you do?" he said.

"Oh!" I tittered. "How do you do, I'm Alice Denham." I got in front.

"Call me Hef," he said, lifting a stiff curtain of a grin.

"You look like an American gothic," I let out. Far more than Gaddis.

Hefner's black crewcut stood straight up over his bony preacher's face with sharp calculating black eyes. His pale face was rawboned, angular, younger than I'd expected. He was slim and well-built, about five foot ten.

"Nobody ever said *that* to me," he smiled tightly.

Hef had the sort of gripping mouth that needs a pipe stuck in it. A few years later he'd use a pipe as a prop on TV. His jaw was staunch and constricted. Hef seemed the soul of propriety.

❧❧❧❧

Taking my elbow, Hef escorted me into a stylish *boite* for dinner. He moved briskly, in a stern almost military manner. In a dark cozy corner with dim lights, I ordered a Bloody Mary and Hef a Pepsi.

"You don't drink?" I said surprised.

"Not often." His eyes softened, as did mine.

"That's admirable." That would keep me from overdoing it.

Teeth clamped on pipe, Hef said, "Your story won me over—hard-hitting stuff for a girl."

"Thanks, I'm so glad." Now I felt easy.

We ordered steak, filet mignon for me. In those days of yore, everybody ate cow. Chicken was Sunday with the family.

Various people stopped by and huddled for a moment with Hef. The owner came over and the sexy young waitresses seemed like friends. He was known here. Hef may have been already famous to the men of America but he wasn't to me. He seemed to wait for a compliment.

Finally he said, "You don't seem very impressed with our operation."

"It depends on what you publish," I replied. "You've published wonderful writers, so far. I hope you keep it up."

Hef laughed. "*Playboy* is a phenomenon, don't *you* know that? We had our second birthday in January."

My mouth rounded in ignorance. I had the wit to say, "Sounds fascinating. Tell me about it."

"We started on a shoestring, only six hundred dollars of mine, the rest borrowed and begged. First, I got the Marilyn Monroe nude calendar—an unused shot—for a mere five hundred dollars from the printers."

"Marilyn for five hundred dollars?"

"Same as you're getting."

"She didn't demand more?"

"She got zip. I paid the printers. They owned it. I saw her model release."

On every commercial photo shoot, a model signs a release that gives that photographer or company the right to do anything legal they wish, including resell the photo forever. The printers had held Marilyn Monroe's nudes till she made *The Asphalt Jungle* and established a name. Then they printed the famous nude calendar and pocketed the profit. Hardly fair.

"Our sales are doubling every month," said Hef. "We can barely print enough copies to meet the demand. It's amazing."

"That's almost unheard of," I said. "You must know how to—"

"*Please men*," said Hef. "If I like it, I figure they do. We're the hit of the business."

"It's the naked ladies," I insinuated.

"Including you," he flipped back, "who'll be one of our finest ornaments."

"I only do it for a living," I got snide. "You exploit it."

"That's why you're here." Hef drained the Pepsi and another instantly appeared. "You gals love to fling your clothes off. Then claim we made you do it."

We smirked at each other, a standoff.

"Maybe you're right," I admitted. "I've always loved it and hated it both. Upbringing versus exhibitionism." No, the problem was to strip *on call*, to keep *on* disrobing for strangers. Like plunging into ice water. "I'm buying time. You're building an empire off women's bodies."

Hef burst out laughing. "You forget this was *your* idea."

"Yes, it was." I blushed fire.

"It'll advance your career too," Hef said sagely. "Wait and see."

"How did you get the nerve to publish a magazine?" I asked seriously. "I'd publish all my own writing."

"*Esquire* refused to give me a five dollar raise." Hef got better looking as he relaxed. "So I decided to put out a college humor mag, like the old *Esquire* with voluptuous girls. It took off. Guns or girls, that's where the market is."

At University of Illinois Hef had put out a successful humor mag, *Shaft*. Then he self-published a book of his own cartoons, *That Toddlin' Town*, satirizing Chicago. Hef was sharp and analytical, not sensitive and cultured. He'd gotten to know major newsstand dealers around the country when he was promo manager for Publishers Development Corporation's gun and girlie mags. He delighted in explaining all this. I always found business processes fascinating.

Out of my Mexican bag I pulled a copy of *Discovery #5* that had my story in it, and handed it to Hef.

He handled it as a rich man does small change, smiled vaguely. "Uh huh."

"*Discovery* is famous in New York," I said. "One day those names will be well known."

At the small Near North Side hotel near the *Playboy* offices, Hef escorted me to my room, carrying my bag. I still had not seen the offices at 11 East Superior Street, and had not met a single soul but Hefner.

"Dinner was lovely," I said. "Thanks so much. And for meeting my plane."

"Aren't you inviting me in for a nightcap?" Hef asked in a proprietary tone.

"Sorry, I have to get my beauty sleep," I said. "So I'll look fresh in the morning." The shoot was scheduled for 10 a.m.

"Pretty please," said Hef.

"Tonight, no. Tomorrow—maybe," I flirted.

"See you at the studio," Hef spun on his heel and was gone.

❧❧❧❧

Next morning gray Chicago glare pushed at the large studio windows. The tall stooped old photographer, Hans, busily tested his color film. His assistant, a leering gnome, peered at me surreptitiously as he moved massive lights around. A young black guy scurried about representing editorial *Playboy*. Hugh Hefner was nowhere in sight.

In the dressing room, Pam the stylist, who looked more like a model than I did, applied pancake makeup to my back, my buttocks, and legs. Pam's mission was to perfect Miss July as a worthy Playmate of the Month.

Of course, I coated the entire front of my body, an endless unnecessary job. Pam explained the motive for all this pasty pancake was to create uniform flesh, like an all-over body stocking.

"Yes, Pam, but it flattens form and eliminates curves," I objected.

Pam pursed her lips, "This is how we always do it."

Normally I used makeup only on my face and neck, my knees, and the broken vein like a jagged radar signal on my left thigh. I aroused my nipples and emphasized my cleavage with Vaseline.

"Now," said Pam, "for a bit of rosy lipstick on the nipples."

"Oh no, you don't." I held firm on this one. "I don't want to look like a candy store."

"But you're Miss Playmate," Pam pouted. "We want you to look delicious."

"I'm a writer," I crackled. Where was Hefner? Wasn't he coming?

"We've never had a writing Playmate," Pam's eyes grew. She reached for a little chignon of curls to plop on top of my head.

"No, Pam, that's redundant. I want to look like a human being."

Pam's chin thrust anxiously forward.

"You've made my hair look perfect, Pam. You're doing a fine job." I slipped into a negligee and slippers provided by *Playboy*.

"We're ready," Pam hollered.

She marched me from the dressing room to the shooting area, as if she were shielding me from the coarse stares of crowds of onlookers. Upon arrival at the edge of the pink paper backdrop, the young gnome assistant wiped off the soles of my slippers with a damp cloth, so they wouldn't leave prints. Pam asked Hans the photographer if he wanted the negligee on. He shook his head, of course.

Then Pam removed the negligee from my shoulders as if she were unveiling the Kohinoor diamond. I almost expected Wagnerian music to thunder forth, announcing my entrance. Would the empyrean open and angels clap? I managed not to snicker.

Everybody was terribly deferential. A nude shoot such as Playmate of the Month is a solemn, grand, even slightly dangerous occasion.

Dead silence, as I climbed onto the bed that constituted the set, trying not to face them head on but failing. Where was Hef? Didn't he want to see? I sat on the downy bed covered with a baby blue blanket draped low around my hips. Masculine artifacts indicated an unseen man around the periphery of the set. A jacket and tie was draped over the headboard, shoes under the bed. There was a man in my celluloid life!

The scene was to be a pillowfight between myself and my unseen implied male lover. A lightning jolt—all the set lights came on at once. Hans peered through the camera, muttered to the gnome, who moved a light. Over my head the hair light bounced, casting deep shadows on my face. They inched it back.

At the penultimate moment, in bustled Hefner with his promo director, Victor Lownes III, a tall curly second lead. My nipples stuck out like early warning devices, as I pretended I didn't notice. When Hef said hello, my whole body blushed. That had happened only once before, on my very first figure modeling job.

"You look as good as your pictures," Hef said casually. "This is Vic Lownes, our promo chief."

Nude but for the hip swaddling, I said, "How do you do?"

"Hi, there," said Vic.

Hef turned to Vic, "Not bad for a writer."

"Not a'tall," said Vic.

Voraciously they gazed at me, and I at them. Reeling with heat, I sat back and basked in a sunbath of lust and hot lights. My legs were tucked under the blue blanket which also hid my nether region.

"Where's your Phi Beta Kappa key?" asked Hef.

"I didn't bring it."

"Here's one to wear," he offered.

"That looks cheap. I don't want to."

"It's very elegant camp," Hef declared and approached to clasp the key necklace around my neck.

"No," I said sharply. "I will not wear it."

"Okay, okay," he backed off right away. Of course, he didn't want an angry model. You have to placate models and keep them in a lilting mood.

"Ready, Hef?" asked Hans.

"Shoot," Hef nodded and we began the shoot.

My first pose I arched my back extremely and lifted the pillow, which also lifted my breasts, smiled rampantly, and threatened to throw. I held it there while Hef tossed feathers to simulate the pillowfight. Hans's camera clicked and feathers flew.

But feathers flew after the camera clicked. We did it again. Feathers flew before. Click—after! Click—before! This should be simple. Once again I lifted the pillow and renewed my iron smile. Feathers filled the air. Kachoo—I collapsed with feathers in my nose, in my hair, prickling my arms. I jiggled with laughter.

"Hit the AC," said Hans.

The air conditioner churned on to blow the feathers off me. Feathers flew backward and landed all over Hef and Vic. Wahwahwah-choo-ha-ha-ha-chooooo, Hef and Vic sneezed. We all fell about roaring with laughter. I laughed so hard I fell over like a tower mangled in bedding. Hef and Vic sagged against the wall.

"Serious, now," old Hans tried. "Get serious, everybody."

That sent us into gales of laughter.

"Oh, really," Pam clucked about. "You're covered with perspiration." Pam began picking bits of feathers off me and fanned me with her stylist's book. Then she mopped my glistening skin with a powder puff, till I had that nice buff finish again. Carefully Pam recombed my hair and glared at me to keep me sober.

Gravely I checked my hair in the hand mirror, spurting giggles, then I caught Hef's eye and we both snortled helplessly. Titillated, turned on.

"Vunce more, everybody," said Hans. "Ready?"

"Here we go, gang," said Hef, and we went to work again with discipline.

I arched, smiled, hoisted the menacing pillow, and the boys tossed feathers on target. Then I tried other angles. My body had gone public. It was my commercial entity and I knew how to display it.

Up on my knees, I bent forward so my breast beacons ballooned hugely. Clickclickclick. Then I squeezed them together by holding the pillow out to the side like a baseball bat. Next pose I clutched the pillow underneath and lifted my breasts like a shelf, a display case. I knew this chest game—lit beacons—backward.

"That does it, everybody," Hans announced. "Ve do another setup after lunch."

"Free?" I asked.

"Freed," Hef replied.

Eyes aslash, I slammed the pillow at Hef, who winged it back. Grinning devilishly, Vic Lownes emptied the bag of feathers on me. Both men advanced on me as I slung all the pillows on the bed at them. I managed to fling the blue blanket up into their faces, as I dived off the side of the bed and marched calmly to the dressing room.

Pam plunged after me with the negligee waving like a royal mantle in the air.

"Tsk, tsk, Pam," I said, "look at those kiddies playing Tent."

❧ 14 ❧

CHARLES ATLAS OF THE SEX WORLD
MARCH 1956

Hefner's bedroom looked like a film studio surrounding a lost island of a bed. A floating bed where two unimpressive figures huddled against the technological storm on the walls. In the semidark, it felt like a movie spaceship with complicated electronic panels and apertures with various buzz signals and colored lights.

Although I was in it, I couldn't decide whether I wanted to go to bed with Hef or not. We lounged in silken robes from the costume department of the spaceship. The wall played jazz, first Ellington and now Brubeck. I sipped tequila neat and slugged Hef's Pepsi once for a chaser.

I coughed, "That's loaded with bourbon."

"Sometimes at night Pepsi needs flavor," Hef said without a grin.

"It's okay," I chuckled. "I won't tell."

"How did you become a writer," Hef asked, "a sexy little big-titted Playmate like you?"

"Hard slavish work—the same way you got to be a *Playboy* publisher." I glanced at him closely. "B'gory, you believe your PR!"

"Believe it? I *am* it—I create it, and I take no small pride in the fact. My ideas, my image, my taste. *Playboy* is *me.*"

"Your outer skin?"

"I like to think of myself as the quintessential urban man," said stolid preacher Hef. His face seemed better off in the semidark when he didn't have to use it for expression. His stiffness was less visible. "Let's watch movies." Hef fiddled with dials and lights and switches on a bed panel.

Psychedelic images and patterns cavorted on several screens, casting shadows on the walls. Image-weary as I was, I tried to duck them by squirming around and facing Hef.

"Yessirree, I'm the proud father of *Playboy. Playboy* changed my life," Hef's sermon wound on from his lectern, the bed. "I live the ideal life of the urban bachelor. Here in my lair during the week and on weekends I drop in on the wife and kids."

"You're married?" I'd never heard that. "You have kids?"

"Christie and David, girl and boy."

"Ohhhhh."

"You don't find married men attractive?"

"They're taken."

"Precisely," said Hef. "How can I be a married swinger? It destroys the image. Free and swinging, not trapped—that's the image."

I tried to be helpful. "Why not use Vic Lownes for your stick figure?"

Hef smiled tightly. "*I am* the publisher. Vic works for *me.*"

"Get a divorce and play the swinging *Playboy* then." I leaned over to peek at his chest under the robe.

"Exactly what I plan—heh, heh," Hef scowled through laughter at my presumptuous irony. "We're practically separated now," he said. "The marriage was bad almost from the start."

"Sounds familiar," said I. My own nuptial excursion was so painfully brief I seldom mentioned it.

Hef put his arms behind his head and gazed up at the mirrored ceiling that gave him back the image of the ideal urban bachelor. Till that instant I hadn't noticed a mirror covered the entire ceiling. Who stares at bedroom ceilings? I frowned, feeling I was still modeling for an unseen aerial photographer.

"Now that I've got *Playboy* she wants me back. Now that I've pulled away and got some better stuff going. When we were first married—Millie wouldn't even *sleep* with me before we were married—she didn't like it any too well. Finally I got tired of it all and got a girlfriend on the side. Then, all of a sudden, she wanted me!" Hef rolled over to peer up my robe. "Are all women like that?"

"Those kind are—the nonsensual. They're turned on by jealousy." Was it real, this appealing naivete? This was only his side of their tale, of course.

On his elbows, Hef laughed his nervous heh-heh. "Used to be, I couldn't make out for trying. In high school, even in college, *no*body would sleep with me—not even my fiancee, Millie. *Playboy* changed my life, all right."

"The Charles Atlas of the sex world," I exclaimed. "From ninety-pound weakling to sex bomb overnight."

"You do have a weird wit."

"That's power. Be glad you have it, Hef."

Hef spun out of bed and played with his wall, changing dials and apertures. The abstract patterns and the jazz disappeared, and a TV screen lit with a movie. Back in bed Hef sat with his arm around me under the robe.

The title appeared on the screen in color, *Switcheroo*. *Switcheroo* seemed to be an orgy of pretty technicolor people by a turquoise swimming pool.

"Don't you like authentic stag films?" Hef casually stroked his organ under the robe.

"Not now!" I stared in attentive shock.

"Especially now." He reached for my hand and placed it on his swelling organ. "They'll arouse you."

I yanked my hand back. "You'll have to do better than that." A pure power play.

In *Switcheroo* two orange and hot pink couples—bad color—were madly eating their partners. The little couples' heads—blonde with black, red with brown—would come up, harkening to directions from the director. Then they switched instantly to lick another part of the same body or another body. Now blonde was with brown and black with red. Flick, flick with the tongue. Heads up again to listen. Switch again.

I laughed so hard I fell off the bed. "That's about as sexy as a car wash," I roared. It did turn me on, though, sort of raced my motor with nonspecific generic greed. It made me hot in a cold way.

Hefner frowned. "That's supposed to be sexy."

He was as displeased with my levity as I was with his lack of tenderness. He wanted cold sex and I wouldn't give it. I wanted passion and he wouldn't give it.

"I feel sorry for the women who do these things," I said, "don't you?"

"Nobody stands over them with a whip," he said. "Don't bring me down."

"Who's that fellow in the red wig?" I squinted closely at *Switcheroo*. "Is that you?"

Hef showed no shock. "Of course not," he said mildly.

Something electronic was always on. The movie faded as the patterns and jazz returned, Stan Kenton this time. Hef was a self-contained entity. He didn't reach out to the woman. The purpose of her hand was to stroke his phallus.

The next time Hef reached for my hand and embraced his organ with it, I was curious and disliked him enough to start playing it. Okay, I'd try going along with it for once. After a while he rolled over and began kissing my breasts. Hef had a spare muscular frame, a good body. He was quite substantial and provided a hard undeviating plunge, rhythm as unvaried as a metronome.

Hef was rigid, yes—and there's something to be said for that—and accountable. He had staying power. A good ride, a steady canter. But I was left with no particular feeling, no personal feeling of connection, of uniting.

Hef had traded sexual failure for sexual power. Wallflower to playboy, swung from one end of the pendulum to the other. He'd missed the vast curving middle where people relate, where humanity takes place. He was afraid of *not* controlling and losing it all. There was a buzzing recording sound. Something electronic was always on.

❧❧❧❧

Promptly at 1 p.m. the next afternoon we wended our way to the *Playboy* offices. We were both up early. Hef often arose at 4 p.m. and worked from midnight to 8 a.m. In his pajamas, slugging Pepsi. I often arose at 2 p.m., modeled between 4 and 9 p.m., and wrote from 11 p.m. to 6 a.m. We were night people, inspired by night air. As we both struggled to get out of bed at noon, I felt closer to Hef. Most people think those are insane hours. Weird habits bonded us.

We walked down the stairs. Hef's bachelor pad was on the top floor of the white brick brownstone at 11 East Superior. Hef introduced me to the staff.

"The pillowfight sequence was my idea," said Art Paul, balding innovative art director. "How'd it go?"

"Great," said Hef.

"Hell, it was my idea," said Vince Tajiri, photo editor.

"Feathers float," I smiled. "You can't fling them."

I met A. C. Spectorsky, the elegant urbane editorial director, who'd written *The Exurbanites* and two other nonfiction bestsellers. Spectorsky, known for his wit, bought stories by Moravia, Steinbeck, and Algren. *Playboy* reputedly paid two thousand dollars to these names while *Esquire* paid only four hundred dollars per story.

Jack Kessie, associate editor, was on long distance and slammed his office door.

"He's talking to our hottest ad prospect," Hef explained. "Class advertisers, that's all we want." Hef had told me they refused girlie mag advertisers. They desperately sought and held out for the big time—sports cars, fashion, status ads like Schweppes's.

Commander Whitehead and Hathaway Shirts' eye-patched gent. "They're scared of our sex association. But with our circulation, they've got to fall."

"When we get one more biggie," said Art Paul, "the rest will dive in."

Kessie opened the door, ecstatic. "We got it, we got it!"

The whole staff yahooed and cheered. They were a friendly bunch.

Hef swooped into Kessie's office. "Take care of the five thousand dollar contract," he called out to the staff.

The centerfold shoot, my story included, paid five hundred

for the one day. The *Playboy* contract paid at that time five thousand dollars spaced out over a year.

To achieve this munificent sum, the Playmate had to agree not to appear in any other magazine in less than a one-piece bathing suit! Whoa! I made a living in bikinis and less. Also to do *Playboy* sales meetings and promotions several times a month in New York, and Chicago, if they should deem to fly me in.

"Will I be paid extra for those?" I asked the young editor who was delegated this job, whose name I didn't catch.

"No, it's all included in your monthly stipend."

"What does "do" the sales meetings mean?"

"Model, perform skits, entertain clients," he almost blushed.

"Entertain?" I knew this ploy.

"Make them feel good, uh, make them happy." He looked at me for help.

"You mean, have sex with them?"

He couldn't answer. His eyes slid away.

"N-O," I said. "Not on your life."

"Then you'll only get the one-time fee," he begged. It was part of his job to convince me.

I almost felt sorry for him, pimping like this. "That's okay." I'd rather have a clean five hundred dollars than a dirty five thousand. I signed the model release for the smaller amount. Feeling free.

∾∾∾∾

Before I left New York, I'd been interviewed for a model shoot in Barbados. The ad agency producer turned out to be old Chuckie from Chapel Hill, a C student in English.

"How'd you get this job?" I asked.

He shrugged, "What do you mean?"

Old Chuckie, who condescended to me, the Phi Beta Kappa A student (female) who couldn't get in the door. "You'll do fine," said Chuck. "Three-day shoot, all expenses, a thousand bucks."

"Great!" I grinned eagerly.

"You'll have to *keep the client happy*."

"You mean—?"

He nodded.

"*You* say that to *me*? I went to college with you."
Chuck blushed. "Part of my job."

❧❧❧❧

Spectorsky stopped me and invited me for dinner in New York two months from now, in May.
"Charmed," I said, and gave him my number.
He clicked, bowed and tease-kissed my hand.
"I didn't sign the five thousand dollar contract," I said.
"I don't blame you," Spec replied.

❧❧❧❧

In an ebullient mood, Hef took me to lunch and then to my flight at O'Hare.
"I had a great time," I said, which was true.
Neither of us mentioned the contract I'd refused to sign.
"I'll be in New York next month," said Hef. "We'll get together."
"Phone in advance," I smiled.
"Of course."
We kissed decorously on the lips and waved goodbye.
On the plane the constant electronic buzz came back to me. Suddenly I wondered if, with all those apertures on the wall, that mirrored ceiling, I had been filmed in bed with Hef, the unsuspecting star of a new blue flick. No, just my wild imagination. Wasn't it?

৯ 15 ৩

CENTERFOLD
SPRING - SUMMER 1956

Hef phoned from Chicago. "How'd you like to see *My Fair Lady?*"

"I'd love to." I felt lucky that I had so many dates I never missed a good play.

"I'm bringing the color proofs."

"Great." I forgot to warn him about the humble nature of my dear old dump of a studio. But then, all independent women were poor, weren't they?

৯৩৩

Hef and Vic Lownes and I spread out the color proofs on the largest flat surface, my desk.

"One whole color set came out blurry," said Hef. "Hans says the film was bad."

We each gazed and picked favorites. Neither man liked my

choices. They narrowed theirs down to two shots where my breasts looked the biggest.

"But my tummy shows," I objected.

"It's a nice tummy," said Commander Hef.

"Righto," said adjutant Vic. As Vic Lownes was tall and sartorial, well-bred and decadent looking, he seemed more the playboy than earnest preacher Hef. Hef clearly ruled.

My Fair Lady, based on Shaw's *Pygmalion,* was the hit of Broadway. Sauntering in my black moire sheath made me feel a glittery part of the celebration of art and success that was nighttime Manhattan. Rex Harrison and Julie Andrews twisted and trolled the Lerner lyrics to Loewe's music, capturing the effervescent Shavian spirit. We sat with Vic and his young Playboy Bunny in the first balcony.

Maybe I'd actually like Hefner if I let my guard down. I kept watching him during the play. We held hands, became absorbed in the play and indifferent, squeezed hands and laughed. Of course, he was no egalitarian. But he possessed one of the finer male characteristics I was aware of: he liked my writing. What's more, he had the power to put it in print. Why not go for power, for once?

But it was obscene to like a man for what he could do for me. Idle speculation, because he lived in Chicago and I lived here. Unless we fell madly in love, it wasn't worth the commute. How could I fall for a man who didn't reach out but contracted like a black hole?

After dinner I invited them to my place for drinks. My Noguchi paper lamp on the bookcase created a soft glow in the dark. After a while Vic and his date began kissing and clutching, and so did Hef and I. But then they began squirming, and I whispered to Hef they'd have to go back to the hotel. I wasn't about to do stuff with another couple in the same room. They left amicably enough.

Hef and I fell into bed and went at it. But not before we went electronic and turned on the record player. I put on Thelonius Monk and we were both mollified.

࿐࿐࿐

Spectorsky took me to dinner at the Oak Room of the Plaza. A thoroughly enjoyable evening as Spec was wise, sardonic, and fun. His European style flattered me and made me feel worldly. He gave *Playboy* cachet, which is probably why the wily Hefner hired him. We talked about de Beauvoir and Sarraute and various European women writers.

"Hef wouldn't know the names," said Spec. "He's focused on big boobs."

I laughed. "*Not* big brains."

Spec was a gentleman. He didn't try anything, which made me feel delightfully unencumbered.

෨෨෨෨

At last the July 1956 issue of *Playboy* hit the stands. There I was, the pillow fighter in full living color, swaddled in my baby blue blanket, face and auburn tresses at their best angle, bare breasts huge. All three centerfold pages of me folding out. Feathers flew about. Two that seemed smack in front of my nostrils had been retouched lighter. Two very white feathers had been painted in to partially hide my peek-a-boo nipples.

Quickly I switched to the contents, where there were tiny arty cutouts of me and two featured men. I flipped to my story, "The Deal." There it was, indeed, with its own full color illustration by LeRoy Nieman. Linda, the impoverished painter in my story, looked like me, and the repulsive old gambler looked handsome, as his outstretched hand offered her sheaves of greenbacks. They were layered in bright Impressionistic color in the crowded bar of a Las Vegas hotel. The cowboy-handsome old gambler in the illustration was the precise opposite of the venal conniver in my tale. What did I expect? Men's magazines flatter men.

Quickly, I read through the story to make sure they hadn't altered it. Phew, it was precisely as I wrote it. For a headliner above the story in big print, they'd lifted a line from my old gambler: "A thousand dollars for a single night."

Then I leafed back to the middle where there was a black-and-white feature with shots of Hef and me looking over my story and several of me alone. A news photographer had shot them at night by a bare bulb in Hef's office. He looked gaunt and I harsh. I'd mentioned the bad lighting, but Hef said it had to be shot then and it was the best they could do. *Playboy* wasn't yet sophisticated and slick. Then there was a small text saying I loved sex but not commercial sex, that I was a Phi Beta Kappa writer who modeled for a living. Predictably innocuous. This was followed by the stripped-down centerfold.

๛๛๛๛

Nobody with a college degree had ever been seen in a magazine with her clothes off. I was one of the first respectable nudes. Before *Playboy* it was strippers in pasties and g-strings, bondage and whips, Tempest Storm and Bettie Page, mostly black-and-white. Before *Playboy* it was sleazy to be nude in a photo. Before the Living Theatre, it was dirty to be nude on stage.

Playboy and its imitators—*Nugget, Quick, Escapade, Stag, For Men Only*—showed pretty velvety girls in bikinis and shortie nighties. Girls you could take home to Mother, if only they'd put on some clothes and deny it was their layout.

Playboy advanced the sexual revolution by showing Nice Girls, whose centerfold proclaimed their sexual freedom or sexual ease. *Playboy* tainted the sexual revolution by proclaiming to its male audience their sex object status. No *men* were nude in magazines. The sexism of nude women in a magazine for men carried on a venerable chauvinist tradition.

From Manet's *Picnic in the Grass* with its nude woman and clothed gentlemen to his *Olympia*, to *The Rape of the Sabine Women* and the abduction and slaughter of willing naked nymphs and goddesses in Renaissance paintings, to Rubens's cavorting naked cake-dough nymphs, spilling flesh in idyllic pastorales. I especially liked Lachaise's powerful dark nude on tiptoe in the MOMA garden. That was art and beauty.

In the thirties *Look* magazine had made it on shots of Hedy Lamarr nude in the film *Ecstasy*. *Life* had printed bare breast shots of Joan Crawford and Claudette Colbert. *Esquire* had begun as a girlie mag but now shunned its past and went posh. Hefner filled the commercial T & A gap.

Playboy put women on a pedestal, but as a tasty dish. Yet if she became a star, like Marilyn or Hedy, she was a sex goddess, a power. Then, too, our natural exhibitionism flowered forth in glory. Or our desire to be merely natural, in our birthday suits, on the world's beaches. A two-edged sword: sexism versus freedom. Both there.

As I knew how huge *Playboy's* circulation was, I felt exposed, flattered, and cringing all at once. I felt immensely pleased that so many people might read my story, "The Deal."

❧❧❧❧

I phoned Hef in Chicago. "The layout looks great and the story too."

"Glad you like them" said Hef, who sounded busy.

"May I ask you to please mail me five copies? To show off."

"Of course, be happy to."

"How *are* you?" I asked.

"Fine. You?"

"Just swimming along."

"Heh heh," Hef clucked, "that's good,"

"Oh, by the way, I mailed you two new short stories about three weeks ago. Have you read them?" I asked.

"Haven't crossed my desk yet," said Hef.

"I do hope you like them—or one." The response to my writing always made me anxious. "Let me know."

"Of course."

Silence.

"See you before too long, I hope," I said casually.

"Possibility," said Hef. "I've got to—"

"So long," I sang out.

"S'long." The phone clicked.

As I felt Hef liked my work, I was reasonably confident he or Spec might pick one of my stories. When another week had passed without a phone call, I wrote a polite bubbly letter, asking Hef to peek under his desk for my wandering manuscripts.

❧❧❧❧

At last, a letter from *Playboy*. I opened it eagerly. Oddly, it wasn't from Hef or even Spec but from an editor I hadn't met, or whose name I'd missed, named Alan Ravage.

Dear Miss Denham,
Thank you for showing Playboy your fine new stories. Playboy was delighted to choose you as our July Playmate and enjoyed publishing your story, "The Deal." However, you should not expect us to publish you again as Playboy wants no woman writer's name associated with the magazine.
Your stories will be returned separately.

Cordially,
Alan Ravage, Asst. Editor

(I am paraphrasing the letter because I ripped it to shreds.)

First, though, I seethed with fury and immediately phoned Hefner. Hef wasn't available. Please have him call me, I said, gazing at the insulting letter.

Bopping the letter, I bustled down the hall to the back apartment and pounded on Nancy King's door. My confidante, Nancy King, was a soloist with the Metropolitan Opera Ballet Company. Nancy had a long swan neck and high ballerina's head with black hair pulled tightly back to reveal facial light, huge blue eyes, and a dancer's superb shape and posture.

"Come in, come in," said Nancy.

"Look," I socked the letter. "Look how they used me."

Nancy read the letter, frowned. "They *did* publish the story, though."

"Yes."

"Alice, you do this pinup modeling," said far more proper Nancy, frowning. "Those people are not reliable. They're—"

"Sleazebags," I said.

"They'll exploit you, if they can. Why don't you do something else? For money?"

"I'm buying writing time," I near sobbed. "Most money for the least time, hateful modeling."

"Rudy's on his way," said Nancy. "Let me ask you, because it bothers me. When he comes here, he doesn't want to talk and have tea. All he wants is to go to bed. Are your dates like that?"

"You're his mistress, Nancy. The rest of his time is taken," I said. "My dates take me to dinner, plays, parties. They're single."

Nancy sighed. "I wonder if it's worth it."

"Look who he *is*," I said. Nancy was the mistress of Rudolf

Bing, famous director of the Metropolitan Opera. Nancy was not too proper for that.

಼಼಼

Back in my apartment, I shrieked with rage.

That was when I ripped the *Playboy* letter to shreds, sobbing.

Hef didn't call. I phoned twice more and Hef was always either out of town or unavailable. Of course, he never called back.

I'd been used.

Did they publish the story just to get my naked body in a clever feature? I knew it was a good story but Hef hurt my confidence as a serious writer. I had naively expected equality based on literary standards. Into rejection I plunged, a steep dive, and surfaced angry.

That was the end of my friendship with Hugh Hefner.

People tell me that rejection letter would be worth gold today.

Ultimately my story was published six times, twice in anthologies, and became the movie *Quizas*, which won two film festival prizes.

"Why a Phi Beta Kappa Posed in the Buff" shouted the headline in the *Daily News*. There was a big head shot of me alongside photos of Ava Gardner and Gina Lollobrigida.

Feature writer Jess Stearn, who also wrote popular nonfiction books, had interviewed me. Jess was an easygoing affable fellow who shared my disdain for both of our jobs.

"A first," said Jess. "Sensational. Our kind of feature."

We pored over my model portfolio and picked a good head shot. As it was shot by Peter Basch as a favor and I hadn't signed a release, I felt free to let the *News* use it. I phoned and asked, and Peter was pleased.

"Tell me your true opinion of *Playboy?*" asked Jess.

"It's run by guys ten years out of college who still act like college boys." Why else was it so wildly popular? Jess quoted me. He also said I was a serious young writer.

಼಼಼

Hugh Hefner and Norman Mailer were both better young, before they matured into megalomaniacs. I knew them just as they began to develop the ability to manipulate others, but were still basically straight-arrow young.

Hefner, I felt, suffered a failure of nerve. With his lofty success status, he could've dated the most gorgeous and interesting women in America. He bragged that he'd never dated a woman over the age of twenty-four. Hef began to look rather silly, an aging man with his nymphet clones. No celebrity should ever believe his PR. But Hef *was* his PR.

In *Lolita*, Nabokov captured the chauvinistic male psyche in all its infantile egotism, in Humbert Humbert's dense lack of awareness. Exactly what Hugh Hefner—another HH—embodied and exploited with his *Lolita* carbons. Precisely what Marilyn Monroe consciously catered to with her baby-doll sexiness, a baby girl face atop outrageously adult curves. Both Hef and Marilyn showed off for the boys.

Men often ask me about Hefner. What's he like? Did you sleep with him? They envied him. Women *never* do. Women ask about James Dean.

అఅఅఅ

Many moons later at PEN, I bumped into ex-*Playboy*-staffer Jack Kessie and his wife. He told me I'd been one of their most popular Playmates, and that *Playboy* had mailed out photos of me for years. Nobody had bothered to let me know.

In Frank Brady's biography, *Hefner*, he quotes a *Nation* article by David Cort, which says:

"One month *Playboy's* Playmate was the lady author of a story in the magazine. As a male writer, I must protest unfair competition."

My dear fellow, you needn't have worried.

However, I became the only Playmate of the Month ever to have a short story published in the same issue of *Playboy*.

Today, at eighty, Hef is still at it. Maybe his blondes offer an infusion of youth.

❧ 16 ❧

FAMOUS FOR 15 MINUTES
SUMMER 1956 - 1957

Doubleday, the envelope said, with Ken McCormick above it. Amazed, I ripped it open. Editor-in-Chief Ken McCormick wrote that he was impressed by my *Playboy* story and hoped I was working on a novel. Would I please phone?

I dashed up the stairs with the letter, and pounded on Nancy King's door. "Look!"

Nancy read the letter and grinned. "That's just what you want."

"Exactly!" I hugged her and danced down the hall to my *pied-a-terre*.

The next week Jack Leggett, senior editor at Houghton Mifflin, wrote and the following week, Random House editor Joe Fox. Each expressed interest in seeing my presumed novel. I was delirious with joy.

Hefner was right.

Hef had said being in *Playboy* would help my career.

❧❧❧❧

Ken McCormick invited me for a drink at the Pierre. I wore a Lord and Taylor cashmere coatdress a French dressmaker had fitted around me. Silver-haired Ken was handsome, long-jawed, an older man whose breeding showed through his affability. Ken was a charmer.

"Remarkable story," said Ken. "How far along are you on your novel?"

"I suppose I've written a hundred pages," I sighed, "of which maybe fifty are good."

"Normal progress," said Ken. "Show it to me anytime you feel you're ready. One hundred pages would be good."

"I'm still working on the direction." It was easy to confide literary aspirations to Ken. He understood the process.

"That's the hardest part with a first novel," Ken nodded empathetically. "You'll get it," he encouraged me, giving my shoulder a paternal squeeze.

"May I ask you a serious question?"

"Shoot," said Ken.

"Do you think it was tawdry of me to be unclothed in *Playboy*?"

Ken laughed. "It was clever. You got people's attention. You got mine."

My blush was hidden in cocktail darkness.

❧❧❧❧

Jack Leggett, Houghton Mifflin editor, favored '21'. It was the ultimate chic *boite*, but only the first floor bar and restaurant. If you were seated on the second floor in Siberia, you were nobody. We sat at the bar.

Jack was younger than Ken, with a very square head and a yachting tan, dun tan hair. Both men looked Ivy League, as did many editors then. Ken was more suave and Jack more tweedy. He was working on *his* first novel, *Wilder Stone*, so we talked writing and writers. Literary speculation inspired me, made me feel capable and cosseted.

"Will you show me your novel," asked Jack, "when you have enough to show?"

"Of course." I couldn't help adding, "Ken McCormick wants to see it too."

"You might know I wouldn't be first," said Jack. "About your story, tell me this. If she, Linda, doesn't believe in anything, in God, what's to keep her from becoming a whore?"

"The experience itself," I said surprised. "The horror of what she degraded herself to do, for money."

Jack pondered, hand on chin.

"That's what I tried to do," I said. "Show a moral stance develop from the experience of *evading* morality." It shocked me when men didn't understand the point of the story. Women always did.

❧❧❧

Random House editor Joe Fox was extremely tall, about six foot three, with a large frame and rather small oval-shaped head. When we met for a drink, he seemed to be angry, not at me but at the world. Joe Fox challenged.

"You must've had some kind of life," he sneered, "to write *that* story."

"Probably no raunchier than yours," I responded.

Eyes narrowed, Joe gave me a nasty crooked grin. I'd seen him at George Plimpton's, where he belonged to the *haute* literary set.

"What's it like to pose nude?" his eyes lit.

"A seamy thrill." I stared him down.

"Let's hope you have a novel we like," he said sardonically.

"If you don't, Ken McCormick or Jack Leggett might," I said.

As I felt he disliked me, I was surprised when he tried to put the make on me. He made a lunge for me at my door and I wrestled and shoved away. Joe left, acting disgusted. At a party months later Joe grabbed me by the arm and spat out, "I'm going to get you if it's the last thing I do."

My mouth fell open and I jerked away.

When I mentioned that incident to him years later, he denied that it happened.

Both Ken McCormick and Jack Leggett took me out for drinks or dinner two or three times a year during the slow years

I worked on my first novel. Both Ken and Jack were married, and both treated me as a friend and literary cohort.

❧❧❧❧

Fan letters came, forwarded from *Playboy*.
One fan letter came direct. It was from my brother, the Episcopal priest.

> You look sexy and fabulous. Don't worry about what Mother thinks. I won't show it to her but somebody probably will. She'll have a conniption fit but it'll blow over. Dad, though, may be hurt. I'll talk to him.
>
> The story was great! So that's what Vegas is like—wow!
>
> Yr adoring bro,
> Palmer

Then Cousin Mac the lawyer phoned, loaded. "What a vulgar insult to the family. You should be a lawyer, with your Phi Bete brain."

"I don't want to administer injustice," I snipped back.

"I ought to come up there and give you some myself."

"You're drunk, Mac." I hung up on him.

To restore my equanimity, I put on a precious old record of Ida Cox singing "Wild Women" with Joe Jones's band, featuring Roy Eldridge and Coleman Hawkins. Ida belted out, "Wild women don't sing the blues."

❧❧❧❧

"*Why* did you do this to us?" Mother phoned weeping. "*Naked*, in that nasty magazine. Your father almost had a heart attack."

"Mother, I—"

"Are you trying to kill us? What did we do to deserve such a daughter?"

"But the human body is—ordinary. Everybody has one."

"I never want to speak to you again." Mother slammed down the phone.

Then the letters began:

Alice,
Stop your vile life. That story was despicable filth, as vile and disgusting as your naked body in that picture. How can you write such unChristian trash? That is NOT art. We sacrifice everything for you and this is how you repay us. I order you to stop showing your body.

You need God,

Mother

Dear Alice,
You have broken your father's heart. You are not welcome EVER AGAIN in our house. You have destroyed our home. How can you hate us so much? You have demeaned and cheapened us. What our friends in Jacksonville must think! I'm glad I don't have to face their shock and horror.

Repent and save your soul,

Mother

No word from Dad. Mother wrote letters for the family. Dad was the one who concerned me. Suddenly it occured to me Daddy hadn't seen me naked since I was eleven. Here I was, unfolded in full-breasted maturity, before not just every salacious male who flipped through girlie mags, but my own *father*. At last I saw why the family was shocked. It was Daddy I cared about, vulnerable honorable Daddy, who loved me.

That night I dreamt that Daddy died suddenly. I'd never talked to him enough, told him how much I loved him. How could he have—gone? Had I killed him with my rebelliousness, my flagrant exposure? In shock, I woke up weeping and trembling, so sure it had happened that I reached for the phone. That dream—that my father died—would wake me, shaking with fear, several times a year for the next ten years. Till Daddy died, of his third heart attack, with me beside him.

It was wrenching but I made myself write him.

Dear Daddy,

Please don't be hurt. I'm only modeling because it gives me more HOURS to write my novel than a regular job would. Please understand. My generation doesn't think nudity is so awful. I didn't intend to offend the family. Your good opinion means everything to me. I hope you can mollify Mother.

Your loving daughter,

Alice

I mailed it to his office.

To calm down, I put on Elvis Presley, the white hope who sang black, and sang along with "Blue Suede Shoes" and "Hound Dog." His rock & roll bump and grind had proved too much groin for the Sunday night *Ed Sullivan Show*. Then, more to my taste, Clara Haskil playing Bartok.

My childhood friend from Jacksonville, Prudence Wise, was here in town as roommate and secretary to movie star Grace Kelly. I didn't look her up because I was ashamed of being a pinup model. One day on the bus I saw Prudy and her mother when I was dressed as a whore. I'd been told to dress sleazy to try out for a small documentary film. I heard her mother say, "That *can't* be Alice," and they turned away. Blushing fire, I stared out the window. I can't keep doing this, I thought, mortified. I'm ruining myself.

Grace Kelly of the fantasy kingdom of Hollywood married Prince Rainier of the toy kingdom of Monaco.

Finally, at long last, a brief note from Dad.

Dear Alley Oop—

My shock and disappointment are personal. Our generation, our family, is conservative by nature. You have every right to go your own way, which I respect. Your ole dad doesn't LIKE you but he still LOVES you.

Your affectionate father,

Simkins

PS. The story—you know more than we'd like, but we can't protect our grown children. I did admire with amazement your writing style.

David Markson and I were both developing our first novels. Any writer or period that blurred in my mind, I'd ask encyclopedic David about and he knew. Also, with his total recall of baseball statistics, David might've won big moolah on the TV quiz shows.

When the July 1956 *Playboy* appeared on the stands, David bought numerous copies and gave them to friends.

"As you now grace my studio wall," David declared, "I want it autographed." Silly though it was, I was flattered.

"Miss Denham, will you autograph this for me?" hobby photographers asked. "Be sure and read my story," I was wont to reply. Guys wanted my autograph, imagine! My bookings increased, I made more money.

Before long my Playmate shot was taped to my own wall. Somebody swiped it. The second copy remained in my model portfolio under plastic. The third went to my agent, John Cushman. Several went to the safe deposit. Too bad I couldn't autograph a copy for the family. Wouldn't it be wonderful if I actually *looked* like that for over two seconds? Somehow they'd caught my absolute pinnacle of facial expression.

David's Village party uniform was a blue button-down Oxford shirt sans tie and khaki pants, which all the guys wore. I wore my Mandarin Chinese sheath dress with sequins or my black fishnet Empire dress over a black bra-slip, both from Saks. I wore a garter belt, stockings, and high heels. I dressed well back then. Sometimes it was BYOB. Tonight the host supplied vodka. Wine was for meals. Parties were at 9 or 10 p.m., after dinner. Peanuts, as well as potato chips, meant fancy. I was perfectly satisfied with David Markson and thought no more about it. It didn't occur to either of us to be faithful. No one expected that.

Then one day a letter came from David.

A letter, how strange. I opened it and at the top was the famous quote, "In my Father's house are many mansions," and below that, David wrote, "And I can only live in one."

The mansion David chose to live in was inhabited by Mag Man's gorgeous literary blonde, Elaine Kretchmar. David and Elaine were getting married. He wanted me to be the first to know. Then he phoned.

"It's a shock to me too," said David. "Just out of nowhere on our first date we decided to marry."

"Your first date?"

"Yes. You know what she said," David was thrilled with excitement. "She said, 'Anything you want, David, any way you want it.'"

"That means—?"

"Elaine wants what I want, any way at all. She'll help support my writing, till it's time to have children."

"Sounds like a good deal," I said sadly, being heaved aside.

"She made only one demand," David tittered with delight. "She said your Playmate picture had to come off the wall."

The sexy Playmate with the fabulous short story, whose working novel three publishers wanted to see, had been dumped. By her favorite lover, with a chortle.

৯৯৯৯৯

Next week I bumped into Joseph Heller walking home from work, and invited him up for a drink.

"Welcome to the dear old dump," I said.

"Looks about right," smiled Joe. Joe and his family lived in the immense Apthorpe apartments on Broadway between 78th and 79th.

"Bet you have space," I said.

"We need it, with two kids." I handed Joe a vodka and he said, "You look morose."

"David and Elaine are getting married."

"I know. Hot news, a legal hitching."

"Joe, but why? I'm as good as Elaine." As Joe was older and married and paternal, I made him my male confidante.

"Alice, do you want kids?" Joe gave me a wise glare.

"Well, I hadn't really—"

"Do you want to be faithful?" Joe persisted. "Do you want only one man for the rest of your life?"

"What?" Certainly David wasn't the only man I was sleeping with. Though the main one.

"You don't want to be married, Alice," Joe Heller pronounced. "You want romance. That's different."

"How?" Though divorced, I was so romantic I thought they were or could be the same.

"Look," Joe took my hand. "When people want to get married,

only then do they look around for a permanent mate. It starts with wanting marriage."

"Is that what you did?" I asked.

"Sure," said Joe. "You look at people differently. I'd been through the war. I wanted to settle down."

"Thanks, Joe." I felt like a child. "I must be very immature," I blushed.

"Not at all," Joe's eyes brightened, flirted. "You're an adventuress. Don't knock it."

❧❧❧❧

David Markson waited a month after marrying Elaine before phoning me to chat blithely away. Any way you want it, David, probably didn't include screwing old girlfriends. We didn't, we gossiped. Couplehood at first makes people fear they've lost the world. Then they socialize with other couples, and mismatched single folk fall away.

Before long I discovered how to use married men—for fill. When I had to have it and no one else was around, I'd let Wayne or Robbie come by. Married men were my Small Friends. They didn't enjoy the status of single men, such as the Wall Street trader who had a guru and wore a gold earring, the first I ever saw on a man. For months on Friday night I dated an ad agency exec with three roommates. All four turned out to have wives in the suburbs. That was Saturday and Sunday.

Do you suppose adultery is the cement of marriage?

The way David and Elaine wanted it worked out when his satirical western, *The Ballad of Dingus Magee*, bought by Frank Sinatra, was turned into the film, *Dirty Dingus Magee*. Then they had two kids. Elaine worked for agent Knox Burger then opened her own agency. She would one day sell my second novel. Elaine Markson became one of the hottest literary agents in New York. David, by then her ex, evolved into an offbeat experimental novelist known to the cognoscenti, especially for his brilliant, innovative *Wittgenstein's Mistress*.

❧❧❧❧

In 1957 Albert Camus, novelist and French Resistance hero, won the Nobel. Over here Jack Kerouac's naive *On the Road* was considered daring. The nation was finally rid of hate-baiting Senator Joe McCarthy who succumbed at age forty-nine. Russia launched the first earth satellites, Sputnik I and II, while we had a desegregation crisis in Little Rock, and Ike sent in the paratroopers. Leonard Bernstein's *West Side Story* was Broadway's official welcome to the new Puerto Rican immigrants. Bernard Malamud's *The Assistant* was published, as was Faulkner's *The Town*.

❧❧❧❧

Minute Maid went on the Big Board. In my orange tutu and orange bonnet, I posed for the papers—click click—with the president of the stock exchange. The orange juice company hired me to represent Miss Minute Maid for a year. As my forebears had owned orange groves in Florida, I felt involved with citrus. In their print ads, I tried to look as much as possible like an orange blossom.

With Jack Lescoulie and cast of the *Today* Show from NBC-TV, I did a cutesy, inane skit in the Minute Maid industrial show at a Connecticut country club. Industrial shows are sales meetings with show biz and jokes. I performed with the other products—Teddy Snowcrop, a hip dwarf who drove a Jaguar, and old Southern Colonel Morton, a benign Russian Jew.

Teddy, who was reading *On the Road*, asked my opinion. "Reminds me of college—all the boys bragging about taking off for Boys' Town in Nuevo Laredo."

Colonel Morton chuckled, "The red light district?"

"Yep, Boys' Town. The open style is sort of fun—lyrical and drooling."

One night our trio acted with Sammy Davis, Jr., in another show at a Manhattan hotel. That night at home, key out, my door gaped—ajar. My door had been hacked and cantilevered open.

I'd been robbed. Dresser drawers spilled open onto the floor, closet thrown around. My clothes trailed the floor like junk.

I phoned the family and Mother answered.

"Mama, the family jewelry—all gone. They got it all—your diamond and ruby ring, Aunt Alice's aquamarine and diamond

145

ring, Aunt Sara's emerald and silver bracelet. They took *all* the good stuff and left the junk." They may have seen me wearing them. I was so used to these family mementos that I wore them everywhere.

"Come home," said Mother. "You shouldn't live in that awful place."

"Oh, Mama," I wept.

"Come home, darling. Dad says so too."

That night I pushed the dresser against the door, expecting huge men to crash in. I felt exposed, in midair, without walls. Anybody could break in and destroy me. My room was a giant photo projection everyone could see.

Then I remembered Mama had said, come home. Mama still cared about me. Mama was never as mad at me as she wanted to be. Nor was I. We were both too adamant. Mother-daughter love/hate is heady stuff.

Half the people I knew had been robbed. Welcome to New York! I'd been initiated. I stayed.

❧❧❧❧

Comedian Jack Carter took me to a party at Sammy Davis, Jr.'s place. Sammy up close was no taller than I and, incredibly, thinner. Next day he phoned and asked me to model for him. I told him my fee was $50, if he meant figure modeling. Sammy said, "I usually pay models with autographed photos of myself." I declined.

❧❧❧❧

"Jump in that hole in the ice," directed Al the photographer.

We were shooting a swimming pool ad in New Jersey in the dead of winter. I wore my new baby blue strapless bathing suit with waist-cincher and ruffly highcut bottom. They insisted I swallow a shot of brandy. The pool was almost covered with ice. I was to wave merrily from the turquoise water while two children ice skated.

They eased me into the ice water while my eyes turned to shock and my expression froze.

"Tread water and smile," called Al. "Don't get your hair wet."
Then he yelled, "Skate, kids."

I treaded water and grinned and waved, with an iron expression of fear. I was freezing from the legs up. The kids skated.

"Relax your face," the client hollered.

Once more I grinned and waved and Al click-clicked.

"Pull me out," I bellowed and swam to the side.

They wrapped me in huge towels as I shivered and we went inside where I swallowed more brandy. We did the clever but pointless ice water scene once more. They rewarmed me again. Then I posed kneeling on the diving board fishing with a rod, smiling placidly. They had the sense to use that one for the ad.

For those few shoots that wanted small, I was in great demand. I posed sitting in a Frigidaire to show how roomy it was. Then I posed on the hood of a Jaguar to make it look huge. My one hundred and five pounds dented the hood. They popped it back out.

A full page nude ad in the staid *New York Times*! I scarcely believed it when Hess's Department Store of Allentown, Pa., shot me nude on a park bench. The park bench was inside a studio at 480 Lex. Next to it on another bench were two men ignoring me and gazing with adoration at a woman gowned by Hess. I was pouting, holding a book covering my private parts. For this delicate situation, my nude scene was shot separately from the clothed models. When the *Times* printed the fullpage ad, a bikini had been sketched on me.

480 Lexington Avenue was the photographers' building with photo studios on each of the twelve floors. Gorgeous models jammed the elevators. The operators ogled and joked. The maintenance men staggered, starry-eyed. Male paradise. These tall, leggy models were *all* prettier than I was.

෨෨෨෨

As I poked through famous old Brooks Costume House, musty and mysterious and huge as a movie studio, a dolly filled with eighteenth-century gowns almost clipped me. "For a Broadway show," yelled the designer, checking them out on the run. "Dere you are," the seamstress called, "get in dere for to pin."

Brooks was entirely emigre women—escapees from the Nazis and postwar Europe. "Madame du Barry today! Vell, vell." She pinned and tucked. "Very exposed, dey vere." She added a chiffon fill-in atop the low-cut bodice. All this was for a commercial artist who'd paint a paperback book cover from my color photo. Last week I was a Tahitian princess for a huge movie poster illustration. The art director for the Hartog Campaign looked at my portfolio, glanced at me, back at my photos. "You photograph better than you look," he said. "I know, everybody tells me that," I smiled blithely. Hartog shot me very high fashion with lots of cleavage in their men's shirts line. The ads appeared every month in *Esquire*.

At Eve's Rental Studio on West 56th, I bumped into the famous Bettie Page, who looked tired, not young. Reputedly, she'd only pose bare-breasted the week before her period, when her breasts swelled big enough. A photographer told me, "She does dirty stuff." I said, "I don't believe it." He showed me a shot of Bettie naked, legs spread, urinating into a can. I felt let down. She didn't have to lower herself so.

At Robert Scott Studio, I bumped into actress Ellen Burstyn, which wasn't her model name, and Candy Loden. As Barbara Loden, she starred in Arthur Miller's *After the Fall*, his 1964 play about Marilyn Monroe. In pinup mags I often saw photos of L.A. model Raquel Welch. Raquel was hefty, hippy, and bosomy. Once the baby-fat melted and she slimmed down as an actress, she looked incredible. Years later she'd option my second novel about those days, which she also lived.

Hefner played around and played around, started several other magazines that failed, put Vic Lownes in charge of the Playboy Clubs, stationed in London, till all of them, including the one on 59th off Fifth, failed. In the so-called Mansion in L.A. he partied and porned till his sixties when he married a young Playmate of the Year and had two children. The marriage broke up because she got bored, a staffer told me. As one of the first five hundred Playmates, I appeared in the giant *Playmate Book* when it came out a few years ago. In 2004 I appeared in the fiftieth anniversary issue, with *all* the Playmates, each of us postage stamp size. In 2006 a new *Playmate Book: Six Decades of Centerfolds* by editor Gretchen Edgren has just been published. We're all there.

It's Hef's good luck that his daughter, Christie Hefner, has even a better business brain than Dad, and is now CEO of Playboy Enterprises.

But back to 1956.

People assumed *Playboy* had plucked me from the millions, for my questionable beauty, to anoint as centerfold, as Playmate of the Month. Whereas *I* chose *them*, to get a story reprinted.

Three publishers wanted to see my first novel. Now all I had to do was write it. I never forgot what Jimmy Baldwin had told me: "More people have talent than the will to sweat out the learning process."

Writing was a delicate archeological dig, sifting to shape treasure. Hard but thrilling. If it went well, I felt luxurious. To discover words for living was ecstasy. Don't laugh. For me, the ecstasy of revelation. I love to analyze, speculate.

If, for example, Jimmy Dean had married Pier Angeli, would he be alive? Would she have tamed his wild streak? That time I saw him, when he told me about Pier, he seemed to want to let down, let it go. Grow through love. We were all wild. Jimmy just got caught.

I kept missing Jimmy. If he were here, he could say instantly if my writing was good or bad—if I'd achieved what I wanted to say, captured the *voice*.

๛๛๛๛

It was only six months since James Dean had died.

His buddy, composer Leonard Rosenman, and I began dating. Lenny had done the music for both *East of Eden* and *Rebel*. We both missed Jimmy.

"He was such a boy," I said.

"A mad fool kid," said Lenny, who was Jimmy's size with gobs of straight black hair, blackest eyes, and a wacky humor. Unlike Jimmy, Lenny was cultured and well educated.

"Sadly."

"Jimmy didn't know how to handle rejection," said Lenny. "He went wild after Pier Angeli dumped him. All because her mother thought he was too wild. Then he went out and proved it. I had to take a gun away from him, out there in Hollywood."

"Lenny, no! Was he being theatrical or—?"

"I doubt if *he* knew."

"Jimmy thought he was immortal," I said.

Jimmy was our bond. Lenny and I were playful joking lovers. When he was ten or eleven, Lenny said, he was so small and supple he could suck his own dick. Of course, he grew out of it. When somebody tells you such astonishingly convoluted trivia, you never forget it. Lenny moved to Hollywood where he continued to write inventive, serious music but had his great success, of course, doing scores for movies and TV.

"Have you seen Chris White?" I asked.

"We had dinner a couple of times," said Lenny and sighed. "She should have Jimmy's luck."

After starring in a TV family series that flopped, Chris White went to Hollywood too, not sought but seeking. She had a small role in Clint Eastwood's *Magnum Force* but found it tough to get parts. It was harder for actresses just as it was for women writers.

Chris became what some call a Jesus freak, testifying on corners, acting out to gain converts for the fundamentalist group she worked for.

The Beats idolized James Dean as the original rebel. The literary world would eagerly greet new offbeat writers Jack Kerouac and William Burroughs, Paul Bowles and Samuel Beckett. But it was conventional wisdom that no woman could write fiction with the scope of a man. Even though it was clear that Katherine Anne Porter, Flannery O'Connor, Virginia Woolf, Simone de Beauvoir, Jane Bowles (Paul's wife, by the way), Christina Stead, Jean Rhys, Nathalie Sarraute, and Dorothy Richardson did. They were called the Exceptions that Proved the Rule.

It upset me that male writers and reviewers seemed to expect our sex to empathize totally with men, to pretend we were misogynistic men when reading. They trashed women so I felt miserable.

In our Manhattan totem, the Sunday *Times Book Review*, I read an essay by Pamela Hansford Johnson, dutiful wife of boring C.P. Snow, that declared women were destined to be minor writers. Angrily, I tossed off a letter to the *Book Review*. It made me sad when women volunteered to be little girls.

Sometimes I wondered if, like Ellison's *Invisible Man*, we were invisible women.

❧ 17 ❧

FAMILY CIRCLE
1957 - 1958

Harry Evans, editor-in-chief of *Family Circle*, claimed to be younger than my father, who swore Harry was older.

"I forbid you to accept invitations from that man as old as your father," Mother ordered long distance.

"It's a job interview, Mother. Daddy arranged it."

"How's Harry?" said Dad. "Give him our best."

At the *Family Circle* office where I demurely appeared, I was interviewed by a reedy, bitter fellow, Harry's second-in-command, whose typing I interrupted. He informed me right off there were no openings.

Then he slid his eyes at me, fingers paused above the keys. "All Southerners are stupid, aren't they?"

"Harry's a Southerner," I said.

Maybe there was an inner office dispute. Maybe he thought he should be editor-in-chief. "Oh, Harry's a social butterfly," he dismissed him.

Brow arched, I didn't mention Uncle Ling and Charlie Merrill, also from Jacksonville. *Family Circle*, founded by Harry in 1932, was owned by its distributor, Safeway Grocery Stores, of which Uncle Lingan Warren was CEO. Safeway was founded and owned by Merrill Lynch, so Uncle Ling worked for Charlie Merrill. Harry had lived in Grandmother Denham's big house when he came to Jacksonville from St. Augustine as a young man.

How could I expect *Family Circle* to like me? I didn't fit in. Harry was society's extra man in those days and he was about as dashing as Jerome Zipkin, a later version. Harry knew everybody and he introduced me to them. Harry looked like a chipmunk with freckles, narrow-jawed, about five foot six, in his mid-fifties. As he'd been a tapdancer-entertainer when young, he was a fabulous ballroom dancer.

At the Reed Whittemore's elegant spacious apartment, I sat on a sofa chatting with a comfy matron from Spain.

"Come watch Harry's trick," someone called.

Guests crowded around carpeted stairs to the floor below. All assembled, Harry removed his white tux jacket but not his black tie, rolled up his sleeves, and walked down the stairs on his hands. Everybody clapped.

"That was scary," I said, as Harry toweled off. "Who's that nice lady I talked to?"

Harry chortled, "That was Mrs. Angier Biddle Duke."

For the charity ball, I wore a floor-length off-the-shoulder ivory evening gown paid for by Harry. "Go to Saks and charge it to me," Harry had said. The saleslady who fitted me had ignored Marlene Dietrich to wait on me. Marlene and her daughter stood in the center of the salon and saleswomen fled. When I asked why, she said Marlene, who always wanted to appear in new gowns, wore them once and returned them next day.

We dined and danced and twirled among famous social faces. Manhattan had a certain polish back then, a gleam of sophisticated style. We chatted with a very tall friendly fellow, who talked writing with me. "Nice guy, that Bill whoever," I said.

Harry doubled up, "That was William Randolph Hearst."

As the rich circled the dance floor, they searched till they spotted the cameras, danced quickly toward them, and ogled, smiled ravishingly, smiles turning to iron as they tossed their curls for five minutes, hoping to be captured for the society pages. A little fancy elbow work from competing couples and they

Playmate of the Month, July 1956.

Story conference in Hef's office.

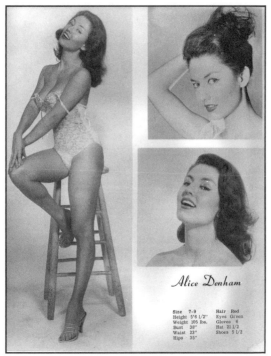

Composite models leave this with photographers and clients.
Denham always lied about her height.

Photographer Leon Gast went on to make the Oscar-winning film about Muhammad Ali, *When We Were Kings*.

Denham posed for camera clubs from Philadelphia to Connecticut.

Left: What a huge fridge (ad).

Right: Queen of the Circus, wearing $1,000,000 worth of Harry Winston diamonds.

Ad for a swimming pool maker.

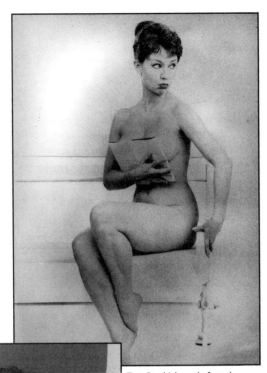

Top: Bookish nude for ad.
Bottom: Figure modeling.

At the Capitol with Congressmen John Conyers, Tom Foley, and local bachelors I interviewed for my *Washingtonian* magazine article, "The Sidesteppers."

Denham posed for dozens of record album covers, movie posters and paperback covers.

Writers workshop at Yale with Barbadian novelist, Austin Clarke, and others.

moved along, faces falling into neutral. What good did it do to be rich if you had to work so hard to get attention? They all seemed afraid of being wallflowers.

We dined at a table for four with the Whittemores, who'd hosted the cocktail party.

"I just finished shooting an Ingmar Bergman movie," I announced. "I was the star, Mai Zetterling, nude."

Everybody perked right up.

"The American distributors decided Bergman's new film, *Illicit Interlude*, needed spice," I explained. "So they hired me to do a nude swimming scene in the woods, climaxed with a steamy embrace with the male lead, impersonated by Jerry the distributor."

"Skinny-dipping?" ogled Harry.

"He wore trunks and I wore my bikini bottom. We shot it in a New Jersey lake. Then I had to do a scene running nude down a hill, which they shot profile as I ran."

"What does Bergman think?" asked Whit.

"Bergman doesn't know."

"Were you embarrassed?" asked Mrs. Whit.

"Of course." I blushed.

When the charity ball hit the society pages, two couples were pictured, the Whittemores, Harry and me.

When I saw rushes of *Illicit Interlude*, I watched my run down the hill and was amazed I never once saw my naked breasts or below, so carefully did they cut and splice.

෧෧෧෧෧

Harry was eager to read my novel-in-progress. I gave him a carbon, refused to go to El Morocco till he'd read it.

"I can't make head nor tail of this," Harry looked chagrined, handing it back. "I marked some grammatical mistakes, though."

"I was making up words, Harry, "like Joyce in *Finnegans Wake*." I frowned, checking through the first chapter and saw he'd turned experiment back into mag-speak. Well, what did I expect?

"If I know your parents, all that sex will—"

"Shock and horrify them," I grinned.

"I was a movie reviewer," Harry apologized. "Not quite a literary critic."

At Elmer's, as they called El Morocco, we drank champagne cocktails seated in our curving zebra-striped banquette above the dance floor, with the in-crowd. Tiny table lamps lit the satiny dark. People watched us dance the cha-cha and meringue and tango. Harry was such a deft leader, I floated. A deb with date danced by, calling out, "Harry, dance the next one with me?" "Sure, darling," Harry smiled his lopsided pleased snaky grin.

We table-hopped and Harry introduced me to Cary Grant and Esther Williams, Jack Benny, and both Gabors. Out on the floor again, I danced past Marilyn Monroe in a plain black short gown with spaghetti straps. Marilyn looked incredibly beautiful and bored, as she danced with a fat short producer, then returned to her table where there were three other short fat producers in tux. Marilyn was far more gorgeous than her photos.

꙳꙳꙳꙳

As Harry was content to be my Dutch uncle, I told him about Oleg Cassini, who'd phoned my model agency to see me. We called these job interviews go-sees. In his fancy East Side townhouse Cassini leafed through my photo portfolio, stretched out on his Victorian sofa.

"Hands behind his head, Harry, Cassini invited me to join his harem. I'd get clothes, he said. I'd start off as number four and work my way up. 'You'll meet people,' said Oleg. 'But you have to be ready to go out when I call.'"

Harry roared at that.

"You don't want to use me for a shoot or a show?" I didn't tell Harry this part.

"You know you're not a fashion model," Oleg had countered. "But you're clean."

"What?"

"Worst smell in the world, you want to know what it is? Upperclass Italian women."

"You like to be provocative, don't you?" I crossed my arms.

Oleg leaped up. "Let me show you the rest of the house."

I followed him up carpeted stairs to a huge bedroom with canopied bed, onto which he flopped. On a glass-topped dresser was an inscribed photo of Grace Kelly, once his lady love. "Did you ever meet Prudy Wise, Grace's secretary?" I asked. "I knew her as a child in Jacksonville."

"Probably, dark hair and eyes, right?" I nodded and he sighed despondently.

Back to Harry Evans. "This is what he told me. 'You have no idea how I loved Grace Kelly. I adored her, I wanted to marry her, of course. But Mama wanted a prince. A mere fashion designer wasn't lofty enough.'"

"Everybody was wild about Grace," said Harry, "but he was hardly in her league."

I didn't tell Harry that Oleg unbuttoned his shirt and I saw his pinkpink slightly fatty chest. As I was used to muscular young men, I bopped back downstairs, grabbed my portfolio, and fled.

"Here's one for *you*." Harry told me society gossip. "When Jack Kennedy decided to run for president, Jackie was fed up with his philandering. She wanted a divorce, so Old Joe settled a million dollars on Jackie in her name, to keep her!"

We tittered then Harry buzzed my cheek. "Past my bedtime," he said. Then he kissed me fast and lightly on the lips.

"I had a great time," I called as he whipped down the stairs.

જાજાઉજાઉ

Bob Evans—no relation to Harry—later head of Paramount, claimed to be interested in my writing. He was young then and fat and still a member of the family firm, Evans-Picone Sportswear. He had a screenplay idea he wanted to show me over dinner, he said. Would I stop by his place? I did not like men who didn't pick me up. But I went.

"What a shot, your *Playboy* spread," said Bob.

"Where's the screenplay?"

"Relax." He handed me a cocktail. "I don't like to dine out," Bob said in his scarlet-walled apartment, patting the space beside him on his scarlet sofa.

So Bob Evans cooked steaks the color of his mahogany furniture and we sipped red wine the color of his walls, and he tried to put the make on me, sans proper dining in a candlelit East Side French restaurant. Evans was a spoiled glossy and gelid garment center prince. He'd forgotten the screenplay.

When he emerged later as a slim handsome movie mogul, I was astounded.

やみやみ

Harry Evans took me to the Blue Angel to see comedian Lenny Bruce, famous for his foul mouth. At the bar he introduced me to Truman Capote, a regular. Elfin Truman greeted me with wan disinterest.

I wasn't aware that Tru had lived in Paris with my cousin, Denham Fouts, after *Other Voices, Other Rooms* was published in 1948. After Denham, "the best kept boy" had sent him first-class fare to Europe. Neither Harry nor I knew that Truman was, in a sense, connected to the family circle.

Aunt Sara and Uncle Ling still lived mostly in California in their Burlingame house, though they kept the apartment at the Sherry-Netherland. Harry lived in the Delmonico, an East Side residential hotel of the sort Dorothy Parker favored.

"I can't marry," said Harry. "If I weren't a bachelor, nobody would invite me."

やみやみ

"We want to come visit you," Mother phoned. "Can you get us a hotel nearby?"

"Sure, Mama. I'm thrilled." An inspection! Since the break-in, they wanted to see for themselves how I lived. Oh boy.

"This doesn't mean your father and I have forgiven you for being naked in that vile magazine."

"No, of course not!" I booked them at the nearby sedate Hotel Wellington.

Did they understand studio meant I lived in one room? I bought flowers, cleaned in a frenzy, but I couldn't change the neighborhood. My stomach knotted with tension, as it always did when I faced Mother.

When Mother and Dad climbed the dark crumbling stairs to my apartment, I'd never felt so ashamed in my life. They both looked horrified. Proper pretty Mother, in good suit and nice lady hat, and Dad, sartorial in English cut, had never walked into such a seedy place. I was mortified at how I'd disappointed them in life. I was poor.

I sat in the circle chair, Dad sat at my desk, and Mother sat on the bed.

"My marble cafe table is new," I flushed. "You could sit there."

I served iced tea, their favorite, with sliced apples, cheese and raisins.

"You'll never finish that book," Mother sobbed. "You need a *job*, so you can leave this dreadful room."

Dad looked stunned. "The building is in bad shape." He tried to react mildly.

"The worst place I've ever been in," Mother burst into tears. "A slum!"

The phone rang. "It never stops," I apologized. "Hello?—Hi, Hunt.—Not tonight, no. My parents are here.—They'll be here tomorrow too. Call next week, Hunt.—So long. Have fun."

"Who was that?" Mother asked.

"Huntington Hartford."

"The A & P heir?" asked Dad.

"Safeway's rival, and Uncle Ling's. Not that he works."

Mother glared, "Why don't you marry someone like that?"

"He's a bit of a jerk, Mother. Nice but somewhat dim."

"You're so uncharitable," Mother sniffed. "He's *rich*."

"Hunt is into handwriting analysis," I explained. "He had me write a sentence he could analyze. Hunt told me I'm a genius because of the long tails I put on the letter *g*."

Nobody chuckled. They looked glum.

Mother and Dad felt so sad about me. Dad said, "I can help you get a government job, in Washington."

"And you can marry one of the rich boys at home," added Mother.

"Mother," I sighed, "I'm with people who stretch my brain, not shrink it at the country club."

"You infuriate me!" Mother yelped. Then she asked, alarmed, "Do you make enough to eat?"

Now I laughed. "Look, I'm okay. I expect to make enough by August to go to Mexico for a couple of months. To write." Their doubting faces frightened me. "Look," I pontificated, "this is my one pass through this arc of the universe. If I don't do the writing I love, what value a life?"

The audacity of my pronouncement seemed to reach them.

Daddy, sweet Daddy, kissed my cheek then hugged me tight.

"It's your life to lead your way, Alley Oop."

"Alley Oop, stick stack stoop, dominicker tintoed bowlegged goop," I clucked. "Remember, Pop, when you used to call me that?"

Even Mama smirked. "Still a goop," she said. "Crazy."

I wanted to take them to dinner at the Brittany, but they insisted on taking me to the Hotel Wellington dining room.

❧❧❦❦

Where was my Modigliani nude print—my reposing woman with Chinese vase curves and pubic triangle? I phoned home.

Mother confessed, "I took it because it was dirty."

"Mother, it's art and it's beautiful," I said. "Send it back."

"It's filthy, like that *Playboy*."

"It's art and it's mine. Send it back," I said in a nasty tone.

She did.

❧❧❦❦

Cancer got me. I got cancer. I met a rich fellow who was angry at himself for flaunting about Europe and not becoming an MD after Harvard. He sent every woman he knew to a cancer surgeon he'd gone to school with for a free examination. Dr. Thomas phoned me, "Your Pap smear came back positive." "How could it? I had a negative two months ago." On Monday Dr. Thomas did a biopsy and it too was positive.

I phoned Marianne, who'd modeled before her marriage to Punch.

"Punch," she said.

"Yes, Punch." Punch was too big and hard for both of us.

"Go see Alice," Marianne would say, because they had an open marriage.

The next morning I'd throb with pain I hadn't felt in the heat of things. Dr. Thomas said there was bacteria in male semen that could cause cervical cancer in women. Probably the thrust had caused small tears that allowed it to enter.

"I'm in shock, Marianne. I go into the hospital on Thursday."

"Why don't you come here for lunch, Alice? I miss you now that I'm home with the kids."

"Darling Marianne." I went downtown to their penthouse and we played Monopoly with the kids.

On Thursday Dr. Thomas operated on me for cervical cancer that had not yet metastasized—spread. I had a cervical cone, not a hysterectomy, which meant I could still have children. I was caught about as early as humanly possible. I was saved by a flip of fate, a fluke. Had I not met the rich guy? Had I not worn hard-toed shoes that night in Las Vegas when the man almost choked me to death?

"Most young women your age aren't being checked," drawled Dr. Thomas, who looked like a Southern sheriff. "If you hadn't come to me, you'd be dead in two years."

"You saved my life," I hugged him. I was still stunned, also weak with pain.

"I'm gonna save those breasts too, don't you worry."

Was I that vulnerable to cancer? It sickened me with fright to think so. Why me, why me? All young women ask the same question.

෧෨෧෨෧෨෧

I phoned home. "Mama, I had cancer. But I'm okay now," I sobbed. "Get Daddy on."

"It's too soon," said Mama. "How could you?"

"All in a week. I was diagnosed, operated on, and stayed five days in the hospital." I explained the whole process. "I'm in shock too."

"Come home and be safe," moaned Mother. "That awful town did that to you."

"Are you sure you're *cured*, baby?" asked Dad.

"Dr. Thomas says so." I gave them his number to phone.

I wanted to experience everything human so I'd be, as George Bernard Shaw said, all used up when I died. But did I mean so early, so often? A romantic notion but it helped me recover from the shock of cancer. Now I'd had what all women fear and far too many of us grow inside, in our invisibly endangered bodies.

෴෴

It was summer and I recuperated on Fire Island at Seaview, on the deck of Marianne and Punch's beach house. Six weekend guests came, among them Gary Morton, a rough comedian with toupee askew. As I lay in pain in a deck chair, Gary dumped a bucket of cold water over me. I screamed in shock. Later he phoned to apologize and asked me out. I said no. He married comedian Lucille Ball.

Fear, frozen terror of cancer striking any moment, would hit me like a crashing wave. I'd tremble violently, huff and puff till it subsided. All my life.

❧ 18 ❦

LSD LITERARY LADS
SUMMER 1959

The most ballyhooed literary publication of 1959 was Philip
Roth's witty adolescent *Goodbye, Columbus*. Though he blamed
everything on the college girlfriend with the diaphragm, which
item caused delicious ripples of shock. With the National Book
Award at age twenty-six, Roth was anointed as the great white
hope. Next most talked-about novel was *Mrs. Bridge* by Evan
Connell, about the submissive life of a Kansas City suburban
wife.

That same year Norman weighed in with his desperately clever
Advertisements for Myself, and in 1958 Jim Jones had published
Some Came Running. Neither caught the new wave like Roth
with his satiric Jewish tales or Connell with his rigid midwestern
WASPs. On Broadway, *A Raisin in the Sun*, by Lorraine Hansberry,
recreated black American family life. The brilliant Hansberry died
a few years later in her early thirties of cancer, a tragic loss. The
same cancer I had, but hers was not diagnosed early.

In 1958 Boris Pasternak won the Nobel for *Doctor Zhivago,*

which the USSR forced him to return. Over here in 1959 D. H. Lawrence's novel, *Lady Chatterley's Lover*, was banned for obscenity by Postmaster General Summerfield. That same year legendary jazz singer Billie Holiday died.

We added two states, Alaska in 1958 and Hawaii in 1959. With money from cheering Americans, Fidel Castro defeated Cuban dictator Batista then visited New York. Far too eagerly Fidel became a Cuban Communist dictator.

≈≈≈≈

Visiting Palo Alto, I met writer Evan Connell at a party thrown by Dick Alpert. Through colleagues at Stanford's Behavioral Sciences think tank, Harvard LSD gurus Timothy Leary and Dick Alpert tested LSD on volunteer writers to see if it enhanced creativity.

The gifted Evan Connell was trying it. Evan was the most strikingly handsome writer I'd ever met. He was tall, noble, with strong perfectly proportioned features and observant eyes, black as his hair. The royal bearing of a Indian chieftain. Was he descended from Sacajawea and Charbonneau? He was no part of the snarling rivalry that consumed Manhattan literary life. Evan had published an inventive book of short stories in 1957, *The Anatomy Lesson*, that I liked even better than *Mrs. Bridge*.

"Aren't you afraid of LSD?" I asked.

With a shrug, almost a smile, Evan dismissed it. "No," he said.

He meant he was more powerful than acid. "I wouldn't touch it with a ten-foot pole," I declared.

Dick Alpert bustled up with a copy of *Playboy*, with my July 1956 centerfold and story. Evan said, "Will you sign mine?"

"How did you like my story?"

"Much," he replied.

We drank tequila steadily, as couples danced by. I love to dance. Evan didn't dance. I didn't care. "Last summer in Mexico, I took multivitamins," I said, "that had benzedrine in them, unbeknownst to me. I felt intensely creative. I did sixty new pages of my novel. Back in New York, I had to junk them; they were bad. Two months' work wasted. That's why I don't touch dope."

We strolled out onto the dark terrace. "In New York," Evan asked in a constricted voice, "do you date famous men?"

"Usually once, till I say no. I went out with Al Capp."

Evan nodded, so I continued.

"I was curious to meet him, since he has an interesting mind. Large hulking fellow with a club foot. Reputation as a tailchaser. You know, wife in the suburbs, keeps a *pied-a-terre* in town. Capp told me he seldom drew Li'l Abner any more, that he'd farmed it out. Sometimes he did the dialogue but often that was done by others. Easier, he said.

"After a fancy French restaurant, he asked me to his Park Avenue apartment for a nightcap, as he needed advice on decor. He gave me a drink, tried to make me sit on the sofa, but I stood so he couldn't lurch at me. The decor was El Morocco ladies room, not remotely like Al Capp. When he rose, I stood by the door and said I had to go. With a sour sneer, he let me out."

Evan almost smiled. "But you, you're—"

Smashed, I put my arms on his skateboard shoulders. "I'm what?"

Evan grabbed me around the waist and kissed my ear. I was ready for a death-defying dive of a kiss. But Evan was proper and we were in the midst of a big bash.

Back at the house, we made instant love. A 69 twirl, we locked. My stroking walls stroked his stoker in my satin slide. Now he was trapped in my lair, I might not let him go, might never unpin my legs. I erupted into Miro spirals and Kandinsky firecrackers, then he came, with silent heaves.

Away from home, away from responsibility, an Amazon of love poured from my secret sources. Of course I was drunk.

ꙮꙮꙮꙮ

Next day in Evan's car we drove to the coast, lunched on oysters at Half Moon Bay, then drove down the Monterey peninsula winding romantically along Big Sur.

"More," Evan said tightly. "More New York."

"Famous men?" This interested Evan more than it did me.

He nodded.

"I had a bit of a thing with Hefner and with Jim Jones." I told him, "Hef was crafty and pornographic, Jones was a solid down-to-earth guy." Etc. I never talked about Jimmy Dean. That was private.

Evan didn't glance at me, didn't react.

I squeezed his knee but his head stayed on the curves, busy driving.

"An agent got me a date with Gary Crosby, one of Bing's blond bland sons. We had nothing in common, as the table chatted Hollywood gossip. I was bored, he was bored. When he brought me home, he offered me one hundred dollars to sleep with him. Like it was routine. I opened the cab door and slammed it on him."

When Evan's face didn't flicker, I blushed. "Well, those are stupid things to talk about." Desperately I said, "Have I told you how much I admire your writing? *Mrs. Bridge,* but especially *Anatomy Lesson.*"

Evan didn't respond. Evan wouldn't talk. Only now did I realize that even last night and all day today, my mouth had been on full blast, and Evan had uttered not ten words. Maybe my jabbering offended him.

I shut up. Every time my mouth opened to speak, I clamped it shut. I waited. Patiently I waited an hour. Utter silence between us. Trying to shatter his silence, I talked about Norman and Adele's parties, about my half-completed novel, how it evolved and fleshed out. "I love to play with style." This ranting exhausted me.

I should stare straight ahead and let it go, give up on him. Tears formed in my eyes. I wheeled to face Evan and said, "Why won't you talk to me?"

Startled, his eyes jumped. "I, I—" Evan gulped. He glanced at me, dazzled or was it dazed? "Must be—huh—the most wonderful—thing—to look like—that. So beautiful."

"Like me?"

But that was the last thing Evan had to say.

I couldn't get through to him. So few men I truly desired to couple with—both of us serious writers—and I hit a wall. Another alienated male writer. Did the modern novel draw men who couldn't communicate otherwise?

✁✁✁✁

"Connell's the strong silent type," Dick Alpert told me when he invited me to Cambridge for a fall weekend. We stayed at the guesthouse on his family estate. Dick was tall and fit, not good-looking but squirming with curly-haired vitality. Should he let his father buy him a chair at Harvard? he asked me, as it looked as if the university would dump him and Leary because of LSD. But then everybody would know his dad paid, Dick said.

"Then don't do it," I said. "Go on the road."

Alpert went on the road to Buddhism, and came back from India as a New Age guru. I can attest that he loved to ram, that Baba Ram Dass.

FALL 1959

Steve Carlin, producer of *$64,000 Challenge*, handed me a script for the show, which he said was a tryout. I was to play a contestant. My category was art and artists. I leafed through it to where I flunked out.

"But how can I flunk El Greco?" I asked. "Everybody knows he was born in Greece." I was to say Spain, when asked.

"Look," said Steve, "we're after the audience's response to the show concept. Do they like *Challenge* or is it too much like *$64,000 Question*?" Tall serious-faced Steve Carlin would've looked more at home with a violin tucked under his chin, than as a TV quiz show producer.

On the NBC stage at Rockefeller Center I answered the art questions correctly, which any fool would know without a script, grinning at the audience. The entire auditorium was filled with enthusiastic folk who clapped each time I was right. Since they liked me, I was tempted not to miss and to toss the script. I was at the four thousand dollar level, my imaginary winnings. But I wanted my actor's pay for the day, which was in the high twos.

Host Sonny Fox, a big ebullient hunk of beef, said, "Now, let's ask our bright young model—"

"Writer," I interrupted.

Audience chuckled.

"—young lady about the birthplace of the famous painter, El Greco. In what country was El Greco born?"

"Hmm, Spain," I said.

Audience groaned, let down.

"Sorry, that's Greece," Sonny supplied me with fact.

"Tsk, tsk, I thought it was just a nickname."

As the audience filed out after the show, several people commiserated with me for missing. We liked you, they said, because you seemed friendly.

I looked at the big sign at the entrance announcing the new show, *$64,000 Challenge*. There was nary a word to indicate it was a tryout.

"Steve," I said, "they thought the show was *real*."

Steve just laughed.

෨෨෨෨෨

That night Willie Gaddis and his wife, Patty, Dick Dowling and I chuckled about my *Challenge*. We met for drinks at Dick's walk-up on Jones Street. Dick was a five foot eight sardonic witty worried Irishman who reminded me of my high school boyfriend. Dick's skin was palest white, his eyes and hair coal black. Both he and Gaddis looked artistically unhealthy. Dick's sisters were actresses, Constance Dowling and Doris Dowling. Dick toiled at Pfizer with Gaddis, where they both were still allowed to work on their novels part of the day.

Patty Gaddis was a small thin blonde, high-keyed and tense. Equally afflicted, I told myself I was intense and oversensitive. Willie Gaddis still possessed his *soigne* aesthetic appeal, winning the cheekbones gambit head on. Gaddis had the highest, sharpest, most concave cheekbone cliffs in town. Bone-thin with deepset eyes, he looked as if he dined on art.

Dick Dowling's specialty was martinis and none of us could resist his fine hand. We talked literature and lit biz, swagged martinis and smoked like chimneys. We rode our mouths on Dick's sofabed in his one-room studio. Possibly the ugliest soiled sofa I'd ever seen, of no discernible color. It looked as if he'd adopted it from bulk pickup on the street.

Friday night, when folks put out old furniture, was great street shopping. I'd adopted small tables and a magazine rack.

We had all liked Evan Connell's *Mrs. Bridge*, so I told them about my date with Evan in Palo Alto.

"There I was, falling all over him with passion," I hollered, "and I couldn't get him to say boo." We all rocked with laughter but it had not been funny at the time.

"Probably he's not the same way with men," I added.

"Or other women," said Dick.

"What does that mean?"

Dick shrugged, Willie chuckled, Patty looked severe.

I knew what it meant—that I was aggressive.

As usual we'd drunk ourselves to virtual starvation and reeled out to dinner at ten-thirty or so.

❧❧❧❧

Steve Carlin wanted me to help him find a Chinese Shakespeare expert. To accomplish this, he took me to dinner in Chinatown. Steve was always busy, busy, dashing about, each new idea swallowed by the next.

At the Shanghai Garden, I said, "Steve, looking for a Chinese Shakespeare expert is like looking for a needle in a haystack."

"It's not that hard," said Steve. "You just ask around." Steve went to the back and talked to the manager. "No luck." He sat down.

On to the second and third and fourth restaurant, where I swirled a drink and waited as he talked to those in charge.

"That should do it," said Steve. "They're going to check around for me."

❧❧❧❧

Not long after that, the news broke. All the TV quiz shows were rigged, just like my "tryout". After Herbert Stempel was forced to lose to Charles Van Doren, he spilled the frijoles. The ascendant hero, red white and blue Charles Van Doren, testified before Congress that he'd been given questions and answers before each *Twenty-One* show. Charles, son of poet and revered Columbia prof Mark Van Doren, was an intellectual fake.

Small wonder Steve Carlin figured it would be simple to ferret out a Chinese Shakespeare expert.

❧ 19 ❧

ABORTION AND MEN
FALL 1959

Fear rolled through my body. Pregnant again! Confirmed by the rabbit test. How could it be? With a magnifying glass I found a minuscule slit in my diaphragm. A thunderstorm of clashing rage, helplessness, and maternal desire assaulted me, as I fell apart on the bed. I couldn't feed a child. I could barely feed myself. Was I still a New Face or overexposed? My modeling days were numbered.

My two current lovers were perfectly worthless chaps, sexy hunks with beanbag brains, but I phoned them anyway. The rich horse-farm scion who liked three things—booze, broads, nags.

"Have it and give it to me," he said.

"It?"

"My old man won't give me a sou. How 'bout if I send you some ergot. Sometimes works."

The out-of-work actor/cabbie who'd sworn he'd had a vasectomy. "Must've been another guy," he pretended umbrage.

Certainly I wouldn't dream of having a child by either. Just as men mess up with a casual date, women get pregnant by the wrong guy. What a fool I felt. Of course, I never let either near me again.

My illegal college abortion had been performed without an anaesthetic by my boyfriend Beau's family doctor in Florida. As he worked alone for safety, no anaesthetic. The pain had been beyond anything I thought my body could tolerate without dying. How could I avoid another such D & C—dilation and curretage— unless I could find an MD teamed with an anaesthetist? Could I even find a doctor up here *willing* to perform an illegal abortion? It *had* to be an MD Suppose Doc Trumbow in Florida had retired?

When I phoned Dr. Thomas, he scolded me. "You know you're not supposed to ask me that sort of thing." He sounded almost angry, then he said, "I'll ask around, kid."

So I phoned Norman Mailer and Joe Heller and my buddy Leo Kelmenson and asked if they knew of a good MD abortionist. None did but said they'd phone around. None of them could come up with information. Norman offered to lend me a hundred bucks if I needed it. I said I didn't think I did, but I'd let him know, and thanks.

A week had passed. Dr. Thomas phoned. "None of us here can risk it. I'm—sorry."

In fear and trepidation I phoned the family doctor in Florida, who remembered me and agreed to do it again. Dr. Avery Trumbow performed occasional abortions because his own daughter had died at the hands of a butcher rather than tell her parents she was pregnant. His fee had gone up, from sixty to seventy-five dollars.

"When are you younguns gonna learn to take care of yourselves?" Doc Trumbow said.

"Doc," I sobbed, "I did."

It was more complicated than that. My sister had almost died twice in childbirth. Mother often told me about her—and my— twenty-six hours of horrible labor, how I ripped and tore her. I came out with a pinhead the doctor had to shape and ears that flapped. We were too small. Grandmother Nena, Mother said, had all her babies on the kitchen table in the Florida wilderness with a midwife. It was so awful her brave husband streamed away in his carriage and wouldn't return till word was sent that she was all right, she lived. I was convinced I'd die in childbirth.

I flew to Florida and walked beside the town lake under tall muscular palms click-clacking an angel blue sky. Then into Doc Trumbow's sunny office, the only outsider in the waiting room. When she heard my name, Doc's efficient nurse ushered me in. Doc Trumbow was tall, stooped, shaggy and patient as an old hound. I shook his large liver-spotted hand.

"Still no anaesthetic?" I asked.

Doc shook his head and handed me a shot of brandy. "I want you to swallow two or three of these."

I shivered as I swallowed the shots.

"You can't make a sound, my dear, because of the patients in the waiting room."

Feet in the stirrups, legs spread, utterly helpless, my body lurched and my arms shook like confetti.

"Shall I hold your shoulders?" asked the nurse. "It might help."

"Yes, please," I huffed.

"You're very tight. Relax," Doc said soothingly. "Calm, calm."

Almost too tight for dilation. "Stop, stop!" I plead.

Doc stopped. "Don't jerk. You could hemorrhage."

After the dilation, Doc Trumbow stabbed me. That's what it felt like. The first pain scraped raw through me beyond pain, appalling my entire body, stretching its range of sensations to the unbearable. I gripped the edge of the slab table. Doc began again. Jab, cut, clip, scrape, pull out, cut again. To be cut up inside without anaesthetic is like hara-kiri, like being impaled. How I hated the race of men at that moment. The clamor of love and sex bled in my body while his remained free. I was my own human sacrifice, killing part of myself to free the rest. My head heaved in shock toward the nurse. The pain was more than I thought my heart could take without stopping. "Stop stop." And the hardly tolerable dwindling began, the searing after the blade. I stared at the doctor, "What was that?"

"Don't draw away," Doc said. "If you can push down on the instruments with your body relaxed, I can work faster."

I tried. I loosened the muscles but they tightened around the first cut. I tried again as the doctor said something that only murmured like the swimming humming room, and I finally forced through the untensing and held it, pushing down on the pain, submitting, boring into it, swallowed by it, within the pain rather than the pain in me, for one infinite ecstatic moment conqueror of the unconquerable, possessor of external circumstance, the microcosm abdicating diffusing and thereby devouring the universe. Till the microcosm, small, could hold no more and collapsed on the edge of the reeling universe of pain which spun and bore me, tossing me on the slicing edge I hung onto, clinging to my fleeing pierced body, drowning in heat white and faceless till I slipped over the edge into orange glue and disappeared.

Doc jiggled my arm. "Wake up, my dear."

～～～～

I'd almost killed myself to regain my autonomy. They say you forget pain. I've never forgotten an iota. Many years later when I read that women were meeting to legalize abortion, to make it respectable and safe and painless, I cried. Every break through the old cruelties makes me sob like a child. I joined the women's movement. Wounded in the battle of the sexes, I felt like a gaping foot soldier, dying in the mud, in fury as well as pain. To be so used, to be meat to society.

No one should have to endure this.

～～～～

Back in New York I didn't breathe a word to a soul. To make life easier for myself, I phoned Leo and Norman and Joe and said, "False alarm." They were relieved.

Illegal abortion was a filthy little secret you kept to yourself. I had no idea other women had them. I didn't dare tell my confidante, Nancy, in the back apartment. It branded you a bad girl, sleazy, unclean. Who would want to be my lover? People suspected that it messed you up inside.

I was terribly alone. I had lovers but no real friends.

A few years later I heard about Dr. Spencer in the small town of Ashland, Pennsylvania. These benevolent skillful doctors were true heroes to desperate women in a dark time. Then I heard the rich could arrange to have it done in local hospitals. I should've asked my Dutch uncle, Harry Evans, society's extra man. But I'd feared Harry might phone Dad.

Years later, in 1967, I read a letter in the *New York Times* magazine from one Betty Friedan. She invited women to join the National Organization for Women to fight for safe and legal abortion. I wept and joined the movement.

The phone jangled. It was my modeling agency. "Where on earth have you been?" shrieked Miss Olivia. "You missed two hundred dollars worth of work—three shoots!"

"Family emergency," I said.

"You can catch the last one, if you phone *instantly*."

I took the info and did. Anything to get out of myself. If I'd missed ten thousand dollars in model jobs, it was still worth it to have it over with.

꙳꙳꙳꙳꙳

Feeling morose, I treated myself to a chocolate soda at the drugstore and listened to Hurricane on guitar. Hurricane Carter, the fighter, trained at Stillman's Gym upstairs next door. He always perched on the last stool at the marble counter and we batted the breeze Southern style, as he gently strummed his guitar. How I adored chocolate sodas Fuji-topped with whipped cream and one glossy cherry in those tall vases. Between the chocolate hit and Hurricane, I felt less mopey.

At Max's Luncheonette at the corner, Max said, "Seen your latest layout?" There I was, a six-page color spread in *Nugget*. The boys kept track. As I ducked into my building, the package room boys at the Hearst building shouted, "Hey, Alice." Mere friendly human noise lifted my spirit.

"Alice," June yelled, Kevin in tow. June and her two-year-old lived across the street in the welfare apartment. "Can you watch Kevin for an hour?"

"Sure, June." Kevin looked like a black kewpie doll. I took his hand and we climbed the stairs slowly.

On third Kevin and I said hello to Mr. Jackson, who lived in the front single room next to my studio. The six-by-nine rooms rented for eight dollars a week. All over town there were rooms working men could afford. Bums sheltered in dollar-a-night Mills Hotels. No one was homeless.

Kevin bobbled about my studio inspecting everything.

"Now I'll do your hair," I said. Kevin's hair was like a soft silkspun net. He knew I liked to do it so he sat very still. Finally, at last, I let myself cry.

Kevin felt the wet tears on my cheek in wonder.

"Sweet baby," I kissed his forehead.

Six years in the city. Yearning flowed through me, a tidal longing for my own mate. The city had taught me sexuality. Now it was time to learn love, to settle down. A woman should at least know which of her worthless lovers had been the ying for her pregnant yang.

❧❧❧❧❧

It had not been Storm Cadwell, the brilliant reporter on *The Reporter* magazine who'd won the Polk Award for the first article on illegal wiretapping. Storm imbibed too freely, favored anal sex, and asked me to marry him. Till tonight I hadn't seen Storm since he proposed to me last May and ran out of town. We met at Costello's, the East Side journalists' hangout. Storm was a sartorial matchstick with a high elegant head and fast wit. We both had martins, as he called them.

"Ole Sport, looking sassy as ever," he buzzed my cheek.

"Hello, freakball," I said.

Later on, bathed in raunchy blue light, we listened to Miles at Eddie Condon's on 52nd Street, which was lined with jazz clubs. MOMA—the Modern Art, on 53rd—was a small friendly building among four-story brownstones. Sixth Avenue was lined with brownstones. Rockefeller Center was the only pinnacle. Skyblockers were so few you could see each one behind the old colonial-style brick houses. We had more light back then.

Storm, having dumped me, wanted to pick me up. I was looking forward, after charming him all evening, to dumping him at my door.

In spite of our sexual problems, I'd considered marrying Storm because he asked. Till he dumped me. Then I realized an alcoholic never knows what he'll do next.

Storm thought I was too sexy. "Sport, I wish you wouldn't act like you *want* it so much," he'd said. "Then I could chase after you."

"But I *am* sexy," I'd said.

"It's not all that appealing," Storm had replied. "You're like a man."

"That's right, Storm."

That's how we escalated to anal sex. He had to find sex I didn't want to do. Then, if he made me do it, he'd have won the chase, cornered me, and conquered.

This did not appeal to me.

"So long, Storm," I said at my door. "Bye, bye."

ﻬﻬﻬﻬ

It wasn't just Storm, or my ex, or the philandering married writers. The conditions of love back then were *not* equal. There didn't seem to be any men like Daddy out there, kind monogamous men. If there were, probably they wouldn't have been bold enough to catch my wandering eye.

"You look like a defrocked priest," I said to the tall intense fellow who flirted with with me at the Egyptian Gardens. His jet black hair and eyes and brow were set in pale clerical flesh. But he was big and athletic and fit.

"Haha, that's close," Stanley Moore laughed with clerical stiffness. "I'm a defrocked professor, a Marxist."

The thrill of this was new to me. He'd waited for me outside the ladies room. I gave him my number and went back to my date.

A few nights later, I dated Stanley at the Egyptian Gardens, the new oasis on 28th Street between Eighth and Ninth, abloom with old dusty green artificial hanging plants. We watched the sinuous bellydancer grind her belly and loop her rubbery arms through the dance floor veils. We drank ouzo, ate grape leaves and babaghanouj, watched the Greek men dance together then got up and joined them. That was the fun of the Egyptian Gardens—challenge dancing, group twirling.

Stanley had been fired from his tenured teaching job at Reed in Oregon in 1954 when the House Un-American Activities Committee called him for questioning about his Communist Party membership. Stanley had refused to say whether he was a Communist or a Marxist, citing academic freedom. With roaring demonstrations, the student body and much of the faculty supported him. But the regents, including his uncle, caved in. At the time he was researching a book on Marxist economic theory on a Ford Foundation grant, which was also snatched away.

"The meetings were so boring I never went," Stanley said. "But I didn't resign." Not to worry about Stanley though. His family was California rich. He taught as an adjunct at Barnard and tried to take as little money as possible from his mother, whom he said "owned the worst kind of capitalistic endeavor, tenant farms."

He told California jokes. "Trouble with Californians is they're Okies who had a car." "My family walked to California. You Episcopalians waited for the railroads."

When we argued politics, I insisted people were far more competitive than cooperative, and he countered that Stalin was a dictator, that there'd never been a real Marxist state. After two years I got Stanley Moore to confess he wanted to be commissar of America. Leader, not led, of course. His fascinating book, *Critique of Capitalist Democracy*, was popular in Japan.

Stanley had a photographic memory. He quoted Byron and Eliot and Hopkins and Marianne Moore, at fragrant length, making a symbolic bouquet of our first encounters.

There will be time, there will be time
To prepare a face to meet the faces that you meet;
There will be time to murder and create,
And time for all the works and days of hands.

murmured Mr. Prufrock, to which I replied in paraphrase:

No, you are not Prince Hamlet, nor were meant to be;
Perhaps you shall grow old and wear the bottoms of your
trousers rolled. But I shall dare to eat a peach, for
I have heard the mermaids singing each to each. I do
think they will sing to me.

How I adored Eliot. Then we slouched on to Bethlehem where, according to Stanley, Yeats's great beast to be born was capitalism.

But Stanley also had a porno-photographic mind. He wanted me to be a sexual tableau for his arousal. He asked me not to wear panties when we went to dinner. Back at his place, with the lights low, he asked me to sit across from him with my legs spread. Then he'd pull his organ out and stroke it. Or ask me to play with myself. Or tell me how he'd fucked sheep on the farm. Or pretend he was a big dog. This was not love.

"Stanley, can't we just touch to turn on?" I said when I grew weary of pedantry.

"Baby is so simple," Stanley chided.

"Touch escalates sensual feeling." Did I have to explain this to a forty-year-old man? "In a natural affectionate way."

"Ah, my pet, so does artifice." I was not yet old enough for artifice.

Stanley was steady as a rock. Every Saturday night for two years he offered me a guided tour to the nonviolent perversities, via the pornographic stills engraved on his brain.

"I believe in politics, my pet. You believe in love."

Tooling around in his yellow jeep, we hung out at the Cedar and Dillon's and dined at Paris Brest and du Midi and the Brittany and Chumley's and the Blue Mill Tavern.

Stanley wouldn't take me to the tony leftist parties in town, because unbeknownst to me, he had a monied left lady. Many of his leftist friends were rich radical chic. I'd had more fun with Storm because we partied with the free-flowing journalistic crowd. When McCarthyism ebbed, in the mid-sixties Stanley achieved a tenured appointment at UCLA, through Herbert Marcuse. He married a Californian younger than I, I who'd considered him rather too old. "She's no intellectual," he told me on the phone, "but I don't want to spend my old age alone."

By the summer of 1962, I was madly insanely in love south of the border. I felt I'd found my mate. But from sixty to sixty-two Stanley provided the stability I needed to spend Monday through Friday nights with my true love, my first novel.

One of his students, Robert Richter, formed a committee of graduates and faculty to petition Reed College to apologize to Stanley Moore. Not till 1980 did they succeed and this apology, the only one offered by a private college to a HUAC victim, made headlines in the first section of the Sunday *New York Times*.

☙☙☙☙

I tried to get Stanley to march in our BAN THE BOMB marches. But he said it was child's play; we had to change the whole system. But to me nuclear bomb testing, above ground and below, was dead serious right now.

During my divorce in Las Vegas, an atom bomb had been detonated outside town on the Nevada desert. The blast had lifted me off my feet and slung me onto my bed. I felt it burn through my body like electricity. When the shock subsided, I ran outside to an open flat rock area and let the huge pretty pink mushroom cloud pass over me. The state of Nevada had recommended people be moved forty-five miles away. The cold warriors ignored this. *Nobody warned us it was dangerous.* Nobody.

Adamantly, I marched with the women fighting bomb testing till finally above-ground tests were banned.

❧ 20 ❧

ART VS. MONEY
SPRING - FALL 1960

James Oliver Brown was a perfect snob of a literary agent. A
Harvard lawyer who dressed like a double-breasted English
MP, complete with bowler and tie-pin, James Oliver Brown
conversed in an envied Anglophile accent. He reminded me of
my Edwardian grandparents.

Jim handled Erskine Caldwell and Jean Stafford, Alberto
Moravia and Louis Auchincloss, and others of the *creme*. Plus
Herbert Gold and my humble self, journalist Dan Wakefield, and
various of our hopeful contemporaries. Jim's office was at 22 East
60th, in the Alliance Francaise building, and his apartment was
two blocks away on 60th, across from Bloomingdale's. Ideal. He
was divorced with ex-wife and children in Connecticut. I'd heard
whispers that he was gay but I never dreamed of broaching the
subject. His affairs were his own, just as mine were.

Jim had liked my rewrite of the first hundred pages of my
novel. Forbidding manner aside, he was kind and sociable,
encouraging, and a good tough critic. With fear and trembling,

I now gave Jim the first two sections of my novel, two hundred pages, much revised, plus my plan for two hundred more. Jim said I'd hear from him in a week.

While Jim read, I had a model shoot, thank God, in Bermuda. Would I be safe alone with this man? Far away from literary anxiety, I eagerly went.

࿐࿐࿐

Turner Welles, my richest client, stood on the sand and shot me lolling in the surf naked, slinging my arms aloft in blissful freedom. Then I dashed about the turquoise water, my upturned face reflecting sun and sea and sand.

Retired from Wall Street, Turner was a proper fiftyish WASP who shot pinups of me about four times a year. Color photography was newer then, porn was illegal and sleazy. Hordes of men, from working class to upper class, shot color pinups and nudes, hiring professional models to sublimate with. Camera clubs, as far away as Philadelphia and New Haven, booked me in spring and summer to shoot outside. On location, at lakes, in woods, at beaches.

White froth breaking behind me, I posed against the sculpted rock that made the cove. Then two cops, guns clanking, spilled over the ridge toward us. In a flash I put on my robe.

"We spotted five men with their noses over the ridge watching you," said one cop.

"No!" Turner and I said together.

"You best put on a suit," said the other. "We want you to be safe."

"Yes, of course," said Turner.

"Uh, both pieces, top too," the cop near-blushed.

"Right away," I said. I never minded covering up more. It was a relief.

Turner and I stayed at the most elegant private beach club in Bermuda. Rose stone cottages sat in tasteful, tropical, English gardens on a high bluff. My cottage was at the opposite end from Turner's. Was he hiding me, or did that make it easier to pounce and run?

That evening we dined and danced at the clubhouse, where Turner introduced me to his rich social set. As we danced Turner preened and grinned with bubbly pleasure at friends. Turner was a perfect gentleman. He never laid a hand on me. At last I understood my mission. I was there to show off as his mistress, to convince his cronies he could still putt.

❧❧❧❧

James Oliver Brown phoned. "I just talked to Ken McCormick over at Doubleday. Let's run it by Ken for his input."

"Hold on," I said. "You like it?"

"You may or may not get an offer," Jim said, busy. "But his support will help us, if he likes it."

"Then you *do* like my book?"

"I like it, I like your writing. But will Ken?"

"Do you think he will?"

"I don't second-guess these boys. Every time I do I get shot down." Jim slowed, "Yes, I think so."

❧❧❧❧

Now began my first prolonged taste of fear of rejection by publishers. Even the famous suffer rejection. James Brown told me dozens of Caldwell's short stories were making the rounds, unsold. Later Katherine Anne Porter told me the same thing. I shivered with fear as I did before diving off a very high board.

Over the years, suave and friendly Ken McCormick, editor-in-chief of Doubleday, had invited me for drinks and asked about my novel. Don't tease me too long, Ken had said, or I'll give up.

Ken McCormick phoned. "I've read your novel and passed it around. We like it, but there are problems."

"Oh!" I was instantly alarmed.

"How long till you finish?" Ken was businesslike.

"Maybe two years," I apologized. "I—I have to work, model, I mean, for money."

"We think your novel should be more commercial," intoned Ken. "We want you to let our editors show you how to make it more commercial."

"Commercial!" Appalled, I hardly dared breathe the word. Did Ken think I was trite, of such small worth that I'd be improved by cheapening my writing with sensation?

If a novel was considered commercial, that meant it was *not* literary. We serious writers disdained bestseller writers as a low breed. They were hacks, we were artists. Most editors published commercial trash so they could afford to publish quality. That was the book world in 1960 when publishers still owned themselves, before the multinationals swallowed them.

"Now I want you to think this over carefully. Doubleday wants to offer you a five thousand dollar advance if you'll work with our editors to make your novel more commercial."

"Five grand?"

"If," said Ken. "Talk it over with Jim."

❧❧❧❧

"Ken's a good editor, if he's behind you," said Jim. "But you've got to want to do it."

"Five thousand—"

"Is a good advance for an unknown at halfway. Don't jump. Think."

For advice I phoned Joe Heller at work.

I could tell Joe was happy to lean back and prop his feet on the desk. "It's your ball," said Joe. "Me, I do things my own way. But if Bob, that's my editor, shows me a better way I grab it." Joe chuckled, "I just turned in the manuscript."

"Lucky you."

❧❧❧❧

In 1960 adorable Jack Kennedy and prissy Richard Nixon debated for the presidency. The old suffragette leader, Sylvia Pankhurst, died. Flannery O'Connor's new novel, *The Violent Bear It Away*, focused on religious fanaticism, which she knew never dies. Fortunately, the Circuit Court of Appeals reversed the Postmaster General's ban on *Lady Chatterley's Lover*. D. H. Lawrence's paean to the mighty penis would be published by gutsy Barney Rosset at Grove Press. One of my heroes, Albert Camus, was killed in a car crash in France. His publisher was driving.

While I mulled over Ken's offer I was crowned Queen of the Circus for the newspapers. I was decked out in a black bathing suit studded with a million dollars worth of Harry Winston diamonds and posed atop an elephant. We shot at the straw-filled elephant compound at the Coliseum. They used only female elephants because nobody could tolerate the male musk.

My Wrigley's TV commercial played on every episode of *Maverick*, the popular James Garner western. Every month for a year and a half I got a nice fat residual check. A friendly client, Jerry Silverman, bought me a TV so I could see it. Jerry fitted his clothes line on me. His sportswear was sized at Misses eight and I was a Junior five but Jerry said he enjoyed my conversation. People didn't look at money as somberly as they must today.

☙☙☙☙

Ken McCormick and I met for a drink. He reached into his pocket and brought out the menu for the Dutch Treat Club publishers' luncheon.

There I was, topless on the cover. I blushed that book people had seen me naked. When I signed the model release for this job, I had no inkling where the photographer would sell it, as the release gave him ownership rights to the photo forever. My chagrin didn't influence my decision, already made.

I turned down Ken McCormick's five thousand dollar advance offer. "I can't do it, Ken. I'd be lost in a forest if I did."

Ken let out a sigh of almost annoyance.

"You may very well be right, Ken, about changing the novel," I felt I was pleading. "But I won't really know till I finish it all the way through to the end, once. I—I'm discovering. Doors keep opening and I learn more."

Ken nodded.

"I'm afraid they'd close." I was breathless.

Ken was clearly disappointed. "I understand, I guess."

"Are you angry?" Ken was a friend, an advisor. I didn't want to lose his good opinion.

Ken's long jaw lengthened but he shook off the mood. "No, my dear, I just hope you're not making a mistake."

"Well, can I—may I show it to you when it's done to the end, once?"

"Sure, sure," said Ken.

But as I had questioned his judgment and that of his editors, hadn't I ruined it?

"Good luck," Ken clicked my martini glass. "Chin chin."

"Salud," I replied.

☙☙☙☙

Back home I got so depressed I felt dizzy. What did I know about novels in progress? Who did I think I was? Some great frothing genius? But I was stubborn. I acted on my instinct. In a sense I felt brave and noble: I had rejected money for art. At the time Doubleday was not known as a literary house.

Later I realized I had turned down an opportunity to *learn* through arrogant youthful stupidity. Turned down a bird in hand for an empty bush.

I had succeeded in adding three years to the time it took Jim Brown to sell my first novel. This is no fairy tale life. Did I think all authority was Mama trying to control me? I didn't trust older adults, they'd manipulate me. No fool like a young one. We in those days believed literature equals truth, commercial equals crap. We smartasses. Life changes.

Self-inflicted regrets teach you how much you don't know.

☙☙☙☙

Outside I heard a crowd roar and ran to the window. There, passing along West 55th, was candidate Jack Kennedy in an open convertible.

"Hey, Jack!" I shouted, and JFK grinned up at me and waved. His face was slightly bloated, from medication he took. But his high spirit radiated smack into my heart.

Later journalist Peter Maas phoned for a date. We'd double date with Pierre Salinger, JFK's press secretary, he said. Peter traveled as a reporter on JFK's campaign plane. He'd told me that at night Jack went to bed with whichever stewardess was on the flight.

"No, Peter," I said. "I have to write at night. Except on weekends." That was my rule, as I was a model by day. Also my encounter with Ken made me feel I could only compensate to my psyche by utter monastic devotion to my novel.

Of course, I was tempted. I was constantly being tempted with evening dalliance.

"Ah, come on," said Peter. "You'll like Pierre."

"No, Peter," I was adamant, "I'd love to, but—"

Next day Peter Maas phoned, chortling. "Ohho, did you ever miss it. You really blew it."

"Blew what?"

"Guess where we ended up? With Jack Kennedy at the Charlton!"

I'd blown two in a row.

❧ 21 ❧

NORMAN STABS ADELE
FALL 1960

In his prophetic bad boy essay, "The White Negro," Norman Mailer glamorized violence, romanticized murder, as if there were no victim. The brave perpetrator was daring forbidden territory, forbidden action. Of course. As a megalomaniac, was he unable to accept the *reality* of the other inviolate human?

Meanwhile, Norman and Adele's challenge games escalated dangerously as his fiction career faltered.

Twelve years and two unloved novels, *Barbary Shore* and *The Deer Park*, separated Norman from his spectacular 1948 bestseller, *The Naked and The Dead*. Other boys spurted ahead of Mailer, Jones and Styron, self-declared contenders for Hemingway's crown. Besides Philip Roth and Evan Connell, in 1960 John Updike raced ahead with *Rabbit, Run*, his finest novel, many said. Joe Heller had yet to launch.

An editor friend, Bob Loomis, told me that back then he and Norman and Bill Styron were on their way to bail an old buddy out of jail, who'd stuck a knife in his girlfriend. Norman was fascinated, he said, and wanted every last slashing detail. Then Norman said, excited, I've always wanted to stab a woman. Occasionally I bumped into Norman and Adele at parties. He often looked wasted. Rumor was Norman was losing control, heavily into drugs, supposedly to spur creativity. I *knew* that didn't work for me. Also he liked to punch guys out, more with fury than heft. He'd been arrested in Provincetown over the summer, drunk and disorderly, then again at Birdland in the fall.

❧❧❧❧

Then in November Norman stabbed Adele.

Norman stabbed his wife, who was known forever after as Adele the One He Stabbed. Mr. Macho. They are both lucky that she lived. They were both bombed, stoned, and Norman had been fighting on the street. Mr. Macho, projector of rage.

It happened at the big bash Norman and Adele tossed on November 19th so Norman could announce his candidacy for mayor of New York. After interviewing JFK, enraptured by his aura, Norman decided he, too, was a politico. The Mailers were subletting at 250 West 94th Street that fall. The candidate did not announce.

That night Norman reeled all the way out of control. He was so boozed up and doped up that he wanted to fight everybody. Guests sensibly began to leave, so Norman went out on the street to fight them as they left. When he stumbled back into their apartment, bloody, Adele supposedly spoke sharply to him, as who would not.

Norman grabbed a penknife and stabbed Adele in the upper abdomen and back. One thrust near Adele's heart was three inches deep and almost an inch wide.

An emergency operation performed on Adele next day saved her life. Norman was arrested, put through a psychiatric examination at Bellevue Hospital, and released on probation. The first thing he did was run to Adele's hospital bed and beg her not to charge him. At the December 21st hearing on felonious assault charges, Adele Mailer refused to sign the complaint. They played kissy-kiss for the press.

Nevertheless, Norman was indicted January 30th, 1961, and on March 9th, pled guilty to third degree assault, was put on probation, and given a suspended sentence. Fame helps. Later in March Norman and Adele separated.

Adele told me later she didn't charge Norman because he pled with her, saying if he sat in jail, his career would be ruined, and he wouldn't be able to support her and their two children. If he was a convict, nobody would want his writing. He promised to support her and the children, married or divorced. Adele stonewalled in court, Norman got off, they divorced, and he kept his word.

There were guys, and not a few, who admired him for getting away with it.

꒦꒷꒦꒷

Once, at the public library, I heard Kurt Vonnegut speak about the exploitative media conglomerate publishing game. Do something sensational, he advised, do somebody in, so you're a household name.

Norman stabbed Adele and gained everlasting fame.

His self-justifying 1966 novel about the incident, *An American Dream*, was vicious tabloid cowardice. Mailer demonized the wife so she "deserved" to be killed by the husband. Women were to blame for everything and macho novelists delighted in doing them in (Mailer), impaling them (Pynchon), trashing them (Donleavy), demeaning them (Roth and Bellow), weakening them (Styron), brutalizing them (Robert Stone, Jerzy Koszynski). Spike the ladies: therein lies revelation.

When male novelists made fun of women, women readers were expected to enjoy the joke. Empathize with the victimized great man. I resented it. Later on, brilliant critic John Leonard would call these Boys' Books.

Norman's violence delayed his run for mayor till 1969, when he'd reestablished his reputation. Back there in the nostalgic mid-fifties, their age of innocence, the worst Norman and Adele did, as far as I knew, was fling off their duds at parties.

꒦꒷꒦꒷

Later, in the seventies, when I bumped into Adele at a book party, she was working at Bendel's, daughters grown.

Adele continued painting, began writing skits about her life, and acted them out off-Broadway and at Actors Studio. Finally she wrote *The Last Party: Scenes From My Life With Norman Mailer.* I phoned to tell her I liked it, she had a real feel for those times, and we became friends. The major media closed ranks, she told me, and trashed her book, the victim's tale. Gloria Steinem phoned, she said, to commiserate, and said that they'll always do that. Protect the great man they're invested in. But I'd read an empathetic review in *The Nation.*

Years seemed to vanish when Adele walked into my apartment in 2000. You'd have thought we were bosom buddies. She still has that dark-eyed sparkle.

"You stripped off your clothes at a party," I reminded her, laughing, "and tried to pull *mine* off too."

"Oh God, did I do that? I probably wanted company. I never knew what I was doing when I was drunk." Adele said she'd long since sworn off booze. "That was my dope. We were always playing games. Norman never did want to be anything but a star."

"If he hadn't been, they never would have cossetted him like they did." I asked her about Norris Church, Norman's sixth wife.

"I like Norris. My daughters are very close to Norris. They're her age. But some of the others, phew." Norman at seventy-seven has two knee replacements, uses two canes and "is an old old old man."

Adele looks pretty and fit and proper and much younger than her age. "Norman doesn't give me enough money. I used to supplement with jobs but now I'm too old. He gives me a thousand dollars a month, I get three hundred from Social Security, and pay five hundred a month for my one-bedroom in a tenement."

In February 2000 Adele sued Norman for increased support. Her lawyer called a press conference, the major media showed, and Adele was pictured in front of her tenement in the *Daily News.* Norman was supposed to increase her support whenever he made as much as seventy-five thousand per year, but never did. He offered her two hundred dollars more per month and she and her lawyer scoffed, and eventually worked it out. Norman and the media celebrated his eightieth birthday in 2003. He and his wife, Norris Church, are living in Provincetown now, in 2006.

Adele never remarried. "I had two real chances. They both had money."

"Why didn't you?"

"I was afraid."

❧ 22 ❧

CATCH-22 MAKES JOE HELLER
1961

When he plopped into my circle chair, Joe Heller did not look his usual gregarious comic self. He hunched forward and stared at the floor.

"I read the review," I said. The Sunday *New York Times Book Review* had dismissed *Catch-22*, saying Heller was an inept comedian, imitative and boring, that the book was not a novel but a bunch of anecdotes strung together.

"We thought we had the fix in," Joe's lip curled. "A bad joke."

"I was shocked," I handed Joe a drink. "With all the hoopla—"

"With all the hype—" Joe clicked my glass, shook his head slowly back and forth.

Everybody liked Joe Heller, he was that sort of guy. Like so many funny people, he was overweight, which seems to add hohoho jollity. At five foot ten he was muscular under the weight. Working full-time and writing before and after and weekends, when did he have time to exercise? I exercised but it was uncommon back then. Every day I did ballet technique and calisthenics, based on classes I'd taken. Between college and graduate school, I'd taught a class for the D.C. Recreation Commission. Like many busy men, Joe was fatter in his thirties than his forties when he started running and shaped up.

"With all the hype," Joe let out a monstrous sigh, "I thought— now, don't laugh—I might be able to quit work and write full- time. That I'd make enough—" Joe looked tired.

Suddenly I felt lucky to have only myself to feed. Smiling slyly, I presented his book. "Will you sign mine?"

"You didn't have to buy it," said Joe. "I was going to give you a copy."

"Dick Grossman gave it to me." Dick was an editor at Simon & Schuster, along with Bob Gottlieb, Joe's editor.

"Enough poor mouth," Joe jacked himself up, grinning. "We got an English sale," he said as he wrote in my copy of *Catch-22*. "Maybe they'll like me over there."

We both rose and Joe gave me a bear hug that lifted me off my feet. Then he aimed an open mouth kiss at my lips, which I deflected to my cheek, and gave him a loud hearty cheek smack.

"Best to Shirley," I called as he leapt down the stairs.

I opened the novel and read his simple message. "With best wishes—for both of us, Joe Heller."

❧❧❧

1961 was a banner literary year. Besides Joe Heller's *Catch-22*, J. D. Salinger's *Franny and Zooey* caused shivers of recognition with its fashionably neurotic Glass family, especially among analysands and their shrinks. James Baldwin published *Nobody Knows My Name* and John Steinbeck *The Winter of Our Discontent*. Henry Miller's clandestine *Tropic of Cancer*—for which I'd paid a ten dollar fortune in 1955 in Mexico City—received its first legal U.S. sex romp from Barney Rosset's Grove Press. Barney had heroically agreed to pay legal costs for any distributor who was sued, and they *were* sued.

My occasional date, Huntington Hartford, who was putting out *Show* magazine, bought Hugh Hefner's failing *Show Business Illustrated*, one of Hunt's usual bad financial moves. Several other magazines that Hef started also failed. Only *Playboy* floated.

Papa Hemingway did himself in. At age sixty, Ernesto declared he couldn't write, drink, have sex, do any of the things he liked anymore. Doing what he considered manly, he took a shotgun and killed himself, as his father had done.

The summer of 1960 Hemingway and I had both been in the stands at Malaga for the *mano a mano* between Luis Dominguin and Antonio Ordonez, Spain's most famous matadors. Balletic Dominguin, ladies' man, and athletic Antonio, crudely strong. Papa, who reported on the event for *Life*, sat with Ava Gardner and assorted celebs. I was with Eloy, the Spanish doctor, during my intellectually thrilling, unendurably romantic first trip to Europe, where I stayed three months. We talked marriage. Were we teasing ourselves? Our last night Eloy stood on the high terrace of his hotel calling my name, till I answered from mine, further down the bluff.

കൈകൈ

"Read it as satire," S & S editor Dick Grossman told me when I confessed I wasn't sure, after a hundred pages, that I liked *Catch-22*. "As black humor."

"Of course, satire is *arched*." I felt rather stupid.

Till you read it as satire, you may think this is superficial, that is exaggerated. Which is why satire *must* exaggerate wildly, as I learned writing my second novel, which was nasty, dire, and loopy.

In *Catch-22* Joe Heller wrote the first absurdist novel about World War II. Not patriotic war with necessary horrors but surreal war, maniacal, killing our own. We all fell in love with Yossarian, the bombadier in the plexiglass nose of the B-25, whose war mission was to save his own life.

With good reviews and hot sales in England, Joe's astute editor, Bob Gottlieb, ran ads every Sunday in the *NYT Book Review*. The ads listed famous male writers, topped by Nelson Algren, each praising *Catch-22* to the skies. Each celebrated name stood out in bold letters on the left, with a succinct quote on the right. S & S ran these *Catch-22* ads for, incredibly, a year. U.S. rave reviews sprang up and momentum built.

๑๛๑๛๑

Next time Joe Heller dropped by, he looked like a slick pouch-cheeked Broadway producer with canny eyes and seductive lips, minus the cigar. He looked, in other words, like himself.

"*Catch-22* is taking off!" Joe hollered. "Second printing just hit the stores."

"I'll drink to that." We clicked glasses. Joe grinned so hard it was ironed on.

"Guess what?" Joe bubbled with joy. "I quit work. I'm writing a film script. For good money. I'm hot, hot!"

"Joe, that's fabulous." Hot hilarious male writers, like Joe, deft with dialogue, picked up film scripts right away. Joe got to join the boys' club, which doled out screenplay moolah. Here I was, in medias res, wildly jealous, because I knew I'd never be hot hot. I didn't know war. I wasn't even male. I was that other second sex.

"Did I tell you it was titled *Catch-18* for years? Then *Mila-18* came out, so we changed it to *Catch-22*. Twenty-two sounded odd to me. You think it matters?"

"Twenty-two sounds natural to me," I said. "Eighteen is too associated with age."

"Man, is Shirley relieved," said Joe. "Greenbacks, at last." Joe was too overjoyed to be sardonic. "I'm meeting writers I've always wanted to know. Like Algren."

"Wow, introduce me, bigshot."

Both Joe and I had stories published in Alex Austin's paperback, called *Great Tales of City Dwellers*. Now Joe was one of the big names.

"Whoops, got to go. Spent too much time with a lady friend this afternoon." Joe giggled.

I lifted a brow.

"Not as cuddly as you—?" he made it a question.

I smiled noncommittally.

"Celebrating—life."

Joe lifted me off my feet in another immense bear hug, with the energy surge of success. He grabbed the back of my head and tilted it, tilted his own, and slammed a flooded open mouth kiss right into my gaping surprise. This time I didn't deflect it. I wanted to taste success.

So Joe played around, like so many others. Somehow I thought he had a rockbound marriage. I had a naive habit of thinking guys were my buddies who actually had a lech for me.

"Best to Shirley," I recovered as he whirled down the stairs.

23

PHILIP PULLS A PORTNOY
1961 - 1964

Book parties were the gyms of the day where I worked out with
my peers, distinguished and unknown, hot and cooling. Over
there stood the heat rage, a fiery aura of honors backlighting his
broad shoulders, tall and handsome, young Philip Roth. Roth
led the new generation of young male writers, those who'd not
fought in or written about World War II.

Philip Roth's book, *Goodbye, Columbus*, had won the National
Book Award in 1960, unusual for a first collection of short stories.
But Roth was eagerly championed by influential younger editors
in the book world, their baby boy with his best foot forward.

Ridiculously overrewarded, Philip had won the *Paris Review*
story award in 1958, a Houghton Mifflin literary fellowship and
National Institute of Arts and Letters grant in 1959, and in 1960,
besides the NBA, the Jewish Book Council award, a Guggenheim,
and an O. Henry second prize. Yo, a seven on his first effort. Not
bad for the kid from Newark.

At six two, Philip Roth was almost as handsome as writer

Evan Connell, tall, dark and lean with tennis muscles. Wavy almost kinky black hair closing in on a high narrow forehead. Skateboard shoulders as well, and black unsettling eyes. Evan's eyes were those of an Indian chief, focused on far and inner horizons. Philip's eyes were laser jets searching for suspects. They glided the room riveting that critic, pinning that whispering editor with author. Philip's eyes accused. When they landed on me for about the third time and stayed, those sexy black darts heated me up like acupuncture. Philip Roth looked hot as a pistola.

Though I'd come to the party with Jack Leggett, author of the novel *Wilder Stone* in 1960, and Houghton Mifflin editor, Jack was my married buddy. Philip, however—wait, what was that at his side with her arm looped through his? Could it be a wife? That small female person as short as myself?

Jack Leggett introduced me, as a writer, to Philip and his wife, Maggie, who was a surprise. Maggie was long-trunked and stubby-legged, with those stumpy table legs, a good sport type. She was the reverse of the slim long-legged ideal that Brenda Patimkin played in her tank suit in *Goodbye, Columbus*. Maggie was brown-haired, not pretty but with a pleasant face, and looked as if she might be the daughter of a high school coach.

"How do you do?" she said sharply, checking me out to see what I might pull. Maggie didn't seem so much devoted as quirky, which was an asset. Otherwise, she'd have sunk into the woodwork.

As Maggie was pulled away to talk by other book people, milling about the brownstone living room, I smiled snidely up at Philip.

"Giving out your number?" said Philip in his sardonic nasty tone. "Maybe we could discuss literature."

"Oh, let's do," I replied archly and gave it to him. Dealing with Philip would be *amour pique*. "Everybody knows who Brenda Patimkin really is," I said. "Did that cause you trouble?"

"Outrage, threats," he snorted, "but ultimately nothing legal. Of course, my parents—"

"Of course," I said. "How does it feel to be attacked by conservative Jews?"

"Did I intend to enrage them?" Philip could not sound innocent. "You see, we second generation are supposed to be team cheerleaders, not critics."

"You can't please straights," I said.

"There's only one who really bothers me," he scowled.

"Who?"

"I'm not saying."

I grinned. Like everybody else, I knew it was critic Irving Howe. I'd found Philip's book a tad naive, sort of Joe College: you're all jerks and I'm Mr. Sensitive. But wild and playful, hilarious style with skillful narrative.

A grandiose poobah grabbed Philip. "You must meet—"

Philip cupped his mouth as he spun away. "I'll call," he whispered.

𖠁𖠁𖠁𖠁

Out to dinner, home to bed with Philip Roth.

Sexual friendships taught me politics, race, class, countries, temperaments, occupations, all useful for a writer. But that wasn't my motive. *By invitation, the world passed through my body.* I was feeling the earth. Sex was my great adventure. Climaxing, I'd twirl through sky at the speed of light, visit far planets, invade the sun, and embrace the universe.

Manhattan was a river of men flowing past my door, and when I was thirsty I drank. The current flowed far too fast but the supply seemed endless. By now my lapsed married-man morality depended on the virtual flow of my sexual desire.

"You Jews fought the Yankees as immigrants, and so did we, as Southerners," I ranted as we spun into my *pied-a-terre*. Booze made me soppy sentimental. "Maybe that's why we get along so well."

"Both losers, eh?" teased Philip.

"Well, displaced." I made us drinks.

"Are you gonna regale me with yo black mammy?" Philip snooped around the minuscule perimeter of my studio kingdom. He tilted his head at the round Paul Klee head above my circle chair.

Roth was clearly a makeout artist. It was in his actions, his movement, and was he ever cocksure. Philip expected. Philip got.

But I wanted to talk literature seriously, first.

"I have a bone to pick with you. You act as if Brenda ended

the affair with Neil because he was lower class." I paused to see if he'd listen. "Whereas I think she ended it because she wasn't yet ready for ongoing sex."

"Hot for it, that one," said Philip.

"A college girl living at home," I insisted, "is subject to her mother, in ways a boy isn't. It's called fear. If Mother had known about my illegal abortion, she'd have kicked me out of the house, forever."

"Interesting," nodded Philip, "interesting."

"He acts like a poor victim," I giggled as Philip snuggled up and licked my ear.

"Maybe he *is* a victim. You girls are so devious." I handed him another drink, both of us into confessional. "Maggie tricked me into marriage."

"What?"

"She was my graduate student. She told me I'd gotten her pregnant. She forced me to marry her. Then it turned out, she wasn't."

"Maybe she thought she was, Philip. Maybe she had a very early spontaneous miscarriage. As I have several times."

"No, she confessed." His eyes were frantic blackbirds, seeking escape. "She did it, she said, because she was so in love with me."

"Lord!" I was shocked with admiration. "She knew how to punch your guilt buttons."

"A shiksa, pulling that. She had me, has me, she thinks."

Gentiles, I gathered, were supposed to be straight arrow. This Maggie was a primal force. "Why don't you divorce her, then?"

Philip wriggled monumentally. "I'm trying to, I don't know" He rose and lifted me from my circle chair.

Maybe one reason he stayed married to her was because her gall so astounded him. But poor victim, Philip, was so acutely in need of sexual ministration, I had to help.

"Come here, baby," he snarled as his shoulders and arms and flat athletic body, plunger impaling my belly, surrounded me in full body grope.

Philip Roth was a sex fiend. He moved from tits to—aaaah!— so fast I was breathless. Speeded up like his talk and his head. But once he got there, he hung in long and steamy. Tepid men never move me. Philip was on fire.

✧✧✧✧

Sex with a married man is a one-night-stand. Adventure, without expectation. Still, I wondered when he didn't call again. Then I heard Philip and wife Maggie had left for Iowa, where he was visiting lecturer at the famous Writers Workshop. Philip always won all the prizes, the fellowship awards, the writer-in-residence plums. Them that has, gits.

Later I heard the real Brenda was very much in love with the real Neil, they were engaged, and *he* dumped *her*. Maybe Philip deserved his comeuppance from Maggie.

✧✧✧✧

It was in 1964 that Philip Roth reentered my life in a prophetic manner and pulled a Portnoy on me. By then I was living on West 69th in an actual one-bedroom apartment.

I'd bumped into him on Columbus, as he was living on West 68th, a block away. Philip, dark and lethal and possibly more mature. Now I had a finished novel to regale him with.

Philip said, "Maybe we could make it a threesome."

"What?"

"My wife finds you as intriguing as I do."

"I thought you were divorced."

"Separated. But we're good friends. How 'bout the three of us getting together?"

I figured he was merely being provocative. "I only do threesomes with two men. So I get all the attention." The sexual revolution was heating up. But I had not yet partaken of quantity arrangements, nor investigated multiples. Nor swung.

Philip chuckled urbanely. "You'd get plenty of attention."

I was silent, angry. I could just see the two of them cutting me up.

"Just joshing," said Philip when I didn't respond.

I remained mute.

"Hey now, I want to see you. Didn't mean to—"

We made a date.

∾∾∾∾

Wrothfully, Philip pounded on my door. "Miss Alice Denham, are you there?" Mother had sent Southern lady calling cards and I'd put one in my mailbox below. "Miss Alice?"

"Come in, come in." Hope, the thing with feathers that perches in the soul, as Miss Emily Dickinson wrote, sat on my hand and sang once more.

Broad shoulders, unsettling eyes, and black gobs of hair wavered at me as Philip entered cuddling booze and mix. There were so many things only another writer understood. I wanted that intimacy and knowledge with somebody close to my age. I wanted to talk about my novel, the lit biz, ask if his editor might be interested.

We circled each other mumbling pleasantries, while I grinned like a giddy child and tried not to notice the chip on his shoulder that now seemed as long as his arm. Superboy writer wasn't quite so golden new, so laden with expectation.

"Nice pad, you've upgraded."

"Indeed." I mixed drinks with his booze, handed him his and sat beside him on my new sofa. "Salud," I clicked his glass.

Philip clicked mine with a sly snarling leer, took a lusty swig, put the glass down, reached for my legs and tried to force them apart.

"Stop!" I scooted away and sat at my cafe table.

Philip fell forward off the sofa onto his hands and knees and crawled toward me. Upon arrival, he tried to pry my legs apart.

"Come on, baby. You won't have to do a thing."

"Why don't you *talk* to me?" I kicked his hands away. "I'd like to get to know you."

"Come on, come on. Don't you know sex is communication?" Philip sat on his haunches, impatient.

"But I don't *know* you." I elbowed him off.

"Sure you know me. You slept with me once."

"But that was ages ago. You never came back so I *didn't* get to know you."

Conversing with Philip was like jumping a barricade that made winsome friendliness more suspect than blithe nastiness.

Evidently he loved to squat down there at crotch level, facing my crossed and locked knees.

"Ahha, vengeance is sweet! Baby won't admit I hurt her feelings." Roth smiled with handsome superiority.

"Listen, I favor revenge. Of course, you hurt my feelings. But you're daft to presume *this* approach will work." He sure knew how to turn a girl off.

"Ohho, she *is* vengeful." Roth stood to refill his drink and tried to jam his hand down my blouse.

"Cut the shit, you clown!" I bellowed.

"Oooh hoo." He scooted away petulantly.

"Don't you ever talk to other writers about their work?" I asked, disappointed. I stood and maneuvered back to the sofa. "I wanted to tell you about my novel."

"Only the young and naive do that. I don't rap about it, I do it."

I kept reaching for some soul in him. "There are so few people—"

"Talk to your agent. He's your crying towel."

"That's not what I meant."

As he passed me, Roth tried to tweak my mound by ramming his paw into my lap. I kicked at him with my leg and sent him flying off balance. He bounced himself off the bookcase with an ape grin, eager to scuffle.

"I've had enough!" I leaped up and went to the door and opened it wide. "Get out of here."

"But, baby," Philip droned in seductive complaint, "what's better than sex?"

"*Real* sex, but that involves emotion." I stood my ground in the hall. "Get out!" I said loud enough for other tenants to hear.

"I'll take my bottles," Roth said churlishly, and swept out past me.

"Oh, *do* take your bottles." So much for enlightening conversation with the prestigious young American writer.

I fell on the bed, weeping with disappointment.

ॐॐॐॐ

Philip felt threatened by women, his friend, sociologist Ned Polsky told me later, and felt *he* had to move before *she* did.

"Philip always felt he had to get the woman before she got him," Ned said, "like Maggie did. He's paranoid but very productive. The writing is the only thing that keeps him sane. He never recovered from the possessive mother."

"We all have that problem," I said.

"Philip feels clutched, hemmed in by women."

"Maggie sure put the hex on him," I laughed. Then wondered if my long-ago mate, Carlos, following on my possessive mother, had done the same to me.

In 1968 I was shocked to hear that the ubiquitous Maggie was killed in an auto accident, crossing Central Park. Was Philip relieved that her fierce clutch on him was over?

In 1969 with his third novel, *Portnoy's Complaint*, Roth joined the Grown Baby Boy school of male writers who never flipped a phrase without claiming to be victims, all victimized by women who don't seem to know they're inferior. Barely burgeoning equality was tough on macho princes.

But *Portnoy's Complaint* was so hysterically funny I howled all through it. Philip to a T—doing *exactly* what he did to me, the morbid whacko sex fiend and nonstop dick diddler with his obscene mouth. How many guys I knew like that, all focused on their whangs and blaming Mom. Mom was either a smothering blanket or a vacancy sign, at fault for everything, high priest Freud decreed.

Never had there been such a whacko funny Jewish mother as Sophie Portnoy, who became the archetype. Philip turned guilt into high-rolling angst-ridden comedy.

You practiced on me, Philip.

❧ 24 ❧

WHERE WERE YOU NOVEMBER 22, 1963?
SPRING - FALL 1963

I know where I was. I was having lunch with Harcourt Brace editor Dan Wickenden. We dined at a French restaurant of muted elegance, waiters darting on soundless balletic feet, when the news broke into it like a crashing wave.

"God knows *why* he wants to lunch with you," my slangy snob agent, James Oliver Brown, had drawled when he phoned a few days ago, "since he doesn't seem all that taken with your novel. But your lethal charm may sway him our way."

Six months ago, spring 1963, I'd tremulously presented my completed novel, *My Darling from the Lions*, to Jim Brown. Every time the phone rang I jangled like an alarm.

"This is the first time," Jim had said solemnly, "that I put my faith in someone on the basis of one hundred pages and got a truly fine novel out of it. It's first-rate, I love it."

"I'm swooning with joy. It's not too wild?"

"Too wild for Georgia. Just about right for New York."

In those tweedy gent literary days, novels were submitted

to publishers one at a time. No publishing house would touch anything but The Original. If an editor suspected another house was also reading, he'd whip the manuscript back to the agent in high dudgeon. We had no copy machines, we had carbons. Remember struggling to make four-five decent carbons? Remember retyping your three-hundred-page manuscript for the fifth time?

On my back terrace I searched the other terraces for a face, suddenly desolate and lonely. No one outside. My new apartment with its separate bedroom was on the fourth floor back of a brownstone on West 69th renovated by Danish Mr. Larka. I bought a carved Mexican desk and a carved inlaid octagonal table from Spanish Morocco. My parents were paying half the hundred fifty monthly rent on my gorgeous new place that I hated.

I missed West 55th. I missed *seeing people* out my street windows, missed the drugstore gang and little Kevin and Max's Luncheonette. Missed my novel as I mooned over the formal photo of my Mexican lover, Lalo, *el arquitecto*, who wanted me to return to San Miguel and live with him in his hilltop A-frame. *Por mi vida de tu amor*, Lalo, he'd scrawled.

Now I was writing in the daytime, working my way into that most treacherous fiction, the second novel. As soon as I moved I seemed to get fewer model jobs. As soon as I finished my novel, my youth was over. Was my age stamped on my forehead? I was officially twenty-five, read thirty-one.

Jim Brown invited me for cocktails at his place to discuss strategy. His delicate round tables were covered with cloth skirts and manuscripts. Jim said we'd try Knopf first, though he figured they'd go into shock, then Viking, then Farrar, Straus, and on. What about Ken McCormick? I asked. Jim decided to avoid Ken, for now, in case he resented my 1960 refusal. Jack Leggett, meanwhile, had moved on, and Joe Fox, I said, seemed to despise me.

❦❦❦❦

That summer *mi amor*, Lalo, met me at Mexico City airport in his silver Porsche Abarth racer. Lalo who had everything, flamboyant rakish Spanish Lalo, playboy architect, Formula One racer, who fought the bulls as a top *aficionado*. Last summer

Lalo had dedicated a bull to me, whirled and arched to the kill like pirouetting Dominguin. At the airport we embraced self-consciously, smiling too hard.

"You wear your hair like everybody else," he said in shock.

He looks crude, I thought at the same instant.

We both determined to overcome the moment.

"*Felicidades* on you book," said Lalo.

"*Finito*, at last. My agent is trying to sell it." Exhuberantly I explained the process.

"You live independent like the man. I admire that." Lalo's affectionate eyes were now, finally, suffused with feeling, no longer withheld. "You are free spirit."

By the time we bumped over the steep cobblestone descent into San Miguel, we were together and easy again. We drove to Lalo's A-frame on Atascadero hill, where he was building showplaces for rich Americans. We watched sunset over the sierras of Guanajuato, the two of us above rosy spires and town domes below.

⁊⁊⁊⁊

Inside it was dark. In the slow silence of evening Lalo removed my clothes with reverence and we embraced, two pale figures in a glass house standing on dark tile.

"I never luf a wooman so moch, Alicia. I never think of wooman for six month."

Lalo kissed my eyes and lips, my nape and breasts. Then he threw himself at my feet and fawned over my ankles and knees, groveling and staring up at me. He kissed my knees and thighs in a wet circular wreath. Then he held onto my legs and climbed me like I was a beautiful flesh tree whose source he adored, and stuffed his face between my legs, and looked up at me like he worshipped me. I stood on the dark tile and wept. There were tears on his face. Lalo carried me to the bed and we feasted as gods, on one another, his penis connecting us, swirling orgasm incense around like a magic wand.

My man, I'd found. We were so easily close, like one force facing the world that summer. We talked about anything, we agreed about everything.

If I married Lalo I could do it all—have a child and

write—because every middle-class Mexican family has a maid, a gardener, and a nanny. In Mexico they say, *"Tienes criada o eres criada* (You have a maid or you are a maid)." In the United States, if a man supported me, I'd have to be wife, maid, and nanny. Back then no American man would take on a woman novelist who wasn't *first* a mother. The Mexican class system could free me to do it all. Yes, and I'd be trapped in the family net, the cloak that walls off the outside world. But, also, protected. For the first time in my fearless stressful life. I could write *more.* I could have my own family, at last. A dream I never expected could come true.

I assumed we'd marry eventually till my Mexican buddy, Rafa, said, "Lalo will never marry you because you're not rich upper-class Mexican."

I scoffed, "We're the same soul."

"Lalo, when should we marry?" I asked, besotted, in September.

"Marry? I never think you want marry. You has you career, you books."

"What's that have to do with it?"

"You Norteamericanas, you can marry two, three time. We Mexicans once for all the life."

"Lalo, you said you loved me because I'm so liberal, so free."

"Yes, but liberal is not for marry. What you know of the home? Nahsing." Lalo wrapped his arms around me. "Pero, Alicia, I luf you. But mi padre, he think all gringas is putas. I have two sisters *monjas*—nuns."

A shock like death went through me. I'd been gored, in the back. Take the flamenco and leave out the Catholicism. It was dangerous fun to understand Spanish imperfectly. Why had it taken me so long to realize I was merely his second-class mistress hidden away in the hills? From the *corrida*, I still have a *banderilla* he placed, dried blood turned brown.

The only two lovers I wanted to marry were Spanish, Eloy the doctor in Spain and Lalo in Mexico. Years before I knew I had a Spanish grandmother. So far, I'd never made it over two years with a man.

When I landed at Idlewild, not yet JFK, I felt precious relief to have escaped my wild urge to escape forever my destiny. Those Sacred Entities, as Emily Dickinson called Words. New York where *I think*, as Doris Lessing said about London versus vacation.

I phoned my dear agent, Jim Brown.

"Knopf says too much sex, " said Jim, "she's too sexual to be a believable wife."

"But I'm talking about the relationship, not the body parts."

"I know. Farrar, Straus says nix, not their kind of novel. Now it's at Harcourt Brace. We'll see."

"Do you still like the book?" I asked, dejected.

"Alice, this agency was built on rejections," Jim chuckled. "Don't fret."

❦❦❦❦

Now, over martinis, I was listening to HB editor, Dan Wickenden, tell me what was wrong with *My Darling from the Lions*.

"Why is your heroine so aggressive?" asked Dan, a nice-looking even-tempered middle-aged big shot editor. "She's not sympathetic. She's wild."

"What do you mean?" I was alarmed.

"Grace is always trying to control things."

"Well, she wants to control her situation with him, to keep him from walking all over her."

"Is that why you say women are like niggers?"

"We don't get enough respect." This is 1963, remember.

"Of course you do," Dan laughed heartily, "when you're feminine, a proper wife. But your Grace suffers, no offense, penis-envy."

My poulet and his filet arrived and we dived in, ordering more drinks. What gave *him*—and Lalo and my ex—the right to define wife and women and *me*? I kept calm.

❦❦❦❦

Then the rumble started in another section of the French restaurant, voices got loud, what on earth? Voices rose to a tumult. The waiter bustled to our table and whispered to us.

215

"President Kennedy has been shot, in Dallas. They say he's dead."

Somewhere somebody screamed.

"Jack was too busy being a movie star," I began trembling.

Dan stared at me with distaste.

"He was *warned* about Dallas, the virulent right wing." But he had to show himself. "He—he can't be *dead*."

We parted outside the restaurant, stunned.

People drifted around the midtown streets in shock. Those jaunty striders, the ones with big grins, obviously didn't know yet. We others looked at each other as if he'd fallen in the street at our feet. The city was quiet as a tomb.

Back home, like the rest of America, I was glued to the TV. A Texas classroom, where JFK had been demonized, cheered the news. With that, I started crying, lurched with tears. I saw, we all saw, Jack Ruby gun down Lee Harvey Oswald in the Dallas police station. As soon as I saw it, I figured they were getting rid of the designated hit man.

My parents phoned.

Mother was weeping, Dad choked up.

"This is the end of morality in America," said Daddy.

❧ 25 ❧

MY DINNER WITH NELSON
FALL 1963

Both Nelson Algren and I were dejected, he because his literary career was winding down and I because mine resisted starting. How was it possible for Nelson only thirteen years after *The Man with the Golden Arm*, which won the first National Book Award in 1950? The downfall of card dealer Frankie Machine, morphine addict, was the first serious treatment of drug addiction in American literature. Quality aside, publishing simmered with fads and power struggles.

After an awful weekend home in Washington, my answering service gave me this inspiring message: "Joseph Heller, Warren Beatty, and Nelson Algren called." Excited, I phoned Joe, "Who's still here?" "Nelson," said Joe. "*Do* have him call!"

The blue letterhead of James Brown Agency always gave me chills. Jim forwarded another rejection letter in which an intellectual editor scolded: "Doesn't she know the wife is second to the husband?" No, she doesn't, I thought. Now my novel, *My Darling from the Lions* was on to another publisher.

Suddenly I remembered when the UNC English Department helped me get a graduate scholarship at University of Rochester. "Why not here at Chapel Hill?" I'd asked my favorite professor, Harry Russell. "Because this college discriminates against women," he'd replied. I'd never had a woman professor. They taught freshman comp, looked down in the mouth. Publishing was the same.

࿇࿇࿇

Last weekend I had faced Mother again. Always on the train to Washington, my stomach ached with anxiety at facing Mother again.

"Why do you make us *suffer* so?" Mother's expressive face was so furious it looked as if she'd created a new realm of existence. "We're paying half your rent because you refuse to *work* like a normal person. You're too old for that nasty nude modeling," she had ranted all weekend. "Nobody will buy that book. It's a pipe dream. It should be a hobby, not a—a—"

"A devotion," I said.

"You must be *insane*," she screamed. "Selfish. Thoughtless. Think of *us*, sacrificing for you." Mama's way of worrying about me was to attack me with her fears.

"I didn't *ask* you for half the rent." She tried to make me cry, break down. "I can take care of myself."

"Baby, we're glad to help," Dad hugged me. "Now we've sold the house, we have money to spare."

The split personality of home was an endless ordeal. Wisely, my sister and her family lived in Florida.

In 1963 my story, "The Deal," was published twice, in a new edition of *Great Tales of City Dwellers* and in Mag Man's magazine, *Man's World*, edited by old buddy Bruce Jay Friedman.

No rental studios, no amateurs had called. I phoned my model agency. Nothing. I'd long been weary of modeling. Now, as Mother said, it was weary of me. I phoned Jim Brown and said I needed freelance editorial work. He said he'd check around but they usually wanted someone with experience.

Now that I was getting older, being poor was becoming less artistic, less devotional.

Because Nelson Algren was famous, I expected him to look younger. In his mid-fifties, Nelson stood at my door winded, as everybody did now that I lived on the fourth floor. Nelson was tall and thin and gray. He dressed proletarian chic, gray-green aged tweed, gray-green checked shirt and brown-green knit tie, loose.

I offered him a drink and he sat quietly on the sofa till I brought it in, gazing at the books and my carved desk.

"Salud," I said and we clicked glasses.

"Nice place," he said noncommittally.

"You look like a leftist professor disguised as a racetrack tout," I said, to break the ice.

He hooted, "Not bad."

Nelson had a long Swedish face, though sallow and etched with disenchantment. His large brown eyes, once smouldering, had seen too much. He wasn't sardonic, or anything with a clever social twist. He talked tough and bitter and well.

Of all the writers I'd known, of whatever class, only Nelson had personally suffered the thirties Depression. Only Nelson rode the rails. He didn't identify with his Swedish or his Jewish parentage. His people were the bums, whores, derelicts, pimps, drifters, junkies, gamblers, and rummies at the bottom of society, portrayed so tenderly in *The Man with the Golden Arm*. To the poet of the Chicago slums, these were the real people and those of us above were phonies who lived off their sweat and degradation.

By 1963 Nelson's social protest novels had been pushed aside by affluence. The novel of the moment was Mary McCarthy's *The Group*, about her Vassar classmates. Everybody agreed it was a lousy book and talked about nothing else.

"*Your* name helped launch Joe Heller," I said. "At the top of the ad that ran for a year in the *Book Review*." How I loved to sip booze and talk lit.

"Fine book, my good buddy." Nelson spread his long arms along the sofa top. "I'll never write another novel," he said dolefully.

"Why?"

"Here I slave over a novel and the publisher tosses out five thousand copies to drown. You think they'll place ads for me? Nah, they *use* me. A shill for the younger guys."

Publishing was a New Faces game just like modeling. I sprang up and made us another drink.

Nelson pulled a book out from his jacket. "For you," he smiled wearily.

"*Who Lost an American?* by Nelson Algren," I read. "You're getting published."

"Ah, it's nothing—sort of touring the world's cities. Won't make money. I never make any money off books."

"What about movies? *The Man with the Golden Arm*, with Sinatra?"

"Maybe six grand. Sold it to this guy and he resold it to Otto Preminger. You think he'd pay me more? Oh, no. Paid Sinatra a hundred thousand, made a million. Cheap motherfucker wouldn't even let me do the screenplay." Nelson glared at me for vindication.

"That's not fair." Obviously still a sore spot after all these years. "How can anyone not honor the creator?" I asked innocently.

"Ahhaha, you're a comedian." Snuffling a laugh, Nelson squeezed my shoulders.

Algren had night skin. He was the color of the dusk in my living room. Before we disappeared I turned on my leaded glass lamp across the way. Now he reminded me of the Card Game painting of Van Gogh, the lean figure on the left. I suggested the Fleur de Lis but Nelson wanted to go to a Third Avenue bar.

"It probably won't have anything but hamburgers," I objected.

"S'okay," said Nelson. "I have to see a guy there."

მ≈ტ≈ტ≈ტ

We were the only customers at the Irish bar, as traffic roared past the plate glass. Once Third Avenue was lined with Irish bars in small brownstones, the huge dark shadow of the El making for seamy night-crawling. Manhattan bars were all green then, as Irish bartenders were masters at bar atmosphere. Once the El came down, the bars looked too plain and bright.

Nelson and the bartender leaned together talking track and

gamblers and nags. Finally the bartender hung on the phone, and Nelson remembered me.

"I read about you and Simone de Beauvoir in *The Mandarins*," I said. "Her marvelous book."

"That old bag, she was crazy about me," Nelson smirked.

I grinned.

"Didn't care a thing about her, old Frenchy. Wild about me in the sack."

"You're lying," I laughed, remembering Simone's fine line that no one can have really great sex who isn't willing to get a little dirty.

"Wanted to move right in on me in Chicago, but I wouldn't let her. Writer needs, you know, solitude, not some broad—" He wafted me a sneaky eye.

"Oh, I know what you mean." We went through this elaborate charade of being monastically dedicated writers, who could not possibly live with another. "Must have been dreadful for you, Nelson, to have her hanging on for dear life."

Nelson stared at me as if I'd flipped out. "Lying, did you say?"

"Come off it, Nelson. You cared a great deal about Simone. You were in love with her, weren't you?"

Nelson grinned sheepishly, lowered his head, glad that I'd caught him. "Simone is probably the most important person to me. I loved her, yes. But our paths split." He gazed mistily into the bar mirror. "Yes, Simone. I owe her a letter right now."

She was clearly his big subject. He liked to worry it. "What was she like?" Imagine, in the sack with Simone.

"Simone loves to let go and live. But an amazing insight into human injustice, toward women especially. She understands—"

"*The Second Sex* changed my life," I spewed out. "Simone taught me about discrimination—that's it's not *me*, not my fault, it's male dominance, male bonding. Even personal life is political, like it or not."

Now we were talking seriously. "I was always proud of Simone," Nelson said gently. "To this day I consider her my closest ally."

"Simone is a hero to me," I blushed. "She showed me what I was writing about. She gave my problems universality. Here's my favorite: 'Art is an attempt to found the world anew on a human liberty: that of the individual creator.'"

Who was more French than Simone, mired in her culture and language, as she was in Sartre? Who was more proletarian American, more lyrically brute Chicago, than Nelson? Land and language are often a writer's greatest love. I was grateful now that Lalo had pushed me away, reverting to patriarchal Mexican form.

"Simone is the only person whose literary opinion I value. If she says it's good, screw the critics."

Now Nelson looked to me like a Swedish seafarer, a crusader for noble lost leftist causes, like I imagined the mysterious B. Traven looked. Customers arrived and dined in booths. But we stayed perched at the bar, ate cheeseburgers, slaw, and chocolate pie. A fast food feast we topped with Irish coffee.

Back in my fine place, we sipped Kahlua, both tired. I was tired because Nelson was too old for me, Nelson because of his hectic pace doing lit biz, he said.

"Would you like to sleep on the sofa?" I asked. "It pulls out into a bed."

Though I felt guilty for not wanting him, he didn't seem to mind too much. We kissed goodnight and I went into my bedroom and closed the door. When I woke up next morning, he was gone.

The next year Nelson broke with Simone forever when she wrote in her autobiography that he was a contingent love, an interlude in her lifelong pact with Sartre. How that must have hurt Nelson. In 1965 Nelson married an actress in her thirties but it lasted only two years.

❧ 26 ❦

SELF-LOATHING
WINTER 1964

"Welcome to the neighborhood," Joe Heller phoned. "What happened with Nelson?"

"That's ancient history, last fall," I said.

"I've been in Hollywood," said Joe with the raucous delirium many writers show for that slush fund they disdain.

"Hotsy you," I got snide, as I was low, crawling along on my belly in the dumps, in the damp dungeon of my nightmares.

"Invite me for a drink and give me the lowdown." Joe's raspy Brooklyn accent and earthy manner hadn't changed with the wild ongoing acclaim for *Catch-22*.

❧❦❧❦

I wandered my polite apartment, searching for a face. Outside on the terrace I searched the back terraces and windows. No one, midafternoon silence. Back to my carved altar desk, puttering with my second novel. My first novel had now bounced over to Grove Press, against Jim Brown's advice. But I was enthralled with *avant* Grove.

"They hold books forever," said Jim. "They're not noted for hot advances."

"Jim, did anyone want freelance editing, or part-time, or whatever?"

"I tried," sighed Jim, "but it's hard once an editor has rejected a book. And I don't want to prejudice those we'll go to in future. They'll think you're desperate."

"But I am," I said so low it was in Braille. After eleven years modeling, I got few shoots now I was a hoary thirty-two. So few I switched my writing to daytime. My money was running low.

"Hold on, hang in," said Jim. "Once we get a sale, they'll all want you, the clones."

I'd just quit a bondage movie, without pay. Nobody had told me that it was a bondage movie. The sleazy producer refused to reveal the storyline. But it involved a funicular that ran up a New Jersey hill. Then in my jeans without a top, I was to lie on the slant hill, hands manacled, and writhe bewitchingly for the camera, legs spread, hips heaving. Camera shooting up at me from below. I quit.

Was this my second dark night of the soul? Daily I wandered the hot coal shores of Dante's hell, each burning foot leaping. My apartment was its own bondage movie. It had no life. *I* had no life. I was suspended over my novel.

๛๛๛๛

In 1964 Hemingway's posthumous *A Moveable Feast*, about Paris in the twenties, was the most appealing memoir of literary youth I'd ever read. It made me ache to be there, and them, and then. Saul Bellow's *Herzog* brilliantly captured the neurotic self-centered Jewish intellectual we all know and are intimidated by. Gore Vidal, my lunch date, published *Julian*, his best, I thought, about the Apostate.

Gaps appeared in the shroud of conformity that flapped over America. Just small rips, but there. First Henry Miller, maestro of lust, and now Terry Southern and Mason Hoffenberg's *Candy*, with its lurid candy-cake sex. The Beatles roared in, cheered by a

World Series of kids. Suddenly men had longer hair than they'd worn since the Civil War.

Always running was heavyweight champ Muhammad Ali's mighty motor mouth. I loved Ali, just as I had Joe Louis, the Brown Bomber. When I was a kid, I hung on the radio cheering for Joe to win every championship fight. I was the only person in the family who listened. My dear photographer friend, Leon Gast, would make the Oscar-winning documentary, *When We Were Kings*, about Mohammad Ali's championship bout in the Congo.

The Twist, at the Peppermint Lounge, was introduced by Chubby Checker. Black and white, we twisted together on the dance floor. It was the sixties. Suddenly everybody was like me. Beyond conformity, liberated. I never thought it could happen. Then, naively, that it would end.

࿔࿔࿔

Joe Heller almost bolted up the stairs, like the young literary lion he was. His big arms captured and bound me in the litany of literary success.

"Welcome to the Uppa West Side," chortled Joe, looking as juicy as a chocolate cherry, with his brown-sparkle eyes and rosy pouch-cheeks, his wavy slick black hair, and, still, his girth. A towel of fat swathed his chin from ear to ear.

"Hey, leggo," I yelled, Joe released me, and sauntered about till I handed him a drink.

"Hey, classy joint," said Joe. "Very uptown. You getting rich modeling?"

"Hohoho," said I. "Family wealth."

"What's with your novel?"

"Making the rounds," I said. "A regular whirling dervish."

"*Catch-22*, babe, I hit the jackpot!" roared Joe. "Paperback is so hot they're using it for *college courses*, your old degenerate Joe. Plus the *movie*, oh yes, a big flick is in the works. I'm so filthy rich I lugged you a bottle of hootch." Joe presented me with Glenfiddich, the only Scotch I can stomach.

"Thanks, rich kid," I grinned at last, envying the sheer energy success gave Joe. "How's the family?"

"Fine, fine, eating regular."

"Salud," I said, and clanked glasses wanly.

"Lemme tell ya about the moooovie!" Joe strode back and forth waving his arms like a director. "It's *great, hysterical!* It's going to be Oscar wrap-up." His voice dropped, "It'll be a miracle if they ever stop diddling and *do* it."

"Oh, what's the problem?" Sometimes I felt I'd spent my entire adult life congratulating successful men by inserting deft questions into their monologues.

"Too many cooks. Too many honchos who want their own way." Joe scowled, bit his nails.

"But you got your money up front?" I know my cues.

"Sure, sure," he grinned, squeezed my knee. "My charmed life is paved with green. Delay money every six months on top of sale price."

I hated Joe because he won it all and I couldn't even get off the ground. A mere trivial woman, what did I expect? Whereas in Russia the first female astronaut, Valentina Tereshkova, had spent three days in space. A woman! But not here, in our male-bonded democracy.

"Joe, do you think your editor might look at my novel?"

Joe scratched his head. "I'm not so sure S & S is into female books."

"Books by women aren't necessarily *female* books. Men will like this book. Will you ask him?"

"Sure, sure. Fill me in about Nelson, kid." Joe motioned with his glass and I made us fresh drinks. "What happened?"

"Not much. Interesting fellow."

"Come on, come on," nudged Joe.

"Nelson seems to feel screwed by the literary world."

"Nelson's done all right." Joe laughed, "Hell, he gambles it away. No family, and he'd just as soon live in a dump."

"The truth is, Nelson's too old for me," I confided, which made me like Joe better.

"But I'm a young stud, baby," Joe strong-armed my head toward him. "How come we never made out?"

"You're hitched." The last thing a woman ever tells a buddy is that he does not appeal to her sexually. Instead you say, "We've been pals so long it seems sacreligious."

Joe opened his mouth so wide to kiss me I thought a ship would sail out, and it did—his tongue. Joe's face was too jowly for a high cheekbone freak like me. I pushed off, sailed away, rose, and adjusted my violet burlap curtains. Joe rose too, spun me around, and pinioned me with a massive clinch and we kissed like movie-star lovers, except I faked it, as I thought he deserved one good smack for fame.

※※※※

"This is Venus from Venus Rental Studio," said a female voice. "Mr. whatsis, oh, yes, Marv Golden, wants to book you for two hours tomorrow."

"Venus?"

"So what's in a name?" snuffled Venus in winged Bronx.

"Two hours for forty," I said.

"I'll sit in the foyer," said Venus.

Venus wore a huge black wig spilling redundant curls, a zaftig shape, and jaundiced eye.

"Mommy, come get me," a little girl piped.

"My daughter, Katie," said Venus.

Katie played on the studio floor. Venus helped her up. Five-year-old Katie had huge alert blue eyes, curly black hair, one leg, and no arms. From her shoulders came two flippers which she used like wings and pointers. Katie had been born that way due to the pregnancy drug, thalidomide. A week later Venus's husband had disappeared.

"How do you do?" said Katie, looking me over carefully. "I think she's pretty, Mother."

"Thanks, Katie."

"I'm going to be a hairdresser," Katie announced. "Can I do your hair?"

"You don't know what you let yourself in for," chuckled Venus, perching Katie in a chair.

"Now, sit here on the floor," said Katie.

I grabbed a prop pillow and sat in front of her.

Venus handed the comb to Katie who grasped it between the toes of her one foot.

Katie combed my long hair gently and expertly, with loving care, humming to herself. It was soothing. My eyes watered. "You're pretty good, Katydid," I tried to be jaunty.

Marv Golden, loaded down with camera equipment, entered and tried to show no shock.

"Oh, hello, Marv," I recognized him from a camera club I'd posed for. We both looked subdued. "I'll just go change," I said. "So long, Katie."

I hoped the presence of Katie would protect Venus in this risky business, just as Venus protected Katie.

"I'm taking Katie upstairs," said Venus. "I'll be back."

"It's not all fun and games," I said, "is it, Marv?"

"Not by a long shot," said Marv.

We smiled like real people.

Before we got uncomfortable, I swung into my cowgirl pose, in my red bandana bikini, tossed my Stetson aloft, and stomped my high-heel cowboy boots. "Yahoo, let the shutters rip," I drawled, with a grin as wide as the West.

After that, when I posed at Venus's, I held art class for Katie and the other kids on the block, a lonely little UN When the weather was good on Saturday, I took them to the park. Katie lorded it over the bunch, and they let her. The rest of her life could hardly be as gentle as her childhood.

Now that I was over thirty, commercial photographers seldom hired me. Only the rental studios and the amateurs still wanted me. Though I was now more skillful, I was becoming an amateur again.

※※※

My life was being rejected. I ached with constant pain at being rejected in my fictional essence, my precious book. A year had passed with no takers. Vindication, proof of existence that I was actually alive on this earth, my pilgrimage on willingly bloody knees to the altar of publication. Failing at my life's work, I wallowed in self-hatred. I loathed myself.

Grimly alone, I banged my head against the wall, hard, again and again. It almost felt good. I scraped the wall with my fingernails. Then I scratched down both arms with my nails till I drew blood. It didn't stop the pain.

A flying leap off the terrace might do it. But it was only four stories. It could leave me brain-damaged. In the kitchen I examined the knives, the steak knife and the long thin carving knife. Did I know a doctor or a doper who knew how many pills? The *banderilla* from the *corrida* when Lalo had dedicated the bull to me? I tested the point on my palm. I soaked the dried blood with my own.

ॐॐॐ

Next day in the mail, a note from John Wilcock, Village party impresario, now a reporter on the *East Village Other*. John sent me the open party list for the next two weeks. I was so grateful I phoned and blubbered at him.

The Village still accepted me. Spiffed up in slithery top and jeans, my body beat with the old energy surge of adventure. I flew down to revisit my turf, my beach, my oasis, the Village.

I met a muscular wiry actor, rawboned and short as Jimmy Dean. He was a rising young star in the new downtown hit. He got me a free ticket and we began dating.

He wanted me to live with him which I refused. One night he came by after the show, a bit looped, and we made love.

"*Why* won't you live with me?"

"I don't want to live with anyone," I ducked.

"But don't you love me?" he slurred.

"Well, now, I—" He was drunker than I'd realized.

He pulled out and tried to force his way into the back. It ached like a blow, like brass knuckles to the soft part of the arm. My body leapt away. "I can't take more than a finger there."

"Oh, yes you can." He held me down with his body weight and nudged at the tightly closed opening.

"Stop! I can't. Please." I shifted my hips away. I had only my arms free.

He pinned my arms. Straddling me, as he was, he slapped me across the face. He slammed my head back and forth, pummeling hard now. Then again he dented the area, it felt like a hot poker, and my hips leaped away.

"You're just another of these cunts that's ruined my life," he snarled and began slamming my breasts back and forth. I freed my arms, covered my breasts, and screamed bloody murder.

Abruptly he tightened his thighs like a vise and stopped to gulp another swig of his drink. Wet with sweaty fear, struggling, I squirmed out from under his weight.

Weeping and yelling, "Help, help, somebody!" I ran out of

my apartment naked to the front apartment and got the husband to help me get him out. His wife handed me a robe.

The rising young star beat me up.

꒰꒰ᜒ꒱ᜒ꒱

Two overweight cops huffed up the stairs. "You can charge him with assault, lady. But you were having sex, right?"

I nodded, arms crossed, in my own robe now.

"No judge will listen to this," said cop #2.

"You weren't gang-raped and slashed and left for dead," said #1 gently. "That gets the judge's attention."

"I want it on his record." They took down the information.

"If he tries anything else, it'll be there." #2 patted my back. "Get some sleep, now."

Next day my face was mottled, swollen, and punctured with red berry marks. It was two weeks before I looked a semblance of normal again. I felt obscurely ashamed that I had not had more sense or taste than to mess with that one. Sometimes it was hard not to be bitterly disappointed in the race of men.

He beat me up and got away with it.

❧ 27 ❧

HOME
SUMMER 1964 - 1965

After his first heart attack, Daddy sat up in the hospital bed looking like an aging schoolboy, Holden or Tom, surprised by old age. With his baby-blue eyes and vacation tan, Dad appeared healthy, his skin with that glow that comes when disease alerts the body.

"Papa," we kissed, nuzzled. "Can't you stand *rest*?" Mother and Dad had just returned from a week at Rehoboth Beach.

"Shock to my system, darling." Dad's voice was as watery as his eyes. "How'm I going to tolerate retirement?"

Daddy always looked staunchly proud and vulnerable at once. Years ago, he'd taken me up in an open-cockpit plane and rolled it. The old flying ace and incorruptible bureaucrat, now aging. Dad was offered discreet bribes with astonishing regularity by senators and congressmen who wanted to get their hands on big FHA properties up for resale in their home states.

Sitting on his bed, I rubbed his arm till he smiled. "Chill of the grave, rub it away."

"How do you feel?"

"Like an army marched across my chest, and I'm breathing between the feet."

"Oh Daddy," my eyes teared, "you've got to be so careful." Ever since I left home I'd had nightmares about his death.

Mother came into the room. "Stop pestering your father. Your father is ill."

Daddy seemed to get smaller, sicker when she spoke. We all did. Mother was still as picky as she was pretty, old Kiss/Kill.

"Want me to stay with you, Pop?" I'd stayed in the hospital with Grandmother Nena the night she died. When a family member is sickest, why go away?

"I'll be all right, baby. I'll just be dozing."

"*Why* must you be a nuisance, Ali?" Mother fussed. Dad and I still tended to ignore her.

Usually Dad hugged me hard, denting me with his chest and arm strength. When we kissed goodbye, his touch was frail. I wanted to protect him. I'd never met a man as good as my father.

"Alley Oop?"

"Yes, Dad?"

"Take care of your mother."

While Dad convalesced at home, he was fine but weak, Dr. Broadax said. Dr. Broadax said he mustn't lift the plastic laundry basket because it gave him chest pain. In 1964 there were no balloon angioplasties, no heart bypasses, no pacemakers, no open-heart surgery. How could I go back to New York with Daddy this ill?

෨෨෨෨

"The gentlemen will have brandy at table while the ladies join company in the drawing room."

"Quaint," I choked, as the hostess rose sweetly and led the ladies into the Georgetown parlor. They crossed their legs and conversed about babies and townhouses. I'd forgotten social Washington's gentility, protocol before substance. Suppressing a yawn, I rose and joined the gents in the dining room.

"Like a cigar?" said the host.

"No thanks."

My date, the legal assistant to the special assistant to the assistant secretary of Commerce, looked askance. I ignored him. I needed contacts for writing jobs. I described my novel, *My Darling from the Lions*, being handled by prestigious Jim Brown, my short stories in *Playboy* and anthologies. I made up a book on the psychological health of bureaucrats, having dated a National Institute of Mental Health psychologist last week. My slightly phony resume impressed them and I picked up names and numbers. Even my date came up with two.

❧❧❧❧

Back in my old hometown. I'd fled New York where I hated myself, modeling made me feel worthless, cheap. I was too old to be a windup toy, a Twinkie, a lustbucket. Here in Washington I boldly proclaimed myself a professional writer, my pen my sword. I became my old self. My parents paid four months rent on my apartment, on the highest hill near the Cathedral. I bought a hundred-dollar car for fifty bucks.

As I made rounds in my good new freelance suit, I felt as I had in my MA scholarly days, my Manhattan early writing days. I offered to write for PHS, HEW, USIA, HUD, NASA, DOJ, NIMH, and local magazines. My first two jobs came from my old buddies, the outsiders, a Jewish woman editor at USIA and a black male editor at HUD. At HUD I wrote articles for the byline of the agency head.

USIA seemed staffed with refugees from harsher regimes. A furtive atmosphere haunted the corridors, as if a bomb factory were hidden in the central core, wired with grievances. I wrote articles for their *Africa* magazine then reduced a soporific biography, *Mrs. LBJ* by reporter Ruth Montgomery, to a thousand-word vocabulary. It became a Washington Square Press paperback distributed in Africa and Asia. Then I reduced *Picnic*, the play by William Inge, to a two-thousand-word vocabulary. Ralph Meeker had starred as the stud/drifter in *Picnic* on Broadway, Ralphie whom I dated off and on for several years.

Public Health Service was a Noah's ark of deviation, where every disability known to man worked. At PHS I wrote up every medical technical specialty for a new recruitment manual. My boss, Alex Adler, was astonished that I completed assignments, as I was their only freelance professional who actually turned in work. I liked easy-going Alex because his stockbroker wife earned far more than he did, and he was proud of her.

My second novel slowed to a crawl. Jim Brown wrote that Grove Press claimed they wanted to publish *My Darling from the Lions* but they never came up with a solid offer. He'd given them a three-month deadline to make an offer or return the manuscript. By spring 1965 my first novel had spent two years making the rounds.

Larry Collins, author of *Is Paris Burning?*, phoned from New York and invited me to translate for the El Cordobes party, while we trailed the matador around Mexico for his next book. "Ought to be one of the great all-time blasts," Larry coaxed. Charge, girl, take off, get high forever! "Can't, Larry. Besos to the matador." Larry titled it, *Or I'll Dress You in Mourning*.

Back home in the polished magnolia suburbs of Washington, I guarded the family from the high ridge above Georgetown, my parents secure in Spring Valley behind. They'd sold the family house, though my brother and I begged and pleaded. As adult children long gone, we wanted home intact on the Christmas card in our memory. They moved into an apartment in Spring Valley and Mother declared, "I'm not lonely anymore."

That was when Mother told me Grandmother Nena had been part Spanish. Nena's forebear in Florida, Aldo Paz, had become Albion Pace when Spain sold Florida to the U.S. in 1820. Nena's name was Almira—to see. My Spanish and Mexican loves had roots.

From my glassy studio apartment at the rise of Wisconsin and Mass. Avenue, I could see the Capitol dome and the tip of our national prowess, the Washington Monument. I watched planes glide down the Potomac to land, and on Sunday, gazed down on white gloves and bald spots strolling placidly to our National Cathedral.

In spring 1965 Daddy retired at the age of seventy. It was hard to believe he had white hair. Then in late spring he suffered another heart attack, though less severe. I was stationed here to guard and protect him, to be near him. At last, in fear, Mother flung her arms around me for support. My brother, the Reverend Palmer, visited often from his Hagerstown Episcopal church. We became almost a family.

"Angel," Mother phoned, "you shouldn't be driving that old wreck. Your father and I want you to pick out a car. A good used one from a reliable dealer."

"A car!"

"I'll go with you to pick it out."

And she did, just as she used to take me shopping for dresses at Woodward and Lothrop, when everybody shopped downtown on F Street.

My parents bought me a pretty used VW I christened Babyblue. Now there was more money, they wanted to make it up to me for having put myself through college. My blonde sister, Bunny, visited from Florida with her two little blonde daughters. In photos we all look precious. We became a family.

๛ 28 ๛

A WEEK WITH WILLIE GADDIS
FALL 1965

Dear Alice,
In one recent evening I 'direct dialed' 4 numbers, 3
in N.Y. and yours in Washington—and got a service
on each one of them. So much for the telephone
company.

My own household has finally collapsed, my effort
of the past 2 years to hold it together unavailing
& Pat moved out with children & so now the long
bloody scene involving lawyers, my demands for
'rights' regarding children etc., none of it new but all
of it new to me and to them and seeming so damned
unnecessary, aren't there enough problems without
adding new ones?

And regarding books, writing—the second book
seems scarcely easier than the first, harder really—God
save us from the 3rd!—but I have a good publishing
contract now and so no need for other work.

Are you ever in New York? Let me know.

Yours,

W. Gaddis
114 N. Highland Place
Croton-on-Hudson, N.Y.

Gaddis wrote with pen tip and ink bottle, in a vertical nineteenth-century script as elegant as his note was casual and straightforward. He must've gotten my address from our mutual friend, Dick Dowling. How I missed New York. So Gaddis was free! But what a pity, with two kids. It couldn't have been easy for Patty to live with a man so obsessed—so *within*—his writing. Now, I ached for New York.

Such a good contract he could write full-time, financial needs taken care of! By virtue of Candida Donadio's famous agenting, and his own excellence. Envy, envy, let me breathe. Be grateful for him. Remember, hope has feathers and my novel may still fly.

Did Willie Gaddis still have his *soigne retrouse* look of a Puritan combined with a seedy elegant boulevardier, a jaunty look with a witty strut to the face? Sort of High Church combined with Paris brothel piano thumper, butt dangling from lip? Or did Gaddis merely activate my imagination?

Fame was different then. Mostly, it was admiration for achievement. Celebrity, though, depended on sensation. Gaddis was famous among literary cognoscenti, not the general public. I began rereading *The Recognitions*, ten years later. Gaddis caught that horrible sensation of negativity, loneness, and inconsequence I had in my twenties. But he missed joy, the bold stroke adventure of sex and people.

How old would Willie Gaddis be now? Probably early forties.

❦❦❦❦

Artistic Washington hung out around Dupont Circle at Duncan and Hazel Hazlewood's, 1841 R Street, which I christened HQ Central. We got bombed in their minuscule front room where Duncan painted at the street window. Duncan Hazlewood, with his dynamic color in overlapping styles, was on the lip of his fifteen minutes of fame.

One night *Washington Post* book critic Bill McPherson came in, with wife Beth, chortling over a satiric western he was reviewing for *Life*. It was David Markson's first novel, *The Ballad of Dingus Magee*, published by Bobbs-Merrill, noted then for avant-garde fiction. "My buddy, David," I hollered and howled over a page or two. Bill gave the book a ripsnorting rave, which helped David get a hundred thousand dollar movie sale to Sinatra, this also with Candida Donadio's suasion. This gave Elaine and David a year off from strife in Florence, and money to start a family.

Lucky me, I was seeing a psychoanalyst as a boyfriend, not a shrink, a distinction which he didn't cotton to. At parties women doted on his huge commanding black eyes, set in six foot two with shoulders and black waves. This impasse—my refusal to be the tremulous female—eventually broke us up.

Dick Dowling and wife, Arlene Donovan, visited from New York. Arlene was story editor at Columbia Pictures, a lofty job that allowed us all to submit novels to her that didn't suit movies. As blonde Arlene was a small, smart, ambitious Southerner like myself, I felt a real affinity for her. Dick Dowling's wicked first novel, *All the Beautiful People*, about cafe society, had told all in 1964. I'd known Dick since his Pfizer days with Willie Gaddis and dated him in 1959, when we often doubled with the Gaddises. Dick, the martini freak, also popped uppers like candy, having a degree in pharmacology. As an Irishman, he sniffed at my fear of overindulgence. We'd been friends and lovers, never in love. Why did it amaze me when *two friends* fell in love and married? Their visit made me long for New York.

Dad was stabilized, apparently, now that he'd retired. Bored, he was making an elaborate Swiss wall clock. If he was out of danger, I was free to check out freelance writing jobs in New York. I arranged to use Arlene and Dick's Gramercy Park apartment, as they were off to Hollywood to peddle Dick's novel. Excited as a kid, I wrote Willie Gaddis I was coming to New York, at last.

෴෴෴

In 1965 the two best short story writers of the era were published, Katherine Anne Porter with *Collected Stories* and

Flannery O'Connor with *Everything That Rises Must Converge*. In 1964 O'Connor had died of lupus at age thirty-nine, after ten years as an invalid on her mother's farm in Milledgeville, Georgia. My poetic mentor T. S. Eliot died, age seventy-seven.

Washington gossiped over LBJ's way of greeting a woman—grabbing her arm up high so he could rub his arm over her bosom. Plus his predilection for calling in staff during bowel movements. Mr. Sound Off, indeed. New names jumped onto the list of women JFK had sex with. Everybody in town could name fifteen or twenty, and point out the house of the Georgetown hostess who'd supplied Jack.

❧❧❧❧

Willie Gaddis stood at the door with his rueful excuse of a grin, his sad staunch smile, still rail-thin with the highest cheekbones in town framing his elfin triangular face and deepset blue eyes.

"Willie!" When we embraced I felt his sharp bones. "You haven't changed. You still have your debonair cadaverous sparkle," I teased.

"You always make me laugh, Alice." He planted a bone-hard kiss on my lips. "Which I desperately need."

I made us vodka martinis and we admired the grand view of Gramercy Park, the quiet green oasis between East 19th and 21st streets. A most desirable apartment.

"You look—better," said Willie, dragging a cig to his toes.

"I gave up modeling." We settled on the sofa. "Well, what happened?"

"A typical story," said Gaddis. "An old marriage—the family complaining that I hide behind my smoking typewriter. They felt cut off, ignored." Gaddis raked his straight beige hair off his wan beige face.

"Like Wyatt and his wife in *The Recognitions*? Didn't you write, `If you want romance, marry a dentist.'"

"Did I? No, not like that, I hope. The only way I know to write is total involvement. How about you?"

"Probably the same. But since I live alone, nobody minds."

Over dinner at Pete's Tavern, booth cozy with red-checked tablecloths, I asked about his munificent contract and whether his editor might take a look at my novel. But as soon as he mentioned the name, I remembered he'd rejected it.

"God, I hope the divorce won't force me back into PR." Willie's world-weary amused sexiness began to reach me, as we relaxed, swilling martinis.

"I'll show you my *Mrs. LBJ* job—English as a fifth language," I laughed.

"Remember the documentary films I used to do for the Army? They paid five hundred dollars." Willie chuckled, "I applied for a grant and when my sponsor saw the figure, he added a zero. 'You work for five thousand dollars,' he said. I got the grant."

"That's great. Have you seen David's book, *Dingus Magee*?" I told him about McPherson's *Life* review taking off from HQ Central in Washington.

"Pure slapstick," said Gaddis. "It was important to that reviewer to rev it up, for his career."

"You liked it?" I doubted it was his kind of humor.

"Riotous performance."

I liked Willie. We got along. My forebears were Puritans as well as Southerners, my brother and two cousins Episcopal priests, and my father prayed on his knees. I was at ease with a strict conscience and moral urgency: it was the other half of my character. Besides, he was frank and forthcoming, not stuffy or snobby like some "learned" writers. We drank and ripped apart the establishment with glee.

"Do you know Ed Doctorow at Grove?" I asked. "I'm having lunch with him."

"I think I've met him."

"They're using my novel for a seat cushion," I sighed.

We strolled back through the breezy wavering light and shadows dancing through tall park trees.

In Arlene and Dick's apartment, there we were, both strangers to the large inviting bed in the large bedroom. What belongs to a couple more than their bed? Feeling like intruders, we undressed on each side, pretending to be casual. As he took off his clothes and I took off mine, his organ responded with its excitable eye trained to the female form. Out of modesty, I kept on my bikini panties, for now.

"I knew you'd be gorgeous," he said, sliding his slim body, only slightly muscled, but sporting a fine centerpiece, under the covers. His wan flesh seemed never to have seen the sun. Then I remembered he'd been ill for years as a child, which had kept him out of World War II. When we embraced, his touch was sure and strong and his skin very warm, warm as a heater. Mother's hands were that way, so warm she could be your glove on a cold day.

Willie made love to me like a husband, easy and natural, without huffing puffing passion. Husbands have bodies that seem well used, accustomed to calm sex, to expect it as the natural culmination to being together. With his reassuring prong thumping against me, he crawled down below the covers and slick warm steaminess liquified my intensity, and then we clenched, we locked, as my greedy silken vise ensnared him. He did it all right, I did it all right. We enjoyed each other, we civilized two.

Gaddis moved in with me for the week of my visit.

❧❧❧❧

Editor Ed Doctorow, who'd soon be recognized as a writer, huddled with me over lunch at the Gramercy Park Hotel. Doctorow looked like David Markson and Herbert Gold combined, a pale fine-boned urban Jewish face with dark eyes and wavy black hair.

"We at Grove like your novel. Your style is breathtaking, at times."

When I broke into a big grin, he continued fast.

"*But,*" he paused. "I don't understand the social context. Who are these people? Who are their families?"

My spirits plummeted. "That's at the beginning, in the first few chapters."

"But it's only about two people."

"It's about their marriage conflict, and the other man and married couple they get involved with. Who are lower-class. That's five."

"Well," he considered, "we like it. Maybe I better give it another read, okay?"

"Okay," I said hopelessly.

Later I met my agent, Jim Brown, at his East 60th Street apartment for drinks, and reported this.

Elegant Jim, in his three-piece suit, swivelled between his lady-skirted tables, spilling manuscripts. "Those people at Grove drive me crazy!" Jim's bulbous patrician blue eyes blazed, like those of my dead Grandmother Denham.

"That's *not* what they said to me. They told me they wanted to publish *My Darling from the Lions. But* their fiction list was already bought for the next two years. So that you and I have to decide if it's worth waiting."

"But, Jim," I felt tearful, "*does* the book have enough social context?"

"Of course. I don't know what he's talking about."

"Well, if he doesn't like it—"

"Barney runs the show. They've had it six months. What do you want me to do?"

"I'm so discouraged," I said.

"Oh, piffle," said Jim. "I'll give them two more months to come up with hard cash, then demand it back. There's a solid literary editor I want to show it to, over at Bobbs-Merrill, Bob Amussen."

"They published Markson's novel."

"You see, originality doesn't make Amussen blanch."

⁊⁊⁊⁊⁊

"Remember when I used to call you the poor man's Frank Sinatra?" I said to Willie Gaddis over dinner.

"I rather liked it," he said.

Dismally, I reported the afternoon's events.

"You should let Jim Brown decide," said Gaddis. "He's hugely respected."

Back at our *pied-a-assignation*, I found Eloy's letter in my purse. I'd picked it up on the way out of my place in D.C. "Want to see script as old-fashioned as yours?"

We both liked the elaborate Spanish stamps and formal square envelope of heavy vellum. I forgot Gaddis could read Spanish, so he read the letter.

"He must care a great deal about you to tell you this," said Willie.

Eloy was the Spanish doctor I'd been in love with in 1960 and 1961 during summers in Spain. We'd corresponded ever since.

Eloy wrote:

Querida Alicia,
I finally found a passionate woman who wants me as much as
I want her. I am happy to tell you we are getting married. So I
won't have to propose again to my old love in New York, after
all. I wish you luck in your life and your writing.

Abrazos,
Eloy

"Do you know what an amazing letter that is?" said Willie.
"The trust it shows."

"We considered marriage. But I didn't want to become
Spanish. I feared I'd never write."

"You must have been very close."

"Yes, I loved him." It had been hard, awful to say no.

It struck me that male writers—including Gaddis—were
good at tensions in relationships, but few understood intimacy,
closeness, the joy of truly reaching one another. Fashionable
modern novels declared true communication impossible, that we
were all consigned to separate cells and could only knock on the
walls. The metaphor of alienation was easier. Despair was chic.

や~や~や~や

Next day I phoned my contacts on *Time*, *Newsweek*, and
Mademoiselle, but there were no openings. I phoned David and
Elaine Markson, but they'd already left for Florence. I phoned Jim
Bryans, who invited me for lunch, and Harry Evans, who invited
me for dinner.

I met Jim, editor-in-chief of Popular Library, at what he
modestly called the James A. Bryans building and we walked to
the Four Seasons, the *haut* French *boite* where he was known. At a
CEO's six foot five, big jocular Jim was as boisterous and canny
as the huge paperback house. He was crazy about Markson's
Dingus Magee novel and eager to see mine when I finally got a
hardcover sale. Jim was a four-star boozehound and big spender
on the power lunch scene, hence well beloved in the posh French
spots. We dined exquisitely and drank to perfection, Jim's five to
my two, his hollow leg barely filled to the calf.

"Why didn't you say so?" boomed Jim, when I said I needed

work. "How'd you like to write jacket copy—front and back covers and page one? Page one is a sensational excerpt of a paragraph or two to snare the buyer."

Jim gave me four gaudy paperbacks as examples and four newly printed but without covers to do copy for, at forty dollars per book. "Read the first twenty pages and the last twenty, keep it simple and sexy."

I did jacket copy for Jim for years. He always sent four, which I always did in one day.

❧❧❧❧

Harry Evans, my old family friend and editor-in-chief of *Family Circle*, squired me to '21' for dinner and proposed.

"I just became a millionaire," said Harry. Harry still looked like a freckled cheerful chipmunk, gleeful with saucy energy at seventy, Daddy's age.

"Daddy's fine, apparently." I told Harry, obviously healthier, about Dad's heart attacks. The scare, the pain, the fright.

"Your father has always been too good," cracked Harry. "It's not healthy to care too much about other people."

"Underneath, always, I worry about him," I admitted.

"If you marry me," said Harry the sprite, "you'll never have to work again. Now I'm a millionaire!"

"I always thought you were, Harry."

"That's what everybody says." Harry said *Family Circle* had been sold to Cowles Publications, who put out *Look* magazine. He'd traded his stock for theirs, hence the cool million. Ironically, *Look* would fade and *Family Circle* would grow in popularity.

"How 'bout it, honey?" Harry got a sneaky snaky look I'd seen once or twice. "I've always had a secret lech for you, baby girl."

"Harry, I—" I blushed. I couldn't go to bed with Harry. Harry was too old.

"I know your whole family. You could write away, without a care for money."

I felt bad, I felt sorry. "Harry, I—I don't want to get married. I don't want to marry—anybody." That seemed the kindest thing to say.

Harry looked crestfallen.

"You know how much I like you, Harry. You're one of my favorite people, I love being with you." I rather overdid it.

"Well. Worth a try." Harry cheered up. He was too bubbly to stay down.

෩෩෩෩෩

Back home at Gramercy Park, I told Willie Gaddis about my day's adventures. "Ironies abound. Here am I begging for work and turning down a millionaire."

We were both aware we were getting far too comfortable in Arlene and Dick's place. So much so that I wished they'd stay in California. But we had one more day to pretend it was home.

We had a nightcap, hopped into bed and made love, and fell fast asleep. Next morning, yawning and turning, we slowly awoke. I noticed small black moles here and there on his torso. When I inspected more closely, I saw they were blackheads.

"Do you know you have the odd blackhead here and there?"

"Why, no."

"Don't you ever look at your body, your skin?"

"Not like that, no."

"Here," I said. "I'll pick one and show you." It jumped right out and I showed it to him. "It's because you have oily skin."

"That's gross."

"No, it isn't. You want me to get rid of them where you can't see them?"

"You don't mind?" he asked.

"No. Pretend we're monkeys and I'm grooming you." So I straddled his back while he peacefully half-dozed and groomed him free of blemish.

We had brunch out then came back to pack up and leave, he for Croton and I for the Washington train at Penn Station. I missed him already, in a family way, Willie and Harry and Manhattan. I wished him well on his divorce, on the trauma of divvying up the family circle of affection and cash.

"I hope you sell your novel soon," said Gaddis.

"I hope so, Willie."

"I'll remember this." We kissed goodbye.

"So will I."

It didn't occur to either of us to fall in love.

❧ 29 ❧

KATHERINE ANNE SAVES ME
WINTER 1966

The great short story writer phoned, at last! My college idol, who'd just won the 1965 National Book Award for her *Collected Stories*, phoned *me*. Astonishing that she lived nearby. I'd pursued her with letters requesting an interview for *Washingtonian* magazine, mainly because I longed to meet her. Katherine Anne Porter, who'd finally made enough money to write fulltime at age seventy-two, from the movie sale of her one novel, *Ship of Fools*.

Browsing in the Savile Bookshop in Georgetown one evening, I had come to with a jolt when I spied a stack of *New York Review of Books* with the note, SAVE FOR KATHERINE ANNE PORTER. I'd rushed to a clerk. "Does she live here?"

Clomping uphill to Lalo's house in San Miguel one day, I realized I'd followed Porter's trail, just as the boys followed Hemingway's to Paris. She was my literary guru, powerful as the ancient Aztec goddess of earth and fire, Coatlicue.

"You tracked me down," said an amused ageless voice with Southern lilt, a flute tone.

"I've been wanting to meet you forever," my own Southern accent bowed in response. Katherine Anne, jasmine and honeysuckle, my lyrical beginnings. At Chapel Hill, her exquisite indispensable stories showed me a woman and a Southerner could be a writer. "I'm *so* glad you called."

She chuckled, "You're a writer?"

"I try."

"What's your life like, angel? What're you doing in Washington?"

"Well, my first novel is making the rounds, I'm writing articles for money, my love life has fallen apart, and I'm always alone."

"That sounds about normal for a woman writer," Katherine Anne said cheerfully.

"How do you stand it? I don't know if I can." We both talked as if we'd known each other forever.

"My first book was published when I was forty. How old are you, angel?" I told her. "Maybe you're a century plant like I am, slow to develop. I learned to write just like a journeyman, five hours a day, maybe more." At age seventy-six, Katherine Anne spoke in rounded soothing tones, like crystal wineglasses striking together.

"That's so reassuring," I blubbered. "I feel let out of solitary into sunshine."

She agreed to an interview, at her house in Spring Valley, at 3601 49th Street.

"Do you like cocktails or liquor or sherry or tea? Every night before dinner, I have a bourbon all by myself—I like that stuff."

"I like that stuff too." We laughed. "I'll bring a tape recorder but I'm not sure how to work it."

"I have one you can use, but I don't know how to work it either. My last husband used to call me a mechanical genius who couldn't work a mixer." We tittered.

How sad that Katherine Anne had a bourbon all by herself every evening. I felt horrendously sorry for those who lived alone. As I did. As if I hadn't chosen it.

The literary boys in New York were my peers, my equals (I thought), but Katherine Anne was my hero. A woman born ten years before my mother, a woman born in 1890, who left Texas to write for a Denver newspaper in 1910, covered Mexico during the Revolution in 1920, moved past towns and men as an independent force. She didn't expect to be taken care of like Mama did. I breathed in the fresh air of her strength.

A miracle had happened, designed especially for me.

෨෨෨෨෨

Staring out my high-rise cell with a view, I worried about my father. Dr. Broadax said he was fine, fine, as long as he placed the pill under his tongue. But last time he and Mother visited, all he could do was sit there and breathe laboriously.

Back in the great immovable swamp of Washington bureaucracy, that vast reservoir for the unemployable middle class of America, huddled on the hot Potomac. Hadn't my father, the civil servant, prepped me for years on the knotted labyrinth of federal futility? Like Jackson Pollock's painting, *One*, a tangle without a tail. Yet Dad wrote federal housing law still used today. FHA's housing loans created the postwar middle-class suburban family.

Furtive fellows scurried through the halls of my apartment, refusing to nod no matter how many times I'd seen them. Spies playing anonymous? On the Wisconsin Avenue bus, military at the secret training school in Rosslyn practiced Vietnamese. Everybody knew the location just as they did that of the CIA in Langley.

Buoyed by Katherine Anne, I plunged into my second novel, everything in flux. It was like walking across the continent on sludge.

The dreaded blue letterhead of the James Brown Agency. This time a conservative editor rejected my first novel.

> Feminist notions have been OUT since Freud discovered penis envy. We agree with Lady Snow (Pamela Hansford Johnson) that women have little to say that men cannot say better. Why should the public care about the intimate details of this girl's life? Though I confess I chortled—the style shimmers. But she is ATYPICAL—are there really women like that? I'd like to know one. Maybe a more literary house?

New York had rejected me. If I couldn't be a novelist there, I couldn't bear to be a claquer, a failure, a mere journalist as I was here. Of course I planned to take a copy of my novel to the interview. I wanted Porter to read Denham.

❧❧❧❧

Katherine Anne Porter was a bird of brilliant plumage. Queenly and vivid, she greeted me in a low-cut green velvet dressing gown that showed off her shapely bosom and waist. Ice-white hair, rich skin, huge glittering emerald matching her gown, surrounded by purple, scarlet and jade furniture and diffused by a gauzy chandelier. My exact colors! We both had the same high taste for exotic clash. At seventy-six, she fluttered with Southern grace, fluffy white hair framing eyes and high cheekbones of well-tempered steel.

"Your shape, angel, it's uncanny." Katherine Anne put her hands around my waist then stood shoulder to shoulder to measure arms, and spun me around. "We're precisely the same size."

"Maybe we're related," I smiled, quite giddy, expecting to have many things in common with my old idol.

"Only now I have a pot belly," she bopped it, "but don't tell anybody. My hair went from jet black to white in a week, during a terrible illness when I was no older than you." Now Katherine Anne had her hands on my shoulders. "What'll you have to drink?"

Of course, we both liked to touch a lot. "Why don't we do the interview on coffee, then relax?"

"Good, angel. My mouth runs on drink."

Of course, we had drinks anyway, bourbon and branch for Porter, tequila for me.

At her marble sideboard, she whirled around. "My father used to flip the catch and swallow a jigger of bourbon before breakfast, then come to the table and say, 'Now, children, remember that any man who drinks before breakfast is a confirmed drunkard.' They'd pour a teaspoon full of wine into our water glasses to make us feel we were at the party."

"Only a Southerner would say that, you tease!"

She sashayed into the living room, pleased.

Katherine Anne's face was strong, noble and spare in the best feminine way—acute wise eyes, high forehead, determined mouth. I could see my grandmothers, the Old South, the organ music of the blood in her face.

As Katherine Anne scooted about her Tudor-style house, talking effusively, I sailed right in. "How do you live alone without crumbling?"

"I love living alone," she declared. "Nobody tells you what to do when. If I feel like getting up at five a.m. to write, I'm not disturbing anybody. The only problem is people, always after me to do something."

"Like *me*," I shot back. "I was raised six blocks from here, off 49th on Butterworth. When Dad and I took walks, we'd pass this house and he'd say, 'That's like the Tudor house where you were born.'"

"Maybe we're kissing kin."

I too had an ornate mirror with gold curls, from Mother, and a round Carrara dining table, hers immense and mine cafe. She perched on her red velvet settee and I sat in an antique purple velvet chair and turned on the tape.

"I honestly thought I'd end up sleeping under a bridge till *Ship of Fools* hit," said Katherine Anne. Her controversial 1962 novel was turned into a spectacular 1965 movie she hated, and with the money from all sources toted up, removed her approximately one million dollars from sleeping outside. At age seventy-two.

"I loved the opening in Vera Cruz, everybody there from the *altagente* to the dogs." *Ship of Fools* was static, though. The conflicts in the first half turn into set pieces. But the style was evocative vintage Porter.

The perfect way to live alone was with fame, spotlight on, mike open for your pronouncements, divertissements, rage and ire.

On Bellow—"All that pity, pity, pity me."

On Mailer—"A smutty little boy."

On Simone and Sartre—"To be born is to become responsible. They didn't discover the principle."

On men and her three admitted husbands—"One of my husbands said, 'You have a previous engagement with a higher power,' and he was right, and he was always trying to break that engagement. That's the way men are. They don't want you to have anything more important than them."

"That sounds like my past. So, what did you do?"

"Leave."

"Salud, so do I." We clicked glasses, on our third drink.

Katherine Anne told me about Mexico in revolutionary days, Paris and Berlin in the thirties, Hollywood in the forties. "We didn't have the twenties in Mexico, we had war. *War*. While in Paris, being gay was all the rage. 'Who is that woman living with that man in the hotel, who claims to be a *writer*?' said Janet Flanner, who wrote for the *New Yorker* as Genet. They were shocked. He was in the State Department. It was better before we got married."

"Your first husband?"

"Oh, no. Number two. We divorced and I spent the forties on contract in Hollywood. 'We have this nice little writer,' the producers would say, showing me off. They didn't give me much to do. Mostly, I worked in my garden."

She told me about her handsome third husband. Albert Erskine, who was twenty years younger when she married him at age forty-eight. It lasted four years. Erskine became a powerful Random House editor. Katherine Anne had been alone for almost a quarter-century since. "I never cared much about age, all that. Besides, after the first one, I never could *get* a man my own age."

"Marvelous," I hooted, confiding girlishly with a woman years older than my own mother, this celebrated grande dame who was far easier to talk to. "My Mexican love, Lalo, didn't want to marry me. Fortunately."

Porter expounded with arms behind her head, feet tucked up cozily in the red velvet sofa. "I always knew what I had to do. I had certain things I wanted to write, and anything that got in the way of that had to go. In marriage you can feel cramped, hemmed in—a loss of freedom. When that happens, it's best to say bye-bye and be on your way."

A garrulous fountain of wit and wisdom, Katherine Anne wasn't easy to interrupt. But I was there to suck wisdom's tit, and she wanted it sucked. "What about money, support?"

"I always supported myself," said Katherine Anne. "No man ever supported me. Even when I was married, I always contributed at least half. If you're going to be an artist, you have to be independent."

"*Felicidades a la escritora independiente!*" I cried in looping glee. Her Spanish, I noticed, was rusty.

"One day, angel, you'll look at a story you've written and you won't be able to imagine how you could possibly have done it, it's so far back."

"Maria Concepcion," her first story. As I looked at her, I felt the story's powerful arching wave. She'd expelled it half a lifetime ago. All her stories impacted in me, gathered and spewed to Katherine Anne as we talked. The power of art is to hold and transmit. Granny Weatherall always there on her deathbed to be jilted fifty years ago.

"When I wrote 'Granny Weatherall,' I was too young to know anything about age. I imagined it all, and old age turned out to be just as I imagined," said Katherine Anne. We were well sloshed, comfy. "The only way I can explain the writing process is that it's like a magnet. Everything you need jumps out and clings to it."

"Yes, things you didn't even know you knew, you remember." Wonder filled our eyes.

Katherine Anne showed me her library with its twelve-foot long mahogany reading table centering a huge Oriental rug. At the end a bookcase contained only her own writing in various editions, translations, and exotic foreign alphabets.

"Just think," said Katherine Anne, arm around my waist, "this one room is bigger than half the places I've lived."

Upstairs, she showed off her elaborate silken bedroom and plain writing room. As thrilled as a young bride, in the only house she'd ever owned.

We had one for the road. Katherine Anne flounced in with my fresh drink, twirled around and said, "Angel, how's your sex life?"

I whooped. "Random. I'm sleeping with a test pilot and a TV newscaster and a mathematical economist, for fill. I'm always horny." I looked at her earnestly, asking.

Porter trilled a chuckle. "When I was your age, the sex drive nearly drove me mad. It was always interfering. I couldn't get a thing done. I'd go to bed with anybody. No, that's not true. I was always selective."

"My sentiments, exactly." I raised a drunken arm. Of course, that was when she wrote her best stories.

Arms round each other's waists, we walked to the front door. "Don't let men tell you what to do, angel. You *know* what you have to do."

Katherine Anne hugged me and I kissed her goodbye on the cheek. Inspired by camaraderie, I bounced down the walk, turned and waved. Katherine Anne still stood in the lighted doorway.

My VW wouldn't start. Babyblue's battery suffered crib death far too often. Katherine Anne still stood there. Gesturing, I kept trying, gave up, and went back up. Katherine Anne didn't seem to mind. She seemed glad.

"Come on in, angel," she put her arm around me. "We'll both take naps then I'll fix you some dinner. Then if it doesn't start, we'll call a cab."

෨෨෨෨

Katherine Anne and I bedded down in her playful baroque living room. She stretched out on the red velvet sofa and I on the green velvet loveseat. Not being afternoon drinkers, we both fell fast asleep.

In about an hour both of us bolted awake. As Katherine Anne broiled lamb chops, I stood in the kitchen sipping Bordeaux. She'd squatted to the wine rack nimble as a girl.

"I never could get published in the *New Yorker*," mused Katherine Anne. "I sent them my latest story, 'Holiday,' and got a note from some young editor telling me to cut it to improve it. Don't they think I know when a story is ready?"

"*You* never got accepted by the *New Yorker*?"

"No."

"Absurd!"

"Story after story I sent them." She gave me a wise glare. "I was not to their taste."

"Too powerful, probably."

"I'll tell you how my hair went white in a week. The plague— the flu epidemic of 1918—swept the nation and killed one hundred thousand people. I was a reporter on the Denver paper, in love with a young biologist." She was suddenly misty-eyed. "I've never loved a man so, before or since. He didn't *read*—he didn't have to—Alexander was luminous and poetic and in love with nature. I caught the flu and he nursed me. I was close to death. Then when I came out of it and survived, I discovered he had caught the flu, and died!"

"That was your story, 'Pale Horse, Pale Rider,' wasn't it?"

She nodded, whispered, "How I loved him."

"They still ask about my sex life, discreetly." Mood changed, Katherine Anne guffawed. "What does an old woman do for sex? You lose the urge, that's what you do. And it's like coming out on a lovely fiddler's green—peaceful, at ease. When somebody asked Socrates what it was like to be old without sex, he said, 'It's like being released from the teeth of the tiger.' That's exactly it."

"You don't miss it?"

"I've had almost no sex life for the past twenty-four years. Haven't missed it since I was sixty, sixty-five."

Always something to learn.

"But it's always there—the attraction—even with an old woman like me and young men. They feel it, and so do I. A warming blaze, a low fire."

Abruptly I remembered to drop my literary child on her doorstep. I showed her the rejection letter from the world-famous editor, whom she knew.

"He hasn't changed a bit," she snarled. "It means you're doing something original that he hates." Her eyes lit, "The best response of all. That means it's only a matter of time, angel."

I gave her a carbon of the first hundred pages of *My Darling from the Lions*. Blushing, I said, "I'd really appreciate your glancing at this. I'd like to tell my agent what you think of it."

"Angel, I'll get to it soon as I can," sighed Katherine Anne. "Somebody's always after me to do something."

"Oh, I know." I was mortified. "Just forget it." I felt hot all over. You can't ask someone over seventy to do you favors.

"Soon as I can, angel. I promise." Katherine Anne put her arm around me and squeezed. She was very kind to me, as I fawned over her the only way you can—naturally.

We kissed goodbye again. Katherine Anne stood in the window again. This time my VW started. This time I knew Porter was lonely.

It seemed unfair that the reward for a lifetime of courage and dedication was loneliness. The sound of one hand clapping against furniture, against pillows. Such a slight sound that you stomp through rooms, kick cabinets, talk to yourself, as I did. In the end many women have to be braver than men, and the bravest women, those who've endured solitary, have to be bravest of all.

In the interview published in *Washingtonian* magazine, I closed with Katherine Anne's blithe warning to artists and all who dare: "If you're tough, you're going to live a tough life."

❧❧❧❧

My boss at Public Health Service phoned while Mother was visiting, Mother in her nice mauve suit, pillbox hat with veil, stockings and proper pumps. As a medical writer, I worked two days a week at PHS. My boss, Alex Adler, offered me a fulltime job as Woman's Coordinator for the division.

"I presume you mean five days a week?—Twenty-one thousand dollars?—I'm pursuing a novel. I can't do it." Alex Adler said he wouldn't take no for an answer. In 1966 that was quite desirable money.

Mother said, "Did you just turn down a twenty-one thousand dollar job?" Still smooth-faced at almost sixty-six, Mother was verging on the grande dame look.

"Yes."

"Here I worry about how you'll *eat* and you refuse to work for twenty-one thousand?"

"It's *my* life."

"You'll never sell that book. Your writing should be after hours, a hobby." Astounded, Mother got louder, "This is *important*—an opportunity."

I was silent.

"You make me furious!" Enraged to tears, Mother huffed out the door.

Maybe I ought to consider it. Freelance writing ate up the time I needed to properly court my second novel. It paid so little I never got ahead, so I could take time off. I'd always wanted to do something absolutely moral, like being a nun dedicated to the Mexican poor. Or something immoral like being a spy, to know firsthand the venal rascality of the world. Or simply toss over my wearisome devotion to art for the glitter of gold, meaning middle-class living, without the anxiety of writing and stress of poverty.

Look how lonely Porter was, both of us in our literary monasteries. Here in my one-room cloistered cell of an L-shaped studio. What did it get me, all this striving? Little beyond my own self-respect.

That night I dreamt I walked through a huge empty Georgetown house I'd rented with my new salary. No furniture at all, only large white rooms without windows. One white-walled room led to the next, without exits. I rushed from room to room. I couldn't get out. I awoke quoting Katherine Anne, "You *know* what you have to do."

Alex Adler called from PHS and upped the salary offer to twenty-three thousand dollars. I liked working with Alex. Woman's Coordinator, that meant women's rights—nun's work—moral and fascinating. I turned down the job.

இஇஇஇ

Katherine Anne phoned and said she enjoyed what she read of the novel. "You write with relish and sensitivity, angel. But how can you write about your own sex life?"

"I don't take it personally." A vast generational literary change. "I throw myself into the hopper along with everyone else."

"How is that possible?"

"We're all just human beings. Through sex, I'm swimming in the tidal waves of mankind. I love to delve into character through sexual relationships."

"Amazing, you young people. You have no loyalties." Did her musical trill belie the comment?

"Perhaps. But I'm fascinated by the way memory and fiction overlap, back and forth."

Katherine Anne invited me for dinner and we made a date. "You can advise me what to wear for the photographer, angel." This was still February and the interview would appear in the May *Washingtonian*.

In blue marker I tossed off a fast postcard to trusty Jim Brown.

Katherine Anne Porter just called to tell me how much she likes my novel. "You write with great relish and sensitivity," said KAP.

Is there hope for,
Alice

Jim phoned and said Katherine Anne might really help and that he'd just sent my novel to the prestigious literary editor-in-chief, Bob Amussen, at Bobbs-Merrill. "LeRoi Jones, David Markson, etc.," said Jim. "He likes edgy work."

❧ 30 ❧

DADDY PASSES
CHRISTMAS 1965 AND FEBRUARY 11, 1966

When we visited my last aunt living in Jacksonville, we didn't know it was our last family pilgrimage. Aunt Mamie lived in a cottage in a grove of floppy banana and guava trees. Live oak and skinny pines hung nets of Spanish moss in a morass so tropical its sunshafts reflected green onto the porch. Daddy's oldest sister, Mamie, resembled Daddy with her high-bridged English beak, her dry wit, mannerly ways, and nicotine craving.

"Light a weed, Sis." Dad inhaled the aroma with delight, though he'd quit five years ago.

"My only remaining pleasure," said Aunt Mamie, age seventy-six and widowed, who'd soon learn she had lung cancer. Mamie had lost her eldest son, Denham—infamous star of gay lore—to opium, her daughter Ellen to cancer, and her husband Louis to suicide. Only cousin Freddie was left. It was she who burnt Denny's memoir when she discovered he was gay.

We drove around to visit all our Jacksonville houses. Dad drove with brother Palmer up front, Aunt Mamie and Mother and I in back. Because Mother refused to fly, Dad had driven all the way from Washington. The Reverend Palmer and I had flown in together, he in sports shirt instead of the vestments that rendered him sinfully handsome.

"You'll be disappointed at your grandparents' house," warned Aunt Mamie.

Grandmother Denham's old fashioned Greek Revival had lost its veranda and columns, its porte-cochere, its charm. The old family home now housed psychiatrists' offices, and the gardens had become their parking lot. Dad recited the litany of its sales, always for more money. The Tudor house across the St. Johns, where I was born, now looked like an ivy-covered chapel. Our modest shingled house emerged as a stylish townhouse. Great parks, steep slopes had shrunk to adult size.

Dad's face looked ashen with fatigue, eyes glazed, mouth hung open. I'd never seen a man so tired.

"Daddy, let me drive. You're exhausted."

Nobody paid attention. Dad didn't respond.

"Let me drive, Dad," I leaned over the seat.

"Leave your father alone," said Mother. "You can only drive that stick shift."

"You drive, Palmer." Palmer mooned, in absentia. "Can't you see Dad's about to collapse?"

Palmer blinked. He never could see, about Dad. "Pop?"

"I'm fine," said Dad, as he always did, eyes at half mast. Speaking of martyrs in the family.

Dad looked as if he would drop dead at the wheel and I couldn't get anybody's attention.

❦

A snowy February night at eleven-thirty, long past their bedtime, Mother phoned. "Your father is having a heart attack. Meet us at the hospital."

My knees buckled, "It's bad?"

"He can't breathe," Mother's voice shivered.

"Ambulance is coming?"

"On its way. Emergency Entrance." She hung up.

My hands trembled so I could hardly button and zip. My father! Vast humbling horror pushed on my shoulders, shot through with a black streak of exhilaration. Life's starkest drama: O God, make him strong enough. He *believes* in You. What's he ever done but be noble and kind and good and sacrificing, exactly as You claim man should be. Jesus, *help* him. I wiped a tear of rage.

Wary of the Beetle in snow, I called a cab and reached Suburban Hospital before my parents. My brother Palmer arrived and we embraced tightly, searching each other's eyes. "How bad is it?" he croaked. "Mother sounded scared," I gasped.

It seemed forever before the ambulance pulled in. Dad was wheeled out on the stretcher, an oxygen mask over his face, Mother beside him. In no time we were in a room. Dad was placed in bed under the oxygen tent with blood pressure dials on his arms. Smooth silver-haired Dr. Broadax, whom Dad trusted, performed various ministrations and adjustments that seemed meaningless.

"Daddy!" I went up and held his cold hand which lay flat beside him, squeezed it to warm it up.

Dad's blue eyes rolled to me. "Weak."

"Don't crowd him," said Broadax, "give him space to breathe."

"Where's Mother?"

"Downstairs signing you in." Mother rushed in. "He wants you here beside him. Hold his hand, it's freezing."

Palmer and I were in mortal terror because we didn't understand how bad it was. We didn't know if Dad was getting better or worse under the oxygen tent. "Doctor?" I asked.

"Ummm," he nodded gravely, engrossed in monitoring, finger pressed to his lip.

Our father rasped for breath, then grew quiet, then struggled again for that most precious element in our lives. We stood around the theatre of death. Time, fifteen minutes, twenty-five, passed. I stroked Dad's ankle and calf through the cover. Mother held onto his hand, his arm. Palmer squeezed his other arm.

Often Dr. Broadax checked the dials and sighed, or raised his brows, or glanced significantly at Mother.

Finally he said quietly to Mother, "We can't get any reading on the blood pressure. It's still at zero."

My blood froze, Palmer's eyes rolled to mine.

"It's not going up?" Mother whispered.

No answer. "Well, not yet."

Dad lay there still as a monument trying to breathe.

Suddenly Dad pulled up on his elbows, stared his blue trust at Broadax and said, "Doctor—can't breathe! What I do?"

Father sank back on the pillows as Dr. Broadax said, "You're breathing, Mr. Denham. You just don't know it."

Open-mouthed, I stared. Dad was sinking. Dad and his trust in healers I knew were helpless. Dad sank and sank.

Broadax checked the dials once more and said, "He's gone."

"*Daddy!*" I shouted.

Mother and Palmer fell into each other's arms, weeping, and ran out of the room.

"*Daddy! Breathe!*" I jumped onto the bed and pressed on his chest for resuscitation, and squeezed his arms and hands and pressed on his shoulders, and shouted at Broadax, "Do something!"

"Daddy, Daddy." I kept pushing for breath as I felt my own father pass away, away inside to his tiniest flicker of light, to a pinpoint, everything slowly ceasing—his warmth, attention, his sight, his hearing. I felt he felt me as long as he could feel. "Daddy, Daddy," I wept onto his chest. It was a slow passing.

Dr. Broadax tugged at my arm. "You can't help now," he said in a professional soother's tone. I elbowed him off, and he stepped outside.

I squeezed Daddy's fingers, sighed heavily, and stood back from the bed. Mother and Palmer were still in the corridor. Mother and Palmer, Dad and Ali. It was always that way. I stood and looked at my dead father.

Suddenly I got very hot, burning hot, as I saw Daddy's face and body form over mine, come down over me like a warm mist, like a cloak, a mantle, a warm engorgement, so that my father's form enclosed mine. I felt the heat of his face and arms coming down over mine and thought, I am now forever partially my father, his inheritor. I always looked like my father. I have my father's face, his nose arch, his lid droop, his planed-off cheekbones. Now that I'd incorporated my father, I would never again be only myself. Now I had to be worthier, true to a nature more noble and less selfish than my own. They ran out. I didn't run. I could never run now because I carried my father's moral responsibility.

"Thank you, Daddy." Finally I left his room, tingling with

grief, careening in the waves of elsewhere. Had Daddy passed his soul to me, a nonbeliever? I did not think such things happened as transubstantiation of souls.

გოგონგა

In the corridor Palmer, wet with weeping, clutched and embraced me so hard he crushed the breath out of me. I hugged Mother, who fell on my bosom sobbing then pulled herself together daintily. Both Palmer and I knew Mother was the one who'd suffer most, who'd have to develop the most strength and endurance. Mother was the one who was now alone. She'd be sixty-six next month.

We sat and talked excitedly, Mother and Palmer and I, even laughed, waiting for the death certificate or whatever.

"I'm going to say goodbye to Dad." I rose and walked a different walk down the hall to his room.

"You can't go in there," said a nurse.

"Why?"

"He's dead."

"I know that. He's my father."

Daddy lay there peacefully, majestically, but so alone. Alone on a deathbed at 1 a.m. in a hospital room in snowy Washington. I kissed his cheek and smoothed his white hair.

"Goodbye, sweet Papa." Why did it always surprise me that he had white hair? For years I'd made it black-gray and Dad fifty-five. He was almost seventy-one when he died. He didn't go, he passed. Death is not an instant but a passage. My father's spirit had leapt toward life, so I didn't mind leaving him alone. Yes, I minded. Nobody admits the permanence of death is hard to believe, even as you gaze upon it.

Wake up, dear Father.

გოგონგა

Both Palmer and I went home with Mother and stayed with her till a day or two after the funeral. Sister Bunny flew up from Florida. Now it was Daddy *was*, not is, not does but *did*. We were very close, we talked about family, we each broke down in turn. The Reverend Palmer made funeral arrangements, with a priest friend, Jim Hightower, officiating. Palmer feared he'd break in the middle of the ceremony. Daddy wanted a closed casket of pine, cremation, no flowers, donations to the Church.

Daddy's rainbow appeared for the Sunday morning funeral.

In the small valley facing the apartment, there was a brilliant perfect rainbow, Daddy's spirit lighting the sky as it rose. No one had ever seen a rainbow there. It was a clear day with no rainbow possibilities. Rainbows don't fit, curve neatly into small apartment valleys like that.

We all saw it, friends and relatives as well. "That's Daddy's Rainbow," I said. Everyone nodded agreement.

Mother put her arm around my waist, "Yes, it is."

The colonial woody Episcopal Church was as warm and familiar as my childhood. Except for the shocking centerpiece, the plain pine casket where Father lay. We sat very close in the pews. Palmer and I held Mother's hands. Bunny and I held hands. We all took Communion, which I did to please the family, but Mother mistook it as renewed faith. The Reverend Hightower performed a simple ceremony, reading Palmer's eulogy.

Suddenly I broke down—the organ music of the blood, pounding through the generations, tumultuous in my veins, pounding its music from the distant past, the multitudinous participants in our lives, from three hundred, a thousand years ago, all the women who had not died in childbirth and all the men who had not died in war, to lead to us now. Captain Arthur Simkins whose house the British burned during the American Revolution. Great-great-great Grandmother Behethland saving her wounded daughter's life after a Seminole attack. Mother and Grandmother Nena swimming in Lochloosa Lake on the orange plantation at Walkee-o-tee, running through the orange groves. Mother the Southern Belle engaged four times. Daddy battling in the blue over France in an open-cockpit fighter plane in World War I. Daddy's favorite boyhood tale of his father, the bank president, sending him as decoy with the bank dick to Cuba with one hundred thousand dollars in cash, to shore up an allied bank that had suffered a cash run. The boy made the detective look like any other doting parent.

Mortality, who can stand it? Since I left home when I was young, I'd had nightmares about this leave-taking, bolted awake weeping, and now it had happened.

Daddy, light as air, now gone.

❧❧❧❧

Back in my own now-unfamiliar apartment, I felt like a new unknown person. Mother phoned and said Palmer had a terrible weeping collapse that went on for three hours, moaning that he'd never never told Dad how much he loved and respected him. Of course he had, in his way. Palmer was like many men: he held too much in, but it seeped out his eyes. While Mother and I raved and ranted and let it spew.

In grief, we were proud of Mother. As with many women who complain and nag about tiny things, she became strong when real strength was needed, only waiting to be shown. Mother told me how long, how worried, how much care, how tired, how alone, how lonely, how awful to be alone at the end when you're old. As most women are. Every day she phoned me sobbing. Now she set the table for one, cooked for one, slept as one, got up as one. Though I tried not to, I cried every day for four months.

How grateful I was I'd stayed in my old hometown.

❧❧❧❧

Several months before he died, Dad said to Palmer and me, "Maybe I should've stayed in Florida and hung onto the scattered property. All my friends who did got rich."

"I'm glad we didn't stay," I said. "It didn't take any guts to stay."

"I wanted to give your mother and you children some security. That's why I took the job here in Washington."

"Father, you did," said Palmer.

"But we'd be rich. And now I don't have anything to give my children."

"Dad," Palmer took his hands, "you gave us all the things money can't buy." Palmer had shown Dad he cared.

Daddy turned to me, "You don't mind?"

Daddy's humility always broke my heart. I put my arm around his shoulder. "We didn't want to live that way, Daddy."

What sort of world is it where a man has to apologize to his children for being good, not rich?

❧ 31 ❧

KATHERINE ANNE RECOVERS
SPRING - FALL 1966

"Congratulations, Katherine Anne." My mentor had won the Pulitzer for her *Collected Stories.*

"Oh, thank you, angel," she bubbled, "everybody's been calling."

"How does it feel to be so famous?" I seethed with unearned envy.

"I have no great respect for fame," trilled Katherine Anne. "If you have it, you know how many people have it who don't deserve it, and how many people don't have it who *do* deserve it, so you don't value it overmuch. But fame has its uses. People listen to you."

"*You* deserve it. By the way, I still like the photo." A full-page shot of her gesticulating faced my article in *Washingtonian* magazine.

"The lines in my face *can't* be that bad."

"Such a glamour girl," I chuckled. When she'd earnestly

asked how I kept my skin smooth, I didn't mention our forty-year age gap.

"Anyway, come to dinner." We made a date.

❧❧❧❧

Spread out across my desk were gaudy bosomy paperbacks. Our palpitating low-cut longing heroine gazes up at our stalwart lean-thighed high-boned hero, he with gleaming black hair, she with soft flowing tresses. Jacket copy for big Jim Bryans at Popular Library, the hack work of the nonfamous: front cover, back cover and page one. These sultry folk lived in flounces and knee britches, in plantations and vistas of the storied past. Page one of *Voluptuous and Virile:*

> "Never will I consort with a married man," Sylvana tossed her tempestuous curls.
> "My beloved angel," Glencove crushed her voluptuousness to his manly chest. "You are the only love of my life."
> Weeping, Sylvana wrenched away and ran full haste from the only man she had ever loved...

I was thinking about my father, who seemed always to ride beneath my consciousness, in my very tissues. Every night before sleep, Dad's face appeared and we talked, reaching through time, around mortality. His misty clear face, ghostly but perfect. My witty and droll affectionate father, whom Cousin Mac called the finest man he'd ever known. Father loved his family, each of us, with a love so tangible we each felt he loved us best.

In my article I'd quoted Katherine Anne on men:

> The truth is that men have always hated this world and tried to get off it. The earliest myth is of man gluing wings to himself and trying to fly, and he's trying to go to the bottom of the sea, and on land he's trying to see how much speed he can make. Because, actually, they hate life and they hate themselves and they don't like this earth and they'd like to leave it... [They] spend billions of dollars putting people on the moon where they have no business to be when we have not yet learned how to keep our water pure or have a decent system of garbage disposal or snow removal on earth.

Then I received a letter from Norman Mailer, one of the younger writers Katherine Anne had mentioned in our interview.

June 18, 1966
565 Commercial Street
Provincetown, Mass.

Dear Alice,

Somebody sent me a copy of the Washingtonian, and Behold! there is a photograph of you looking exactly as you looked—is it 10 years ago? My God. What's happened to you? Where are you? Answer, kid. Give me your secret.

Surf's up

Norman

That made me think very well of Norman. Had he become more gentle?

వ్యాం

In 1966 Indira Gandhi, Nehru's daughter, became prime minister of India. Lise Meitner, recognized at long last, received the Fermi Award for co-inventing nuclear fusion. Meitner had refused to work on the bomb. Margaret Sanger, who invented birth control, died, as did Lillian Smith, author of the maligned early black-white romantic novel, *Strange Fruit*. Truman Capote published *In Cold Blood* and Bernard Malamud *The Fixer*. The Soviet *Luna 9* spacecraft then our U.S. *Surveyor 1* made soft landings on the moon. The moon gave us eleven thousand TV images of its facial terrain.

Miniskirts came in style. I swore I'd never wear one. Next day I swung my gams like a young colt in my new mini.

వ్యాం

On the Capitol steps I posed with congressmen Tom Foley, John Conyers, and John Brademas; newsman Daniel Schorr;

National Gallery director J. Carter Brown, and various local lights for the August centerspread of *Washingtonian* magazine.

To meet men, to get over my father, I'd interviewed twenty-two Washington bachelors about their attitudes toward women. Many didn't want to marry a career girl and waved the old double standard of male prerogative. John Conyers, handsome black congressman from Detroit, said, "Women are deprived and discriminated against in America." It amazed me when a man freely admitted it. Conyers had already introduced an equal rights bill, which was joined by the Equal Rights Amendment.

After I replied Norman wrote again.

565 Commercial Street
Provincetown, Mass.
Sept. 24, 1966

Dear Alice,
This is going to be the shortest of lines. I didn't answer any mail all summer and now am going through it like a reaper in a field of wheat. Actually, this is just to ask you, if you ever get to New York, to get in touch—for the Lord knows, I don't get to Washington very much, since they're not consulting me as a visiting expert unduly—and then, indeed, I won't even be in New York until November at least, when we're going to do a play of *The Deer Park*, off-Broadway. But I would like to see you again, so if you are in New York at that time, my phone number is: UL 5-8966, and I'll keep in mind that you're doing your best to relieve the siege of Washington. Say hello to Irv and Zola and, oh yes, Miss Porter.

Best and all,

Norman

Norman's letter made me feel I still had friends in New York, I was still connected. Here was Norman, who cared whether I existed.

☙☙☙☙

As Katherine Anne had invited me for dinner, I lugged along a half gallon of wine. I was always thrilled to see her again. Also I brought my bachelor article called "The Sidesteppers."

All along 49th Street in Spring Valley, the houses sat atop a ridge of small green hillock. I parked under the shadowy trees and climbed the brick walkway to her Tudor house perched above.

I rang the bell. No answer. I rang again and knocked. No response. Once more I rang and knocked loudly, calling "Katherine Anne?"

Katherine Anne's eye appeared in the peep, looking frightened.

Smiling, I waited. Silence. Mystified, I knocked again.

At last a tall youngish middle-aged man came to the door. "What is it you want?"

"Katherine Anne invited me for dinner."

"I'm her nephew," he said. "She says she doesn't know who you are."

"Of course, she knows me," I said to Paul Porter. "I did the *Washingtonian* interview. She invited me last week."

He looked flustered, pale. "I think she's had a relapse. I'm sorry." He closed the door firmly in my face.

I felt crushed.

As I slid into my car, I glanced back up at the window.

There was Katherine Anne, peeking out at me from behind dark drapes, as if I were an interloper.

My father gone, and now I'd lost my friend, as well.

⁂

A month later Jim Brown phoned. "Bob Amussen at Bobbs-Merrill is seriously interested in your novel." Jim fast-talked, as usual, "He's coming to Washington on business and wants to *see* you."

"You mean, he might—"

"—very well publish it, unless you alienate him some way. So, watch your forked tongue," Jim giggled.

"Lord 'a mercy, after all this time?"

"Now, Alice, he wants changes," Jim's mollifying tone. "Don't fight him tooth and claw."

"No, no, of course not."

"Bob is going to phone you to set an appointment. I have a feeling this is it!"

"Jim, I'd given up hope."

"Never do that."

᷍᷍᷍᷍

"Yahoo ai ai ai!" I hollered. Before I remembered, I phoned Katherine Anne.

"Where've you been, angel?" said Katherine Anne.

I reminded her she hadn't recognized me.

"You were here?"

"At the door, early summer."

"It's all gone. Memory loss, that's what it does." She explained she'd had several minor strokes. "But I'm back now, slightly rocky though."

"I'm relieved, I was worried—"

"Do you know Elinor Wylie died of a heart attack at the dinner table? She turned to her husband and said, 'Bill, is this all?' and dropped dead." Theatrically, "On the way to her execution, Madame du Barry said, 'My life is incredible. I don't believe a word of it.' That's exactly how I feel at times."

"Hot news, news flash," I interrupted her flow. "Bob Amussen is actually interested in my novel!"

"Didn't I say so? He's a fine editor if he's on your side," she was nonplussed. "Years ago when I was first getting published, I was the prettiest little thing you ever saw. You may not believe it, I'm an old woman now, but I had the prettiest black hair and the whitest skin and men were always after me. Well, two famous writers now, making their way with the group back then, sat down and wrote me letters telling me they thought my stuff was terrible and that I was obviously just making out on my sex appeal. You know who they were—Sherwood Anderson and William Carlos Williams. I saved those letters. Fifteen years later when I was still around, do you know they both wrote me letters of apology. I've laughed over that! They liked my stuff, the silly fools."

Her nonstop gab left me breathless. "Sometimes, Katherine Anne, exceptional men don't like competition."

"Angel, I've fought men all my life, and gave as good as I

got. My husbands were all good men and they loved me as well as they could. But I've always had a greater talent for friendship than love."

I wondered if that was true for me, as well.

"Edmund Wilson called me a first-rate artist. I was always proud of that," she chattered like someone who'd been alone too long. "I'll issue that dinner invitation soon as I'm strong enough, angel. Let me know what happens with the book."

"He's coming here, Amussen. I'm going to meet him." I was starry-eyed—my possible savior, my white knight.

Jim Brown had said, "Amussen is tall, handsome, literary, and caring. You'll like him."

୬∙୬∙ଚ∙ଚ

Luckily I caught Katherine Anne before she went into Suburban Hospital, the very hospital where Daddy had died, for five days of tests, October 24 to 28. They tested her brain because of a fractured skull twenty years ago. "The lump has been bothering me," she said.

"Possibly that induced the strokes," I said.

"I asked the doctor my prospects and he said, 'You've had a long and fruitful life, what are you worried about?' It reminded me of visiting a friend who was ill. When they said I could visit as often as I wanted and he could do anything he wished, I knew he was a goner. A few days later he died."

"You sound marvelous, so high spirited."

"Mind and spirit, I suppose I've separated. It never really bothers me what happens to my body. I don't get depressed when I'm ill." Her voice was melodious but weak. "My manager, my lawyer, my accountant are attending the corpse to make my final will."

On the 26th I phoned her at Suburban and asked if I could visit her tomorrow.

"Yes, angel, come for cocktails, about four-thirty."

When the hospital staffer said I couldn't see her because I wasn't a relative, I said thank you and climbed the stairs to her room.

Propped up in the hospital bed, Katherine Anne greeted me in a sheer black negligee over a sheer black nightgown. As I kissed her crisscrossed cheek, she said amiably, "Angel, I'm getting ready to die. I'll welcome it. I've had enough. No one cares but me, and I'm tired of caring."

"Not true, and you know it." But I knew what she meant well enough.

Flaunting, Katherine Anne produced airplane bottles of vodka and paper cups. "They forbade me to bring liquor, so I thought this would do nicely."

"Elegantly," I said. "Salud—health, that's what you need." We toasted, rubbing paper cups.

"My last marriage, did I tell you about Albert?"

"Albert Erskine, the big Random House editor?"

"I was forty-eight and he was twenty-eight. I never cared much about ages, all that. Besides, after the first one, I never could get a man my own age. But he persisted, came with posies and all that, and I couldn't resist him in the end. I'd been alone so long, I couldn't turn down love forever. I told him I'd never known of a case where it worked with the woman so much older than the man. I told him we should live together, and he was shocked. Moralistic, you know. Well, I have no complaints. They were all good lovers. I've had good lovers and my husbands were good lovers too."

My brother, the Reverend Palmer, was only a few years before marrying a therapist sixteen years older than he, and they're happy to this day.

As Porter sat up to reach for another tiny vodka, the black negligee fell aside. In her sheer black nightgown, beneath her strong weathered face, Katherine Anne had large, perfectly smooth, beautifully tilted breasts, twenty-six-year-old breasts on a woman of seventy-six. Naturally she wanted to show them off. Southern women are body proud. I gaped in astonishment and she seemed pleased.

We toasted our second airborne vodka.

"'In my end is my beginning,' Mary Stuart's motto," said Katherine Anne. "I'm going to have it placed in my library at University of Maryland—it's to be a separate room with all my books and pictures of me and my own library furniture, set up as it is in my house."

Many years later I'd visit the Katherine Anne Porter Memorial Room and find my own first novel in her book collection behind glass. They wouldn't let me touch it. Fittingly, a literary reading was about to start, and they invited me to read.

"Then I'm going to set up a trust fund to help struggling writers, so that in my end will be my beginning. And if I had the papers right here to sign, you'd be the first to get help."

"Me?" Pie in the sky?

We drank and talked art and illness. "'We cannot know the truth. We can only approach it through lies,'" she ruminated. "Kafka."

"Picasso said art is a lie that creates truth."

"I can live or die with equanimity, angel. I've had everything I was capable of, given my nature and limitations. I feel thankful."

"I doubt my father felt that way."

Of course, Katherine Anne got well.

ॐ 32 ॐ

SLEEPING WITH EDITORS
FALL 1966 - 68

A lean tentative Scandinavian, Bob Amussen, editor-in-chief of Bobbs-Merrill, entered my apartment with the brooding mien of a poet-priest. This tall melancholy Christian knight, out of an Ingmar Bergman movie, liked my novel. Surely an aura floated his noble head and shoulders.

The first thing he said was, "Dick Dowling died. I hate to tell you but Dick died over the summer."

"What? They were just here, last year, Dick and Arlene. Everything was—"

"Cirrhosis of the liver, age thirty-eight."

"Good God! I stayed in their apartment last fall." I didn't mention Gaddis. "He was, he was so *young*. Lord, how is Arlene?"

"As you might imagine," he shrugged, sighed. "Coping."

"I'll phone, thanks. It feels weird that I didn't know!" This mutual loss made us feel close and easy, but pressured by woe.

Amussen admired my federal panorama view. I made drinks

and he said, "Yes, your novel is exceptional. I've never read a woman who writes about sex as you do."

I smiled warily.

"Amazing insights, good character conflict, your lyricism, well—"

I waited for the But.

"But," Amussen said, "we think it should begin on page two hundred, part three, for tighter suspense."

"Ohhhh?" Did my face fall?

"Don't go gloomy on me," he smiled protectively. "Why don't you reread it from page two hundred and see what you think? Then use whatever you like from the first two parts as flashbacks."

"Okay. *Okay!*" His fine-boned face had moral care etched across it.

We arranged I'd read it that night and he'd phone tomorrow and if I agreed, he'd send Jim Brown a contract and give me three months to make changes.

"I have a confession to make," Bob's pure intensity got to me. "Till I read your novel, I didn't realize I'd always thought of women that way."

"What way?"

"As different, or less, like Carl, the husband, did. Less interesting than men, even though I know it's not so."

"Less important, less competent?"

He nodded. "I'm afraid I treated my ex-wife that way, since I did more important work."

My arms crossed, "You don't do more important work than I do. Or your wife. Or your women editors."

"Yes, I see what you mean." The burdens of literature, truth and justice lay on Amussen's shoulders. Bob glanced into space, turned to me. "Your novel changed my life."

Tears sprang into my eyes.

"Suddenly I understood women weren't put on earth to fit my needs."

By now, of course, I was half in love with him.

❧❧❧❧

That night when I read *My Darling from the Lions* from page two hundred to the end, it moved more passionately, at a supple fictional pace. Bob had taught me something essential.

Next morning, I said, "Yes, yes, yes!"

Bob laughed, "Miss D, we'd be honored to publish your first novel."

We agreed I'd have the changes in by February. "Then I'm moving back to New York, b'gory."

Swooning with joy I phoned Mother and Katherine Anne and my old D.C. friends and Tony the newscaster I dated and Conyers at Congress. I phoned Alex at PHS and the folks at USIA and HUD. Now they *all* wanted me fulltime.

It was the happiest day of my life.

That night in bed, when Dad's face appeared, I told him my news. I was only six months late in a lifetime. Year after year, Daddy had watched me slaving haplessly at my devotion, and he'd died without my fulfilling him. Had he felt I was a dilettante? A fool? How could I bear that he mightn't know? It wasn't fair that Shakespeare and Emily Dickinson didn't know they'd lasted.

Mother said, "I can't stop talking to your father just because he's gone." So I asked her to tell him too, every night.

Don't we all possess more than the sanctified capacities, the recognized senses? I could create warmth in my hands by imagining it. Visualize a feather stroking my back and feel it. Partially deflect pain by placing it elsewhere. Slow my heartbeat with deep long breaths. Make scenes between my characters so real I suffered agony. See after-images—photo retention of light, of people at parties, of travel along highways or through clouds. Blissful scenery passed, and people I'd never seen. I'd been seeing faces, places, before sleep all my life, since childhood when Mother's eyes on the ceiling terrified me.

As I revised the novel, pink stigmata formed on my temples, rosy welts that I knew would stay till I finished. My tense companions as I did perhaps the most crucial writing of my life. When I finished to my own, then Amussen's, satisfaction, they disappeared. Getting published at last, at long long last, there I stood on the portly porch of Significant Lit, at the door, breathless.

SPRING 1967

It's easier to find a job than an apartment in Manhattan. There I perched in the huge Park Avenue office, elephantine plants, skyline, thickness underfoot. The landlord's secretary sat beside me, our chairs on the far perimeter of his massive green marble desk.

This dauphin of realty, New York's finest con game, spread his tiny polished nails on his glimmering huge desk, and bellowed, "Why should I give you this *fantastic* apartment when a *doctor* has offered me twice the money?"

"You accepted my checks." I rose, livid. I'd found a forty-by-twenty floor-through in Greenwich Village, on the same street where Katherine Anne had once lived. I hungered for the place. Casement windows, wood-burning fireplace, one bedroom, 130-year-old Federal.

He slung my checks across the desk to me. As fast, I slung them back.

"I went before the Rent Board, with your representative, and they okayed me." The Rent Board had checked my book contract, various articles. The city had created a new affordable category for freelance professionals who lived and worked in the same space. This gave landlords a 30 percent increase in rent rather than the usual 15 percent. Doctors, sculptors, painters could get larger professional apartments as they needed space. Writers got smaller apartments, called semiprofessional, as we needed less space. Being a writer ensconced in a semiprofessional apartment was as good as being rich.

"I don't know that man," mumbled the multimillionaire realtor.

"He's from your office. I just said hello to him." I knew what he wanted. More money.

"I didn't authorize the agent to give away the place."

"Then why did you advertise the price?" I hollered, vital rage pumping like bellows. I wouldn't give him five dollars more, on principle. Besides, I couldn't afford it.

His phone rang. Grandiloquently he talked, arching back and revolving his overpuffed chair. Gold gleamed—rings, cufflinks, pens, plaques, mementos. His secretary sat silently beside me. But I couldn't see her. I couldn't see him. I was white with anger, a white wall instead of vision. When he hung up, I saw him again.

This royal pipsqueak stood up behind his desk, smiled broadly, stuck out his pink hand. "Congratulations, the apartment is yours."

My eyes narrowed, understanding. "You're a despicable man." Smirking with joy, I shook his hand.

His secretary walked me out, arm around my shoulder. "You were wonderful. He really enjoyed that."

Welcome to New York.

❧❧❧❧

At Max's Kansas City, the chic artists' hangout on then-dumpy Union Square, Bob Amussen and I shared a booth in the woody back restaurant. Red decor lamps hanging over each booth turned faces sallow and food into brown mounds. The Mickey Ruskin drug scene roared in the glass-fronted barroom, with strung-out artists entertaining gawking uptown tourists. Artists attacked the feedbag, free bins of chicken in gravy, snagged a beer. Then hit up the tourists for a few.

Bob stroked my hand as he explained galleys and PR and reviews. "If you alienate conventional critics, well, all to the good." In Bob's brief tenure turning Bobbs-Merrill literary, he published LeRoi Jones's *The Toilet*, Sam Shepard, the *Naked Poetry* anthology, Markson, and now me. B-M's big ticket back then was *The Joy of Cooking*, plus college texts.

Back at his much larger floor-through, he showed me a long dark hall of formal family photographs in serene gold frames. All handsome chiselled women and men, long-faced and solemn. He showed me shots of his striking willowy ex-wife. Bob always seemed melancholy. He was very involved with St. Marks Church as an Episcopalian, not merely a poetry lover.

"I fail to understand how you, such a sensitive person, live without religion?" he asked, kissing my shoulder.

"I believe in art, Bob. My life force, as Shaw said."

We fell into bed. His movements were infinitely slow and somber, so I felt constrained to be serious not playful. To be solemn rather than passionate. Finally he told me why he was low.

"Years ago," Bob said, "my father died of a heart attack while sitting on the commode. Just a few months ago, my brother, my younger brother, walked into a fancy bed and bath display shoppe—the sort of place he never went in—walked over to a fancy mauve basin and toilet set, sat down on the toilet lid. And died."

∾∾∾

Norman Mailer invited me to his block party to celebrate the hundredth performance of *The Deer Park*, the play from his novel, at Theatre de Lys. Bob and I strolled along Bedford Street bolting drinks in large paper cups in the dark, barely lit by colonial casements. We walked through the past of early settlers, night shapes, hollering to chums. Norman and Dial Press had inveigled Mayor Lindsay to close the Village street to traffic. There was Norman! We hug/patted, spilled drinks. I introduced widening Norman to reed-slim Bob, who asked him for a quote for my book jacket.

"Send the galleys along," said Norman, grinning big. Norman was older. He wore a granddaddy black suit with black vest over Falstaffian belly, tie, and cop shoes. He looked about as hip as a clerk hawking cheap menswear on Delancey Street. But it was great to see Norman again. Made me feel at home.

FALL 1967 - FALL 1969

My September novel was rescheduled for November, right before the Christmas coffee-table book push, off-season for serious books. Review copies were sent to my famous writer buddies for quotes.

Norman phoned and said he'd started it. He sent me his new allegorical satire, *Why Are We in Vietnam?*, a hilarious absurdist diatribe against the Vietnam warrior-CEO overkill mentality. It was dead-on, his most original novel. I loved it.

At the special screening of his film, *Wild 90*, I was eager to ask what he thought of my novel. Tout lit and radical chic applauded lightly, politely, as Norman and his blonde actress wife Beverly, actor Mickey Knox, and editor Buzz Farbar cavorted in home-movie fashion. Playing hoods, the boys acted bad Brando pastiche. So far, Norman had dreamed he was Hemingway, JFK, Killer Joe, and now Brando.

"Hey, Marlon!" I yelled back to Norman, and the uptight crowd harrumphed. The only one I knew was editor Aaron Asher. Once again, I couldn't put the names of these mighty poobahs together with their faces, having been in Washington for three years. Norman became addicted to making truly bad movies with his famous friends. The chaotic chic of the *Maidstone* and *Beyond the Law* shoots made trendy magazine pieces, though. Lots of good stills.

Norman invited me for dinner with the gang at a midtown restaurant where we sat at a circle table and everybody deferred to him. Beverly wasn't about. Norman saw me home, sat his sturdy wide legs on my purple striped sofa, and accepted a drink.

What did he think of my book? I put it delicately, "How do you think reviewers will respond to my novel?"

"These people will never accept you, Alice. You're too wild," said Norman. "Don't you know what they're like? They have the temperaments of librarians."

I felt like I'd dropped through the floor. "But surely a person can write about sex, sexual relationships?"

"How come we never got together? I've been attracted to you for years."

"You're always married, Norman." Easy way out. Talk sex, dodge my writing.

"Not lately, so much." Norman still had bright sparkly sage eyes and wavy wild cascades of hair, but also girth. "Maybe we should give it a try. I'm a pushover."

I laughed. "Norman, it's well-known you're spreading your sacred seed, that you won't have sex with birth control."

"But, babe, if anything happens, I'll support the child. I always have."

"It's not a chance I want to take," I said, attempting to be merry. "Even with Abraham, founding father of the dynasty." I couldn't stand it any longer. "What did you think of my book?"

"Your novel is silly."

"*Silly*?" I was mortified, reduced to blushing triviality, a mere female pretender: burn at the stake.

"You may care more about writing than marriage, but that's rare. Most women don't *long* for careers," said the patriarch.

"But, Beverly's a working actress." I was furious. "She's been on Broadway."

"Till she became wife and mother of our two," he waved away her acting success. "Southern girl, like you."

Later I found out Norman and Beverly were separating over the very same silly problem I wrote about: independent career woman married to dominating man who wants her to be hausfrau, not actress self. To serve, not achieve.

"What about the style?" I persisted.

"Lots of angst," he raised brows, tickled his ear.

"Gee, I wonder why." Before I got nasty sardonic, I suggested we go over to the Lion's Head across the street. "I want to show you off." What I wanted was to get out and blow off this mood, before I wept.

Would he give me a quote anyway, now that I'd turned him down? Of course not.

The Lion's Head, across the tall trees of Christopher Park, nestled next to the cramped two-story *Village Voice* office that wrapped the triangular corner. Our literary oasis in the global Village. Over the bar the carved mahogany lion's head thrust out with its sign that tallied the rising weekly body count from Vietnam.

When I walked in with Norman, the pub suspended in silence. A god had entered, prince of the pantheon! Then the Head bristled with electric thrill at sight of the macho giant of the still very male literary world. Norman the magnificent! Lesser lights salaamed, crowded about to chat, to admire, show off. Several whispered to me, "What a coup!" and "You know *Norman*!"

Some wag quoted Robert Service to Norman, "Who's the poet?"

Norman said, "Yeats?"

❧❧❧❧

Katherine Anne had promised me a quote. I'd sent her a precious review copy, and heard nothing. So I phoned her in Washington.

"I'm too old to do myself or anyone else any good any more," Katherine Anne said weakly. "The doctors say the emphysema and bronchitis will do me in slowly. But the doctors say I move too fast, talk too fast, live too fast, that I could live a long time if I'd slow down." She trolled a chuckle, "I'm not interested in living a long time."

I plunged in on a breath. "Will you write out a quote for me—just one sentence? Bob Amussen wants it in writing."

"Angel, of course, I will."

"It means so much," I plead.

"Did you go look at my little house at 17 Grove?"

"What a darling house, all long planks of wood, rather weathered though." It was three stories high, at the corner of Grove and Bedford, wood among all the brick.

"That was my first apartment in New York. One night I saw a murder out front. Two thugs in raincoats with slick black hair hit a man with brass knuckles. I was too scared to call the cops. They came, with a straw coffin, and took him off. I used to sit in the window with the lights off and watch the night life."

"Don't forget, Katherine Anne." I interrupted her flow. "I miss you."

"I miss you, angel. I'll do it."

But, of course, she didn't.

❧❧❧❧

As review copies had been sent to all my famous writer buddies, for blurbs, I phoned Joe Heller and Bruce Jay Friedman and left my number various times. No response. In January 1968 when it was already too late, a card came from Vance Bourjaily and a letter from Willie Gaddis. Vance said he hadn't seen my book, that it probably arrived over Christmas and was stolen. Vance was now head of the Iowa Writers Workshop.

Gaddis wrote:

> Dear Alice—I'm sorry for the lateness of this for I've had your book & started it—But do recall our talk about quotes, at that party I think, and why it's never made sense for me to give one because I honestly can't believe my name would sell a single copy so that— since it is not a name in the public mind like Mailer's for instance—my name on the jacket of someone else's work, or in an ad, flatly would strike me as an advertisement for myself, like the raft of provincial reviewers whose livelihood apparently depends on such publicity—that's from my point of view, & from yours—I'm convinced it wouldn't change your sales etc at all—where publishers get these ideas I cannot imagine—I even recently got in the mail a big book of Aubrey Beardsley drawings—some quite startling— with request for comment—imagine my name selling Aubrey Beardsley! I don't think anyone's figured out the chemistry of book sales—except the fact that the one who sells books is the man in the bookstore—and as I know, there's altogether too much pain connected with it—hang on—all I know that counts is luck & I certainly wish you that—I'll keep an eye for reviews—

> Willie Gaddis

> 25 Park Trail
> Croton-on-Hudson N.Y.

A polite rebuff that broke my heart. A quote from Gaddis could've been a gold-engraved invitation to the ball, guaranteeing serious review attention. Not sales but critics with influence. And he knew it. By the time my novel was published, these mundane male dodges still rankled. They mattered. They hurt. Why had I thought I was one of the gang, our gang of writers, when I was the Second Sex? Precisely what my novel dealt with.

&c&c&c&c

The day *My Darling from the Lions* was published, would planets tilt and bow, the sun flare in applause? All was serene. Publishing a first novel is like an earthquake on your own very small street.

I longed to be the legitimate heir of Katherine Anne and T. S. Eliot, to add my flicker to their great spark. Secretly I wondered if I might become rich and famous, today's version of Happily Ever After. Obviously I knew nothing about the book business.

I remembered what Katherine Anne Porter told me about fame. Katherine Anne had said, "I know writers who deserve fame who don't have it, and I know writers who have it who don't deserve it. So I have no great respect for fame. But it's useful. People listen to you."

At night, dreaming, on a high cliff ledge and floating out, out in waves of flying. Then suddenly in a different flat land. Look back and I'm way above the cliff, look ahead to an immensely high peak through the haze and I'm on a plateau in the middle. Between the emotion and the response falls the shadow. The knife shadow that shears anticipation from reality.

Tense and anxious, I read every review as an ironic putdown. The *New York Times Book Review*, our sacred text, said, quoting me on love:

> When Miss Denham is being lyrical, she is capable of some really incredible language. ('The white pain of discovery raced through them with a blinding sear, leaving them groping in the eyeless black. . . with that foreknowledge of doom that plunges after the first intimation of love, with a fierce desire for normality and piddling emotions.')

Was he making fun of me? Years later I realized it wasn't a bad small review. But it was by Martin Levin, in the books-in-brief section. Minor league.

꙳꙳꙳

Most reviews appeared in 1968. In my delicate condition, I searched each review for excessive praise only, reviews from Minneapolis to Miami, from Los Angeles to Boston. The *Fresno*

Bee delighted me:

> First, the characters are well individualized and believable. Grace is a struggling artist and Carl a musician of promise. . . Each is a dynamic, forceful person, often controlled by inner creative drives. Their explosive union does not leave much room for acquiring talent as a wife or husband.
> Secondly, Miss Denham is a stylist who fingers words and phrases with supercharged intensity before placing them, ever so precisely, in position.

I could have kissed the reviewer.

"You're ahead of your time," Bob Amussen said somberly when he sent bad reviews. The majority by women were good. *Playboy* said I had "panache," a chic refusal on their part to get serious. Women reviewers identified with it more strongly and male reviewers always got cute about my Playmate days, mentioned on the book jacket. The conformists of both sexes thought Grace and Carl were far too wild and crazy. They were. They were the sixties in the fifties.

Hans, an émigré German industrialist who'd been an American POW, bought fifty copies for colleagues and workers. I'd never dated Hans, he was a friend, an incredibly kind friend.

How feverishly we all struggle to achieve the dreams of our youth. Now my dream was real, solid, on display at Doubleday's Fifth Avenue bookstore and at Scribner's across the street. How lucky I was to be there when literature mattered, when literary artistry and sensibility ruled the book world, when I knew all those grand, evil, macho literary guys.

❧❧❧❧

Explain yourself, young lady. On CBS radio, I told Mike Wallace *My Darling from the Lions* was about the changing role of women and the conflict between marriage and identity to an independent but loving woman. "What conflict?" said Mike. "You certainly are down on marriage." I replied, "You've been married four times, haven't you, Mike?" He laughed, "Well, yes." When

CBS aired the tape, the part about Mike Wallace being married four times was cut out.

On his popular prime time TV show, Alan Burke performed his comic book Satan act, holding my novel up for his audience. "But women like to be dominated, don't they?" Brows arched to the sky.

"The husband can't tolerate his wife's equality. He wants to be captain, with her as first mate." Swallowing stage fright, I flogged my novel mercilessly.

"Too many captains sink a ship." Burke leered at his female audience, who clapped girlishly.

"It isn't fair," I got hot, "for a man to put himself above his wife."

To my surprise, the audience cheered and clapped even louder.

Amussen had warned me the TV and radio talking heads wouldn't have read their review copies, so I supplied each with five simple questions. They were grateful, especially Joe Franklin. "Why does a writer choose to live in New York?" he asked in his lovable ditsy way, shuffling papers.

"Because I almost never meet anybody stupid here. New Yorkers are smart and tolerant. They care about art."

Joe grinned, motioned for applause, which came in halting waves.

On *Girl Talk*, catfight for the camera with aging movie star Ann Miller and aging designer Rudi Guernrich. "Monogamy is the curse of the powerless," I announced wildly.

Beehive hostess Virginia Graham said, "Shocking," and gave me a wink. "Tell us," she threw her head back, tossing her sprayed-concrete blonde hive, "What drives you as an artist?"

"Writing keeps me sane," I blushed. "Beyond that, I'm in a constant rage about the Vietnam War we seem unable to stop. March, demonstrate—I turned in my demo draft card at a rally the other day. Boys over there stay stoned so they can tolerate the slaugh—"

"All very tragic," interrupted Graham, "but that's another show." She signaled for a commercial break.

When Stewart Klein interviewed me on ABC-TV, he'd actually read the novel and was interested. "Your hero—as soon as they marry—he wants another woman. He gets her, then he wants his wife, as well. Is he typical?"

"Men can have three lives, if they choose—professional, domestic and romantic. Women seldom have more than two."

"Certain inequality there?" Stewart asked in his easy witty way.

"I advise you gals out there to play around because your husbands do."

The audience snickered, having come to be mildly shocked. Thrilled by it all, Alice in Wonderland ranted.

"I recommend *My Darling from the Lions*," Stewart held it up for the camera. "A very unusual first novel."

Stewart was first rate. Once when he hated a movie, he called it *caca*.

The *Village Voice* interviewed me and concluded:

> Alice Denham is a Southerner with all the grace and pliant femininity one would expect. But she's a surprisingly direct and dominant personality. She speaks softly but expects you to agree.

They'd detected my feminism. They ran a model shot that showed me tall and leggy in a lace one-piece bathing suit. You can make anybody tall by shooting from floor level, as movies do for heroic stance. I began dating Ed Fancher, psychologist and co-publisher of the *Voice*. Ed was big blond boyish, husky in early middle age, naturally analytic, easy company. I was surprised when he told me, disappointed, that the *Voice* had never been noticed by the literary establishment.

At a party tossed by Barbara Wasserman, Norman's sister, I shocked Ed and others by declaring women did *not* suffer penis envy. "Nobody wants a dick. Women want the same opportunity in the world that men have. Women want to be recognized artists, MDs, scientists, reporters." In the late sixties only men were allowed to be reporters for *Time* and *Newsweek*; women had to be researchers. Medical and law schools had 10 percent female quotas. No women students were permitted at Princeton and Yale and Harvard and Amherst or any other Ivy college. The best colleges were for men only.

After he read my novel, the head of Comp Lit at NYU offered

me a full scholarship to get my PhD I did not wish to be an academic. I wanted to do the creating, not criticize other writers. I said no, but thanks.

The phone rang every half-hour for three months. Not only media promotion but many strangers of our fair city. An inventor featured in *Newsweek* sent me a copy of the article and asked me to dinner. A fourteen-year-old girl wanted me to do something about how fat she was. Several men sent me their photos, smooth heavy cheeks and ineffectual eyes, and asked me to marry them. The obscene callers rallied their lustbuckets for the big fuck & suck phone-in. "Pardon me," a polite British voice enquired, "but has anyone ever helped you get off over the phone?"

Rosemary, whom I hadn't seen since fourth grade in Coral Gables, wrote congrats, she always knew I'd be a writer. Six boys I hadn't seen since eighth grade in Tampa wrote a Round Robin letter. Friends across the country wrote they related to *My Darling*, but what a daring book. About a hundred people wrote fan letters, saying they were moved. Many women wrote they had exactly the same problem with men. Some said they were making their boyfriends read it.

One afternoon a large detective knocked, showed badge and ID, said he'd picked up a rape suspect with the *Daily News* photo spread article about me in his possession. He whipped out a shot of a slight Puerto Rican. Did I know the man? I did not. Later the detective phoned and asked me for a date. "There never was a rape suspect, was there?" He chuckled, "How else could I meetcha?"

At the Lion's Head a fuzzy young concert violinist asked me to autograph his copy. Smiling not too eagerly, I attempted the air of one inured to literary adulation. "I recognized you from your hair," he said. "When I was at Julliard, I used to masturbate to your pictures."

Two men proposed to me on the first date, a lawyer from San Francisco and a doctor from Boston. I thought they were both crazy for proposing to me on the first date, but the lawyer was crazier. He fell in love with my toes and talked to each of them, personally.

The book was dedicated: *To My Mother and to the Memory of My Father, Loved and Missed by Us All.*

When Mother read my novel, she burnt it.

It was my blue barque sailing home, proof I hadn't wasted my life doing it my way. A sacred book of lives shared, both good and bad, my version of the satin-bound photo albums of Bunny and Palmer and me as children, Dad and Mother as young marrieds, with Dad's love poems pasted in back. In a long letter I explained why I'd used the family—to discover Truth, which was Beauty, wasn't it? Weary Odysseus, sailing home with the wind. Southerners are melodramatic.

My own mother burnt my first novel.

But how could Mother see the artistry and ignore her role? Dad's forebears were writers. At Yale Dad had been called their Southern Poet without Portfolio. Dad wrote for FHA. Mother wrote talented letters. But Mother didn't read. She snacked, a taste of that paper, this junk mag, never solid fare. Bunny and Palmer had written me funny gushy fan letters, each adding, "What will Mother think?"

Mother wrote:

How dare you write about us and bring such shame to our family? Your mind is cluttered with sex. It's a blessing your father is dead. This would kill him. I cannot allow such vile trash in my house, so I burnt it.

You need God!
Mother

I bawled like a baby. I kept butting my head against the wall that was Mother, surprised it hurt. Years later I realized Mother felt I maligned her character before cherished old friends and relatives. How about the difficulty of parenting incorrigible me? Like many writers, I had no sense of shame. About revealing myself or others. I trespassed avidly in search of truth. In college when I discovered shame distorted truth, I discarded it and began to write.

What shocked me most in 1967 was when my drugstore buddy, Rubin Hurricane Carter, was convicted with John Artis of triple murder. Hurricane was number one middleweight contender at the time. There was never a milder man than Hurricane—strumming his guitar, smiling gently, perched on the last stool at the soda fountain, next to Stillman's Gym, while I chatted at him. The only evidence against him and Artis was that these two black men were driving through that area of New Jersey at the time. Nelson Algren, my dinner date, didn't believe it any more than I did, which he wrote in *Esquire* at the retrial in 1974, which was also lost. In 1986, after Hurricane had spent nineteen years in jail for a crime he didn't commit, a judge ruled that racism and withheld evidence had caused him to be jailed unfairly.

⋟⋟⋟⋟⋟

In spring 1968 Joe Heller dropped by and said he'd have given me a blurb, for sure, but he was in Hollywood and out of touch. "You know what I've always liked most about you?"

My boobs, I expected.

"Your delicate face," Joe said. "Such fine bones."

Joe Heller was always a good guy. He didn't have an ounce of pomposity. He was macho, of course, but he was a buddy of sorts, bursting with high spirits and fun. Probably he really would've given me a blurb for my novel, if I'd reached him.

Joe was losing beef now in his shape-up forties. He gave me his latest, the play *We Bombed in New Haven*, and, I fear, it did. I enticed Joe to Sheridan Square Paperback to buy my novel, which I signed. My magenta-and-white hardcover was displayed nicely on its own rack, fronting paperbacks. I introduced Joe to Bob Marloff, eager affable owner and patron of Village writers. The very small street of the earthquake engendered by my first novel extended from my corner to Bob's, crossing the sliver of park to the *Village Voice* and the Lion's Head.

Sheridan Square Paperback was our bookstore, just as the Voice was our paper and the Head our pub, all on pie wedge Christopher Park where little Phil Sheridan's green statue poses for loungers under leafy green maples. Before the homeless took over, the neighborhood sat on the benches and read newspapers in the sunshine.

We thought it would never end.

❧ 33 ❧

GIRL OF THE MOMENT

Jim Brown phoned. "Lancer says they'll double the print order if they can change your title to *Coming Together.*"

"But, Jim, *My Darling from the Lions* is a—an original title."

"Phone Bob and see what he thinks."

"Oh, God," moaned Amussen. "Slaves to fashion, the publishing world." The Sexual Revolution was heating up books.

"They said 165,000 with my title, 265,000 with theirs." In 1968 that was a lot.

"Go ahead," Bob said in solemn dirge. "You want as many readers as possible."

Ever the showoff, I posed nude for the 1969 cover of *Coming Together*, which title hid my breasts. Exposed were my face and my legs from knee down. The second printing featured a miniskirted model stamping her boot on a prone man, and declared it a novel of women's liberation, and myself a leader in the "female liberation movement." *Coming Together* was about breaking up. It sold well.

In 1969 the French version from publisher Fleuve Noir in their "Presence de Femmes" series was titled *Vivre a Deux*, which sounds delightful in French. I hoped the French had translated the theme of liberation as well.

To flog the paperback in 1969 I did a *Cosmo* article modestly titled "I was a Nude Model," topped by a topless shot of me as a bottomless fishtail mermaid. Though I disapproved of body shows to push a serious novel, I courted them. I was schizoid. I looked down on being a nude model and preened for my fans. *They* called themselves fans. I was an exhibitionistic prude. Or simply a pirate, an icon-buster. An advertisement for myself. Absurd to make a big deal about bodies we all possess. Don't you remember when we ran around the forest buck naked as cave women and didn't shave our legs, and were fond of fellows you could hardly see for the hair?

David Markson's new novel was *Going Down* and Dan Wakefield's was delicately called *Going All the Way*.

As the sex wave churned and swelled across America, an established book editor offered me a twenty-five thousand dollar advance if I'd write a book on the Swingers. I'd heard there were swingers, people who swung. But I hadn't a clue it was a national sex club where couples exchanged partners.

"Of course," said the big-time editor, who was a tweedy easy-living country club type. "We'll have a great time. We'll go around the country swinging and interviewing."

"We?"

"You'll have to join and participate. As my partner."

"*You're* a Swinger?"

"Yes, I love it."

I said no.

❧❧❧❧

One evening my Palo Alto friend, Professor Pat Suppes, took me for drinks at the East 60s brownstone of mighty Random House head Bennett Cerf and his wife Phyllis Wagner. Pat and Phyllis were in the educational TV business together.

Bennett, a charmer, showed me his upstairs studio and handed me a new book of poetry. "Glance at this a minute."

I did. "It's drivel."

"We've sold twenty thousand—the worst stuff I ever read." It was Rod McKuen's first book.

"Why didn't your novel come to us?" Cerf asked, as I lent him a hardcover.

Blushing I said, "I have an enemy there—Joe Fox."

Roaring with laughter, Bennett said, "Don't you know everybody hates Joe Fox? But he's a brilliant editor."

When Cerf finished *My Darling*, he phoned. "We would've published this novel. Only I would've made you take all the sex out."

As I desperately needed money, Jim Brown sent my novel to his client, Jean Stafford, asking her to recommend me for a Guggenheim Fellowship. Posing as her own nonexistent secretary, she replied from Long Island:

> During Miss Stafford's prolonged sojourn in Iran, I am handling her correspondence and I take it upon myself to tell you, in no uncertain terms, that Miss S. is not in the habit of reading books about f—king, with the photograph of the author in her birthday suit on the front cover. After a lifetime of working closely with Miss Stafford, I have come to adopt all her opinions and I think I may safely say that she would undergo (as I did) a most grievous curdling of the blood if she were to read the passages particularly recommended by Miss Alice Denham.

Bob Amussen and I dined at Casey's, ne plus ultra 10th Street restaurant owned by K. C. Lee, rich party giver and artists' friend. K. C.'s father had reputedly cornered the tungsten market in Taiwan. Rich Bohemians K. C. and Marshall Allen loved to entertain seedy needy artists.

Nearby were Ginger and Bruce Jay Friedman, Bruce who'd evaded my calls pleading for a quote. Norman and Buzz Farbar and dates were at the next table. My grudge level was so low I charged over and greeted them like old buds, and introduced Bob Amussen. Bob and I had become lovers and literary co-conspirators, our temperaments too diverse for love.

As I already had a date with *Voice* editor Ed Fancher, I invited Norman to science writer Gay Luce's Christmas party. Gay wrote the popular *Sleep* book about rapid eye movements and dream research. In his funereal black suit, Norman came solo and we danced. Norman was a clompy dancer. He was disarmingly humble and friendly with everybody. Norman was clearly exploring for his next mate.

Saul Bellow was so famous everyone at David and Elaine Markson's party gave him a wide berth. No one dared to go up and chat with him. He and his youngish companion inspected books in the Markson dining room while the crowd convened in the living room. Finally I approached as the young woman left to refill their drinks. We chatted. I delivered my first novel credentials.

Bellow put the flirt on me. "I'd like to stay in town and get to know you," big swoony black moon eyes, "but I've got to leave," he apologized. As if I'd asked. Shepherded by a solemn young woman who acted like a curator, cautiously displaying a precious object that mustn't be disturbed by the vagaries of the world. Important males are often trundled about this way. Bellow was still handsome and knew it.

❧❧❧

"You're the girl of the moment, a literary *succes de scandale*," roared big Jim Bryans, Popular Library editor-in-chief, over dinner at elegant Chambord.

"But I need serious money," I replied. I still did jacket copy for Jim, four paperbacks at forty dollars per book.

"How'd you like to write a mystery?"

"I've never read one."

Jim sent me two to read, arranged for me to see the NBC-TV pilot of *The Ghost and Mrs. Muir,* and told me to dream up a mystery plot involving the leads, the widow played by Hope Lange and the ghostly sea captain, acted by Edward Mulhare. Yawning, I read one mystery then came up with a twisting plot. At the Pierre Bar Jim and I cranked up the plot on champagne cocktails, and I wrote it in six weeks. I had one rule: don't think, write. It was harmless fun like dancing. I was able to live on the money for six months.

When copies of *The Ghost and Mrs. Muir* were published in November 1968 a mystery book club wanted to buy rights to print another one hundred thousand copies. With Hope Lange and Edward Mulhare adorning the cover, it was a TV tie-in to PR the new show. Then NBC, which had sold the literary rights to Popular Library, was sued by the estate of the old English novelist who'd created *The Ghost and Mrs. Muir*. I knew there'd been an old movie but I had no idea it was based on a book. Jim Bryans told me they couldn't accept the mystery club offer: they'd been ordered to cease and desist publication. I got fan letters. People still tell me they enjoyed it. Out there somewhere are the original one hundred thousand copies.

When Peggy Fleming won the world championship in figure skating, an NBC producer asked me to write a quickie biography of her, which I refused. I had no interest in skating. As if that mattered. I wasn't too sharp at making a living. It took desperation to drive me to fast books.

⚜⚜⚜⚜

Look editor-in-chief Bill Attwood wanted me to write a column in 1969 alternating with Betty Rollin and Gloria Steinem. But staff nixed it. Three women—really! Two male writer friends cast me as a dominating woman in their novels, which pleased me greatly. Gracias, Lamar Herrin and Geoffrey Wagner. Desperate for money again, I won four hundred dollars as a TV contestant on *Snap Judgment* and five hundred as an imposter on Gary Moore's *To Tell the Truth*.

Then, in 1969, I had a movie offer. Independent James Lipscomb, who'd had a big success with his shark movie, *Blue Water, White Death,* had optioned *My Darling* and now he wanted to buy all the rights for twenty-five thousand dollars and make the movie. Jim Brown said absolutely not, never give away all the rights. The trick about one solid offer is you expect other producers reading the novel to knock down the door. No? I said. Jim was theoretically right, except for this: ultimately, no one else was interested. Lipscomb had dropped his option and gone his way. So far, I'd turned down fifty thousand dollars out of principle. Hmm. Were my principles finer than I was? It could only have helped to have a movie. If I'd been morally able to swing, probably I'd be famous.

❧❧❧❧

According to the *New York Times*, Schoenberg in 1968 and later, plus this from Alex Ross:

> Perhaps most impressive of the group, Al Hansen's "Alice Denham in 48 Seconds" hits on a powerful ordering principle: the letters of a name are reduced to pairs of numbers (A=1, L=12, I=9, C=5, etc.), and each pair determines the pace of events (1 event in 12 seconds, then 9 events in 5 seconds, etc.)... Surprisingly, the number system creates a vibrant, pulsing rhythmic field.

Composer Al Hansen phoned and said he hoped I hadn't minded his using my name. He dropped by, a pale fit sixties hippie painter who also created Happenings, performance art partly determined by chance. Originally, "AD in 48" had been performed with John Cage in his New School class, then at Brooklyn Academy of Music, and finally the Paula Cooper Gallery in Soho.

Al promised to invite me next time. But the invitations came from Europe where his avant-garde Fluxus art was welcomed. He'd moved to Cologne. Moondog, the Viking beggar-composer, moved to Europe, as did experimental jazz.

❧❧❧❧

At Yale, in Calhoun College where my father had lived, there was a wall plaque of the St. Elmo Society, to which he'd belonged. I moved through homey worn Gothic splendor, carved altar chairs, stained glass windows, arches and faded Oriental rugs, all humanized by generations of students. Austin Clarke, Toronto's famous Barbadian author of *Survivors of the Crossing*, had invited me to Yale to read to his writing classes. Austin, having recently become a Beautiful Black—the new term for acceptance—was in demand as a visiting professor.

Afterward the students cracked open cases of beer and sat on the floor around my priestly Gothic chair and asked questions.

They smiled, they liked sitting on the floor, they didn't mind my being above them in the chair. I liked their ease. About a third were women, even then. The students were avid, funny and rumpled, furious about the Vietnam War.

In the afternoon session I gave them technical help on their manuscripts. As soon as I showed them on the page how it could be done, they understood. After the mindlessness of flogging my novel on TV, it was a revelation. A sheer pleasure.

There I stood in my father's shoes, accepted in the place where he was accepted, too naive to realize it was provisional, that I was only there because another outsider, recently permitted indoors, had slipped me in. Still, how proud I was to be there, Daddy, at Yale.

❧❧❧❧

Out my Village window, the old sailors' church plays its Angelus, its gift to the square. Gulls soar high up, rose slivers tilting to the sunset as they fly down the Hudson. Evening rush hour in the sky drones overhead with jets flying upriver to land before dark. Suddenly I remembered when Dad took me up in that open cockpit plane and rolled it. Pop the old flying ace. Tired after work, Dad used to say, "I want to get on that slow boat to China and when it's almost there, turn around and head back, and when we see the Golden Gate, turn around and. . ." The point was, stay afloat. That was my struggle, in the literary macho boys' club of my era.

Dad's boat had blown to shore. I'm sailing on, Dad, writing as my windhover.

Always fresh shoots spring from old roots, once again blossoms.

Memory is the palace of the mind.

❧ 34 ❦

AFTERMATH

"What do you broads want?" a guy yelled, as Lucy Komisar, Claudia Dreifus and I, and ten others from NOW harangued the crowd, outside Lindsay headquarters. Mayoral candidate John Lindsay had ignored our women's civil rights platform.

"*You* know what we want?" I passed a black guy.

"*I* know what you want, sister," he replied.

As the crowd jeered louder, aides flew out the door. "What is it you want? What can we do for you ladies? Come inside, please." Smiling, we sauntered in and our demands were met. We also picketed Judge Anthony Scalia's Village office when he opposed legalizing abortion. Of course, he ignored us.

❧❧❦❦

My dear bro, the Reverend Palmer, phoned in alarm. "Ali, Mother will see your name in the paper, saying you had an illegal abortion!"

"Well, Palmer," I sighed, "she'll just have to see it."

In spring 1970 we placed full-page ads in the *New York Times* and the *Washington Post* admitting we had all had illegal abortions. Our two hundred names and the names of many prominent women were listed, professions or titles or names of books after each. Imagine, the most respectable women, the few powerful women in the nation, confessing to illegal abortions. A brilliant ploy, a sensation.

On March 9, 1970, New York State legalized abortion and I broke into torrential tears. We fought for it and, to my amazement, we won! Women would never again have to suffer as I had. We were naive enough to think that was it.

❦❦❦❦

Would I spend tonight in a jail cell? Fearing jail, I rose in the elevator to the *Ladies Home Journal* floor. I joined the flow of a hundred women from NOW and nine other movement groups as we invaded the immense offices on Wednesday, March 18, 1970. We easily barricaded editor John Mack Carter in his huge corner office. We demanded relevance in a magazine targeted to women.

Carter, a curly-haired Irishman, appeared in a blue shirt, media arrived on tall shoulders, cameras held aloft. Holly Forsman and I guarded the door of the jammed office, both of us looking fierce on the front page of the *Village Voice*. Women sat on every inch of floor, leaned against walls. Many of the female underlings smiled secret smiles all day.

Signe Hammer and Susan Brownmiller read our demands to editor John Mack Carter in his crammed office. Enough gooey desserts, lace-collared dresses, how-to-keep-your-man. How about equal pay for equal work, sex discrimination, legal abortion nationally, unnecessary hysterectomies, 10 percent female quotas in law and medical schools? Half the articles were written by men, using female bylines.

They read the demands again. Then Marlene Sanders and the ABC film crew strode in. "Carter, what is your response?" Marlene thrust her mike in his face and his voice temporarily vanished.

NOW's president, Jacqui Ceballos, spoke with her usual steely poise. For seven hours, we discussed, harangued, got promises, squeezed into his hot tense office.

Suddenly John Mack Carter climbed atop his desk to be above us.

Tiny dark dynamo Shulamith Firestone of New York Radical Feminists pulled him down. "That's *just* what we *mean*," she said.

I read Media Women's demands on ABC-TV. After eleven hours, the *Journal* agreed to give us eight pages in their August 1970 issue, for which they'd pay ten thousand dollars. Swimming through the open floor of offices, talking to staffers, was actually a lot of fun.

❧❧❧❧

Walter Cronkite CBS-TV News interviewed three other feminists and me in March 1970. This was the women's movement's first appearance on national TV. Reporter David Culhane taped me at home, at my marble cafe table, my novel propped up on it. First, they scrolled four or five model head shots then cut to me, looking older.

David Culhane said, "Didn't you *really* become a feminist because you were too old for nude modeling?" I got angry.

The camera cut to a full screen closeup of my eyes, making me seem a witch, as I said, "I became a feminist to fight for women's rights. Read my novel." I jiggled it.

When I phoned NOW to apologize for being less than smashing, they said not to worry. I should've had their media kit. Rule #1: never show anger. Rule #2: answer any question with exactly what you wish to say, ignoring the question, as politicians do. I was too politically naive to know how savvy NOW was.

❧❧❧❧

Several years later, in her Falls Church kitchen, Mother said casually, "Did you have an illegal abortion?"

"Yes, I did." I waited.

No comment from Mother.

"Thank God, now it's legal," I added.

300

❧❧❧❧

Desperate for money, as usual, I wrote a novelization of *Adios, Sabata*, a spaghetti western starring Yul Brynner, for Jimbo at Popular Library. I worked directly from the murder-riddled movie script. As it was the camera angle that mattered, the script merely said, "He shot, they shot, guns shot, bullets shot."

The bullet whizzed, slammed, banged, hit, sliced, caromed, zapped, zoomed, blasted, bore, cut, laced, ribboned, ricochetted, rammed, socked, pinged, crashed, jumped, carved, toppled, wasted, leveled, sailed, arced, flattened, jarred, tore, ripped, pierced, killed him.

It was my job to make this endless shootout entertaining, hence my list for the gunplay.

What I wondered was how America could relish fictional and movie violence with the killing fields in Vietnam and street murders at home? Yet it would come to pass that in mass market a book without a tasty murder was like spaghetti without sauce.

Another six months of life paid for to aim at my second novel. I needed sustaining *unobtrusive* work. In fall 1970 I got an adjunct job at John Jay College of Criminal Justice teaching Creative Writing to cops.

With Dan, an ex-Marine captain, I protested at the big anti-Vietnam war rally in the Central Park bandshell. We strode up on stage and turned in our surrogate draft cards. Then as we left through the back exit, we were photographed by a phalanx of FBI men.

❧❧❧❧

The sexual revolution, a gism of release from the war in Vietnam, spewed forth with the chic Swedish sex movie, *I Am Curious (Yellow)*. Middle-class people sat in Eighth Avenue porno theaters staring into genitals the size of cars. Dan took me and it exhausted, repelled, no—mechanized us so we didn't have sex.

In Michael McClure's avant-garde play, *The Beard*, Billy the Kid went down on Marilyn Monroe. Those unwilling to get into group sex or orgies were square. Monogamous couples were wimps. My orgy invitations always came from blokes I wouldn't date.

Sex clubs appeared. Jon, my cartoonist friend, invited me to go see. At the Underground, folks arranged orgies. There were six of us, including Barney Rosset. In Jon's bathroom, we three women took turns inserting our diaphragms. Already this staged orgy was on automatic. The others were high on grass. I wasn't. All six of us on Jon's round bed, stiff as frozen fish. I felt the woman next to me. Cold as ice.

"You mechanical toys play with each other. I'm going home." And I bolted up and left.

Years later at a Grove book party, Barney Rosset's white ring of hair was red, his face younger. One of the early male face lifts? Barney said my outburst ended the evening. "I didn't want to stay anyway," said he.

෨෨෨෨

At Plato's Retreat, couples had sex on the mats—mattresses— in an open gym while others watched their buns rise and fall. They resembled a fishscape in the dim light, slowly moving pale undulant creatures. "Never saw so many cracks," commented my date, Rod, a magazine reporter. At Plato's I watched two gals sucking off guys in the playpool. Rod and I dropped our towels and swam laps in the bigger pool.

Almost everybody we met were reporters. The best mags in town leaped at this trendy prurience. Another drink; we poured them down, toked a passing joint, as did the other uninhibited Puritans at Plato's, trying to decide. Couples had sex or exchanged partners or simply made out with strangers.

Too zonked to see, I lost Rod. In sarong-towel, I danced with handsome young dude in toga-towel. We hit the mats. I saw no one but him. When he got into regulation pushup position above me, I suggested, "Why don't you go down on me?" He reneged. I got up and walked away, closing my towel around me. Thank God. Instantly I forgot, out on my feet. Time for another drink.

"Rod, you're naked!" He was, walking his apparatus around, completely relaxed. We drank and chatted with his boss, Seymour. Then we hit the playpool, where supplicants floated up to and away from each other like manatees. In the limpid pale blue, a middle-aged couple were going at it, his back to us, her face blushing over his shoulder. We lay on a divan to make out, Rod and I, when I spotted a banquette of voyeur reporters gleefully watching, chins cupped in palms. It was 5:30 a.m. We went home and made out in the sensible morning.

Plato's offered the thrill of sexual jeopardy. Now that love and sex had moved so far apart, did we want to move them even farther? Was losing individuality a release, or was it losing your core? Tout Manhattan was there, searching. It seemed to take everyone a tubful of booze. Exploration pushes people on because, like the mountain, it's there to be discovered. Wasn't America built on entrepreneurial curiosity?

I never went back.

❧❧❧❧

When Jim Brown said, leering, "Maybe feminism will give me a chance to sock one of my lady writers in the balls," I knew who he meant. When I said I needed a feminist, a woman agent, for my new novel, Jim said, "Go ahead. She'll do a better job for you."

"You don't mind?"

"Of course not, my dear. Good luck."

I took my new novel to my friend, Elaine Markson, who had her own agency now. With my help, Elaine sold *Amo* in two weeks to wild man Bill Henderson who was then an editor at Coward, McCann & Geoghegan, Jack Geoghegan's imprint at Putnam. It was so iconoclastic and raw and sexual Bill was afraid, he said, to give it to a woman editor for a second reading, so he gave it to Walter Minton, then head of Putnam. Minton said, "It went down like butter." When I told Bill that Bob Loomis at Random was waiting to see it, a fine offer appeared that spring of 1974.

I felt incredibly lucky that I'd achieved a small measure of acceptance, doing the only work I loved with a passion.

Now it was our turn. Just as the war novelists had been overwhelmed by Jewish male writers, now they were moved aside by feminist writers. We were soon to be elbowed over by African-American writers and immigrants, and always Borges and Garcia Marquez and Alice Munro with her brilliant small-town tales.

Hendo began Pushcart Press with his own book, *The Publish-*

it-Yourself Handbook, and succeeded as few writers have with his *Pushcart Prize Anthology* of literary review stories and essays, and his own remarkable memoirs, especially *Her Father.* Flamboyant raving Hendo was my kind of guy, briefly, between his marriages and my Lion's Head romances.

Once in a while I bumped into the aging bad boys at the Lion's Head, at soirees and book parties. Gaddis apologized for not getting back to me. "But, Alice, I have to take care of myself." He'd married a young editor who tried to sell *JR* to Hollywood. Norman bought me a drink at a PEN event. "Mickey Knox always asks about you," he said.

In 1980 I finally met my man, the one who loved me enough for me to love him.

THE END